The Mexican American: A Selected and Annotated Bibliography

THE MEXICAN AMERICAN
A Selected and Annotated Bibliography

Second Edition

February, 1971

Luis G. Nogales

Editor

Stanford University . *Center for Latin American Studies.*

Stanford, California

The Center for Latin American Studies
Stanford University
Stanford, California

First published, 1969
Second edition, revised and enlarged, 1971

The Mexican American: A Selected and Annotated Bibliography

Second Edition

February, 1971

Editor:

Luis G. Nogales

Assistant to the President
Stanford University

Editorial Consultant and Contributor

Benjamin Martinez, Graduate Student, Graduate Special Programs

Stanford University

Contributors—Graduate Students at Stanford University

Maria Baeza, Latin American Studies Program
Arturo Pacheco, School of Education
Carl Vasquez, Department of Political Science

Stanford University

Stanford, California

The Mexican American: A Selected and Annotated Bibliography

First Edition
October, 1969

Director:

John J. Johnson

Professor of History
Stanford University

Consultants:

Luis G. Nogales

Assistant to the President
Stanford University

Augustin Medina, Jr.

Graduate Student
Department of Political Science
Stanford University

Associates — Graduate Students at Stanford University

Susan B. Drake, Department of Communication
Lynn Hunt, Department of History
Ralph Mann, Department of History
Robert Slenes, Department of History
Patricia Stell, Department of Anthropology

TABLE OF CONTENTS

PREFACE
TO THE SECOND EDITION

A number of works not favorably discussing the Chicano and his aspirations are included in this bibliography. In fact, we have purposely included some studies whose theses have been rebutted as examples of the state of public opinion, public policy, and the level of scholarship as it related to the Chicano in different time periods. Had the contributors been writing reviews rather than annotations, many of the studies included herein would have been handled more harshly than they have been. We have included lists of journals and newspapers to which readers may refer for representative comment on studies that have shown a lack of awareness of certain major aspects of Chicano culture.

The second edition of the Mexican American Bibliography represents a substantial revision of the first edition which appeared in 1969. The volume contains approximately two hundred additional annotations. Unpublished dissertations not treated in the earlier edition, are here covered extensively. The number of contributions of Mexican scholars to Chicano Studies has been expanded significantly. The index has been made more useful, we believe, by including bibliographies and by cross-listing of entries when appropriate. Some annotations appearing in the first edition have been modified in order to provide a more uniform format.

This bibliography makes no pretense of being all-inclusive. On the contrary, it is meant to be selective; and the emphasis is very definitely on scholarly publications. It could hardly have been otherwise, given our limited financial resources. Undoubtedly, we committed oversights in not including certain crucial studies. We look forward to producing a more comprehensive third edition and invite suggestions that may help us in attaining that objective.

Many individuals contributed to making this second edition possible. Maria Baeza, graduate student in Latin American Studies, assumed the onerous task of reading many unpublished doctoral dissertations available only on microfilm. Arturo Pacheco, graduate student in the School of Education, did an outstanding job in researching and selecting materials in the field of education. Carl Vasquez, graduate student in Political Science, traveled to Mexico in search of material on the Chicano in the libraries of Mexico City and contributed many thoughtful ideas that made this bibliography a better document than it would otherwise have been. Ben Martinez, graduate student in Political Science, is owed a special debt of gratitude both for the number of his thoughtful contributions and for his diligence and cooperativeness at the editorial end. Manuel Cisneros, senior in Political

Science, provided invaluable assistance in preparing the index and compiling the list of Chicano periodicals. Al Lopez of the Stanford Chicano Press was of immeasurable assistance in designing the volume and cover.

Those of us primarily responsible for the second edition express our thanks to John J. Johnson, who initiated the effort that led to the first edition and who participated in the early stages of the planning of the second edition. We also wish to express our appreciation to Mrs. Janet Dubbs who helped in so many ways with both editions of the bibliography and to Miss Rosemary Sedillo and Miss Lilian Charles for their assistance in producing this edition.

The project was funded through a contract from the Office of Education, Institute of International Studies of the United States Department of Health, Education, and Welfare, and through the Provost's Office of Stanford University.

It is hoped that the bibliography will be of use to Chicano students in fulfilling their educational aspirations and commitment to the Chicano community and it is to them that the bibliography is dedicated.

Luis G. Nogales
Stanford University

PREFACE
TO THE FIRST EDITION

Literature on the Mexican American or Chicano, terms that are used interchangeably herein, is increasing significantly both in quality and quantity. Bibliographies have kept pace with these developments, for the most part. To our knowledge, however, no annotated guide to outstanding printed works on the Mexican American has been published recently. We feel that this bibliography meets the growing need for such a guide. It contains 274 annotations of works we considered to be the best of the approximately 1000 studies originally considered for inclusion, of which 600 were actually examined.

The Guide is designed for use by both the specialist and the informed layman. With but few exceptions, the selections are readily available in college and university libraries. Quite intentionally, the bibliography focuses upon the contemporary interests and concerns of the Mexican-American community but does justice, we feel, to contributions of an earlier generation of scholars and publicists in the field of Mexican-American studies.

Most entries appear because of their scholarly merit, some because they are the best sources in the areas they cover. The social sciences are far better represented than the humanities not because we would necessarily have it that way but because of the nature of the materials currently available. Several theoretical studies are included for those who wish to explore the current methodological approaches and to acquaint themselves with the pitfalls and satisfactions of studying minority groups in general and the Mexican Americans in particular. No set of guidelines could or should rule out the human factor, and in the final analysis the works that appear in this bibliography do so because one or more of our annotators believed that they should. Each annotation was made the final responsibility of an individual staff member and his initials appear at the end of the entry; for a list of staff members, see the title page.

We look forward to a second edition of the Guide which will give fuller coverage to the rich field of government documents, conference proceedings, unpublished dissertations, and works published in Mexico. For the moment, we refer the reader interested in such material to the Advanced Report Number 3 of the Mexican-American Studies Project (see entry F.) and the bibliography of the Inter-Agency Committee on Mexican American Affairs (see entry D.). In the initial stages of this project we relied heavily upon those two works, and they reduced our work load immeasurably.

This bibliography may contain oversights; some books and articles of outstanding value possibly have been overlooked. Also, authors and readers may fault some of our evaluations. For these reasons, we invite constructive criticisms and advice, in the hope that the anticipated second and expanded edition of the bibliography will be better and more comprehensive. Throughout the project, we have been impressed by the increasing number of individuals who have committed themselves to studying and understanding the Mexican Americans, who numerically and culturally constitute such an important segment of the United States society. If this bibliography stimulates others to study the Mexican American so as better to understand him and his place in the contemporary world, it will have served a most useful purpose.

The contributors are indebted to many persons. Luis Nogales, Assistant to the President of Stanford University, and his staff were most cooperative throughout the project. We sincerely thank Mrs. Florence Chu of the Inter-Library Loan Service of Stanford University Libraries who gave freely of her time and her vast knowledge of inter-library loan procedures. To Mrs. Janet Dubbs, Executive Secretary at the Center for Latin American Studies, Stanford University, we say thanks for assistance in too many ways to enumerate. A grant from the United States Office of Education, Department of Health, Education and Welfare, made the project financially possible.

The Staff

ANNOTATIONS

1. Adorno, T. W., et al. The Authoritarian Personality. New York: Harper and Brothers, 1950. 990 pp.

This book deals with the phenomenon of social discrimination, and attempts to determine what distinctive personality traits characterize the prejudiced individual, and what kinds of social psychological factors have contributed to the emergence of the type labelled "authoritarian man." The authors suggest as one of their major findings that individuals who are extremely susceptible to fascist propaganda have in common numerous characteristics which go together to form a kind of "syndrome." The authoritarian personality is said to be characterized by such attitudes as conventionality, rigidity, repressive denial, fear, dependency, and by the formation of stereotypes and ingroup outgroup cleavages.

The authors, in conclusion, state their belief that the systematic and scientific study of the phenomenon of prejudice, such as is undertaken in The Authoritarian Personality, can make a direct contribution to the amelioration of the social and cultural atmosphere which fosters the development of the authoritarian type.—BM

2. Afro- and Mexican-Americana. Fresno, California: Fresno State College Library, 1969.

This bibliography consists of a list of holdings in the Fresno State College library as of January, 1969, including materials on order, which relate to the culture, history, and problems of Americans of African or Mexican descent. The materials listed include books, government publications, Master's theses and graduate study papers, and periodicals. The materials in the last three categories are arranged alphabetically, but the books are arranged according to their shelflist order, thus generally grouping them by subject. The bibliographical citations of the books contain author, title, and date of publication, but do not include the publisher or the place of publication.—BM

3. Alvarez, José Hernández. A Demographic Profile of the Mexican Immigration to the United States, 1910-1950, Journal of International Studies, VIII, No. 3 (July, 1966), 471-496.

The author presents statistical data on Mexican immigrants for comparisons across time and between regions of the United States. He uses data on settlement patterns, evolution of the second generation, intermarriage, education, jobs and housing. In the period of heaviest immigration between 1910 and 1930 there was a "fanlike" dispersal westward to California from Texas, New Mexico and Arizona. Railroad construction and urban industry attracted a stream northeast to Chicago, Gary and Detroit; however, it never amounted to more than 10% of the total immigration. The influence of agricultural recruitments steadily decreased as later immigrants settled disproportionately in the urban areas and outside of the Southwest. Intermarriage with other nationality groups was higher in the rural areas and the urban Northeast which attracted higher percentages of single men than the cities of the Southwest. The highest rates of inability to speak English (in 1930) occurred in the areas of longest settlement (Texas, Arizona and New Mexico); although the second generation completed more years of school, the rates were consistently lower in Southern and rural areas than in Western and urban settlements.—SD

4. American Council on Race Relations. Intergroup Relations in San Diego. San Francisco, 1946. 35 pp.

This report to the San Diego City Council and Board of Education contains comparative material on all ethnic minority groups present in post-war California and devotes considerable attention to Mexican Americans. Unlike many reports of that era, it demonstrates an awareness that Chicanos rejected many Anglo institutions and values. Indeed, the report classes Mexican Americans as "the most isolated group in Southern California."

Race relations are seen in their spatial and ecological dimension instead of in a vacuum. Economic standing is emphasized over the purely social setting. Summaries of such topics as housing and education are standard but the inclusion of other areas—for example, police and community relations—is unique.—PS

5. American Ethnological Society. Spanish-Speaking People in the United States; Proceedings of the 1968 Annual Spring Meeting. June Helm, ed., Seattle, Distributed by the University of Washington Press, 1968. 215 pp.

Spanish-speaking people in America provided the unifying theme for the 1968 meeting of the American Ethnological Society. Twelve papers of varying quality were presented which touched on several aspects of minority life. They ranged in methodology from extremely theoretical quantitative analyses to impressionistic, occasionally emotional reporting. The more relevant papers, in terms of findings, are annotated separately:

Bodine, John J. "A Tri-Ethnic Trap: The Spanish Americans in Taos."

Goodman, Mary Ellen and Alma Beman. "Child's Eye View of Life in an Urban Barrio."

Maloney, Thomas. "Factionalism and Futility: A Case Study of Political and Economic Reform in New Mexico."

Moore, Joan. "Social Class, Assimilation and Acculturation."

Paredes, Americo. "Folk Medicine and the Intercultural Jest."

Shannon, Lyle W. "The Study of Migrants as Members of Social Systems."

Smith, M. Estellie. "The Spanish Speaking Population of Florida."

Swadesh, Frances J. "The Alianza Movement: Catalyst for Social Change in New Mexico."

Waddell, Jack O. "From Dissonance to Consonance and Back Again: Mexican American Correctional Processes in a Southwest City."—RM

6. Anderson, Henry P. The Bracero Program in California, With Particular Reference to Health Status, Attitudes and Practices. Berkeley, School of Public Health, University of California, 1961. 294 pp.

This report originally was confidential, and limited in circulation to individuals and agencies dealing directly with health and medical care aspects of the bracero program. Although it concentrates on health problems, the report touches practically every aspect of the bracero experience: recruitment in Mexico, screening processes at the border, housing, wages and social services in the labor camps in California. The work is based on interviews with Mexican nationals and others involved in the program.—RM

7. Anderson, James G. and William M. Johnson. Sociocultural Determinants of Achievement Among Mexican-American Students. Las Cruces, New Mexico, Educational Resources Information Center, New Mexico State University, 1968. 45 pp.

Some widely-held opinions about Mexican American values are contradicted by this paper, which presents the preliminary findings of a study relating cultural characteristics to school performance. The Mathematics Project conducted by the Southwest Educational Development Laboratory researched the performance of 263 students (grades 7-12) in a Southwestern community. The study indicates that

Mexican American children desire good grades and get as much encouragement and assistance at home as do Anglo children. Educational plans and aspirations of Mexican American children and their families approximately equal those of Anglos, with the child's aspirations becoming increasingly independent of his parents' as he grows older. Retarded school performance is related to low socioeconomic status, use of Spanish and, probably, the minimal self-confidence of Mexican American children. Consistently low achievement of Mexican Americans in school is due not to a low level of educational motivation but to inadequate educational programs. The authors suggest that schools must change their programs, but they do not offer specific recommendations.—PS

8. Anderson, James G., and Dwight Safar. The Influence of Differential Community Perceptions on the Provision of Equal Educational Opportunities, Sociology of Education, XL (Summer, 1967), 219-230.

This is a study of the effect of the perceptions and attitudes of school personnel, from superintendents to teachers, on the provision of equal educational opportunities for Spanish-speaking children. Two communities in New Mexico were studied, one which was 15 percent Spanish-speaking and another that was 40 percent Spanish-speaking. The results of this study showed that there was a common feeling among school personnel that the "Spanish American" children were less capable of achieving in the schools, and that this lack was commonly perceived to be an inherent and innate lack of ability on the part of the "Spanish American" student rather than any failure due to inadequate school programs. The authors also concluded on the basis of their findings that this feeling of innate inferiority was commonly internalized by the minority groups themselves.—AP

9. Anderson, Theodore and Mildred Boyer, Bilingual Schooling in the United States. Austin, Texas: Southwest Educational Development Laboratory, 1970. 2 v. 292 pp. 327 pp.

This two-volume study is a comprehensive and up-to-date work on bilingualism in the United States. The study contains information on bilingual education programs, their history in the United States and other parts of the world, rationale and recommendations for planning such programs, possible curricula, and descriptions of bilingual programs now under way in the United States. A bibliography of nearly 900 entries is included.—AP

10. Angel, Frank. Program Content to Meet the Educational Needs of Mexican-Americans. New Mexico State University, Las Cruces, March, 1968. (Available through Educational Resources Information Center). 21 pp.

This paper, prepared for the National Conference on Education Opportunities for Mexican Americans held in Austin, Texas in 1968, describes five areas of an educational program which must be developed if Mexican Americans are to have a sound education. The author discusses in detail the following five areas: (1) the language needs of Mexican Americans and the use of English as a second language; (2) the problems of cognitive development, specifically in relation to Mexican Americans; (3) the needs for affective development, which, if left unattended, can lead to grave psychological damage; (4) the need for development of programs in inter-group relations; and (5) the necessity of improvement in occupational education programs which in the past have been inadequate for Mexican Americans. Central to all of these programs is the question of whether the program needs and content are to be identified and determined on the basis of Anglo or Mexican

American criteria.—AP

11. Bamford, Edwin. The Mexican Casual Problem in the Southwest, Journal of Applied Sociology, VIII (1924), 363-371.

In this article of the 1920's, the author discusses the following five general questions: (1) Why do Mexicans come to the United States? (2) What occupations do they enter and in which of these are they most efficient? (3) What American conditions tend to promote industrial instability among Mexican immigrant workers? (4) What traits do these immigrants possess, which, if properly developed, would tend to become effective in solving the Mexican casual problem? (5) Are Mexican immigrants economic and social assets or liabilities? The author tries to answer all of these questions, pointing out the failure of the socialization process to keep up with the process of industrialization as a probable cause for the instability of the Mexican immigrant. He says that while there were many who were concerned with promoting industrialization and the use of Mexicans as cheap labor for obvious economic advantages. There were few who were concerned with the socialization of the Mexican immigrant into American life. The author suggests that industry be required to bear the costs of improving the Mexican immigrant's condition, through night schools, community centers, visiting teachers, and social workers, thereby making the Mexican into an economic and social community asset.—AP

12. Barclay, Lisa F.K. The Comparative Efficacies of Spanish, English, and Bilingual Cognitive Verbal Instruction with Mexican-American Head Start Children. (PhD dissertation, Stanford University, 1969).

This dissertation is a report of an empirical study conducted by the author involving 67 Mexican American children enrolled in a 1967 summer Head Start program in Union City, California. The author posited two hypotheses: (1) that the use of a structured language training program, based upon psychological and linguistic foundations, would result in greater development as measured by appropriate tests than would the use of music and art activities for equal time periods; and (2) that a bilingual presentation of the above language training program would result in greater language development in English than would a presentation in either Spanish or English alone. The research was conducted with eight test groups of children and two bilingual teachers hired specifically for the project. A special 25-day bilingual language curriculum was designed specifically for the project, as well as some specific testing instruments to use in addition to the standard ones available. Extensive analysis of the pretest and posttest data, including one-way and two-way analysis of covariance, led the author to reject both hypotheses. Included in the dissertation are the author's review and comments on related research in bilingualism and preschool curricula. The 95-page bilingual language training curriculum designed for this study is appended as are the new testing instruments that were developed.—AP

13. Barnett, H.G. Innovation: The Basis of Cultural Change. New York: McGraw-Hill, 1953.

This book consists primarily of an attempt to formulate a theory of cultural change and of the individual and social circumstances involved therein. The data upon which the analysis is based are derived from a study of the cultures of five ethnic groups, Euro-American, three American Indian tribes, and the Palauans of Micronesia, and of one religious cult, the Indian Shakers. Innovation, i.e., thought or behavior that is new because it is qualitatively different from existing forms, takes place as a result of acute stress and dissatisfaction in the lives of individuals within a society. Evidence is presented which indicates that it is usually the deviant or maladjusted individuals who serve as innovators or who tend to accept innovations.—BM

14. Barrio, Raymond. The Plum Plum Pickers. Sunnyvale, Ventura Press, 1969. 201 pp.
This novel vigorously protests the exploitation of Mexican American migrant farm workers. The setting is Santa Clara County, California, and the plot line is composed of a series of vignettes depicting various representative characters: a Mexican American migrant family, the migrant camp foreman, the grower, and the young unmarried pickers. The author covers many aspects of migratory life, including camp conditions, aspirations for permanency, and problems in the Anglo-dominated schools.—CV

15. Beals, Ralph L. and Norman D. Humphrey. No Frontier to Learning: the Mexican Student in the United States. Minneapolis, University of Minnesota Press, 1957. 148 pp.
The authors studied the partial acculturation of the Mexican student in United States universities. They discuss the changes in the Mexican's opinions about the United States and in his basic attitudes and values as a result of contact with its culture. The authors base their study on interviews conducted primarily with Mexican students at the University of California at Los Angeles in 1952-53. One chapter of the book draws upon secondary sources to discuss the cultural values of the urban middle- and upper-classes in Mexico, and succeeding sections present the results of the authors' research. One of the concluding chapters focuses on the problems of readaptation which face the Mexican student on his return to his homeland.—RS

16. Bean, Walton. California: An Interpretive History. New York, McGraw-Hill, 1968. 533 pp.
This survey of California history treats topics about Spanish and Mexican Americans in the state. Exploration and settlement and early government are covered, and shorter sections deal with agri-business, the bracero program, and ethnic intolerance. Space limitations precluded treating any of the topics in depth.—RM

17. Beck, Warren A. New Mexico: A History of Four Centuries. Norman, University of Oklahoma Press, 1962, 363 pp.
This history of New Mexico is intended for readers who want a brief, yet reasonably comprehensive treatment of the development of the state. The narrative begins with a presentation of the geographical setting and its impact upon those who have made New Mexico their home. The story goes back to the time of the Spanish Conquistadores. It treats the Indian and Spanish heritage and the coming of the Anglo. Finally, it is an attempt to evaluate the meaning of the "new" New Mexico that has emerged in the second half of the twentieth century." This excerpt from the author's preface best describes his work. The history presented gives careful consideration to the cultural impact effected by the Spanish on the indigenous people as well as the impact of the Anglos on the Hispano. In addition, the author presents a basic study of New Mexico's political and economic development. He includes an extensive bibliography of books, articles, and unpublished theses on New Mexico on a wide range of topics covering almost every

historical period since the 16th century.—CV

18. Beegle, J. Allan, Harold F. Goldsmith and Charles P. Loomis. Demographic Characteristics of the United States-Mexican Border. Rural Sociology, XXV (March, 1960), 107-162.

This demographic study compares many characteristics of the populations on both sides of the border. The distribution of Spanish-surnamed persons in the five Southwestern states is plotted and comparisons are made between characteristics of the Anglo and Spanish-surnamed populations. Results of the survey include: the Spanish-surnamed population had more members under 20 years of age, a lower proportion married, higher fertility and unemployment rates. They were also more rural than Anglos in the Southwest. The typology of the Mexican border states was similar to the Spanish-surname population in the United States. The work is based on the 1950 census.—RM

19. Benedict, Ruth. Continuities and Discontinuities in Cultural Conditioning, in Clyde Kluckhohn and Henry A. Murray. Personality in Nature, Society, and Culture (2nd Edition). New York: Alfred A. Knopf, 1969, pp. 522-531.

This article deals with the way in which cultures handle the cycle of growth from infancy to adulthood and explains that there is no one single "natural" or "correct" path to maturity. What is necessary, the author states, is that social institutions and practices be developed which will provide continuity of conditioning and will thus prepare the child for the adult role which he will be expected to assume in a particular society. By way of contrast, discontinuities in cultural conditioning frequently serve as causal factors in the development of maladjustment and personality upheaval.—BM

20. Bergel, Dennis Eugene. Mexican Response to United States' Expansionism 1841-1848. Unpublished dissertation, Department of History, University of California, Berkeley, 1965.

This history treats the conditions under which Mexico went to war with the United States to stop the expansionism that threatened to cost Mexico most of her territory. The author sees the war as Mexico's ultimate but reluctant response to American expansionism. Mexico's inability to ward off American expansion was due to a number of factors, according to Berge. Of greatest significance was the ever-present internal disarray of Mexican politics which served to weaken the Mexican government. Mexicans, Berge argues, had little commitment to the government, though they harbored a fierce commitment to the nation. This dichotomy between nation and government caused a number of weaknesses to become part of the Mexican government at a time when Mexico most needed unity. The dichotomized loyalties were divisive rather than unifying. Loyalty was to religion, cultural regions or political ideologies—not to the strength-giving institution of government.—CV

21. Bodine, John J. A Tri-Ethnic Trap: The Spanish Americans in Taos, Spanish-Speaking People in the United States; Proceedings of the 1968 Annual Spring Meeting of the American Ethnological Society. Seattle, Distributed by the University of Washington Press, 1968. pp. 145-161.

This is a study of the social condition and position of the Hispano population in the Taos region of New Mexico. The superior position of the Hispanos to the

Indians is reversed in Taos because an Anglo artist colony is infatuated with the local Pueblo culture and denigrates that of the Hispano. Although the Hispanos effectively control local politics, Anglos see them as having the lowest group prestige and negative social attributes. The Anglos remain ignorant of the Hispano cultural heritage and allow their enthusiastic study of the Indian to give them a false picture of the community.—RM

22. Bogardus, Emory S. Racial Distance Changes in the United States During the Past Thirty Years, Sociology and Social Research. XLIV (November-December, 1959), 127-135.

The author compares data from survey research he conducted in 1926, 1946 and 1956 to measure "racial distance," or racial antipathy, between Anglos and over thirty different ethnic or racial groups, among them Mexican Americans and Mexicans. In all three surveys virtually the same questionnaire and the same list of racial and ethnic groups were used. The three national samples were similar in composition. The respondents were predominantly white and equally divided between college students and professionals—that is, they were primarily middle- and upper-middle-class, a fact that Bogardus perhaps did not emphasize sufficiently.

The racial distance of Mexicans from the Anglos in the author's samples increased between 1926 and 1946 but decreased between 1946 and 1956; their status rank order among more than thirty groups fell during both periods. The racial distance of Mexican Americans (Americans of Mexican parentage) from Anglos decreased between 1946 and 1956 and their rank order improved.

Other articles by the same author in Sociology and Social Research, XLIV (March-April, July-August, 1959), 286-290, 439-441, analyze the 1956 data in terms of race reactions by region and by sex and offer fuller tabular presentation of the results. Two earlier books and an article by Bogardus discuss the methodology and the results of the 1926 and 1946 surveys: The New Social Research, Los Angeles, Jesse Ray Miller, 1926; Immigration and Race Attitudes, San Francisco, D.C. Heath and Company, 1928; and "Changes in Racial Distances," International Journal of Opinion and Attitude Research, I (December, 1947), 58.—RS

23. Borah, Woodrow and Sherburne F. Cook. Marriage and Legitimacy in Mexican Culture: Mexico and California, California Law Review, LIV (May, 1966), 946-1008.

The first part of this article is a detailed history of marriage laws and patterns in Mexico. Examination of both official and unofficial patterns leads to the conclusion that irregular and informal unions and the consequent procreation of illegitimate children is characteristic of the rural and poor in Mexico. The second part of the study deals with marriage and legitimacy among Mexican Americans in California and is based on the welfare records of Santa Clara County. The authors conclude that the high rate of common law marriage can be attributed to cultural carry-over from Mexico. An appendix of relevant statistical tables accompanies this article.—LH

24. Bosch Garcia, Carlos. Historia De Las Relaciones Entre Mexico Y Los Estados Unidos 1819-1848. Mexico, D.F., Escuela Nacional De Ciencias Politicas y Sociales, UNAM, 1961. 293 pp.

This is a strongly documented history of the political relations between Mexico and the United States preceding the Texas annexation and the War with

Mexico of 1846. Bosch traces in detail the events precipitated by the American politics of Manifest Destiny and the Monroe Doctrine. According to Bosch, the American hunger for the northern territories of Mexico was as much a result of competition with Great Britain as of expansionist philosophies. It was economic entanglement and dependence on the United States by Mexico rather than its military weakness which made Mexico susceptible to the expansionist aims of the United States. The events which occurred within Mexico with its political crises and internal disunity are meshed with the events of diplomacy between the two countries to present a more complete picture of the conditions which resulted in a war in which Mexico lost more than half of its territory.

25. Blalock, Hubert M., Jr. Toward a Theory of Minority-Group Relations. New York: John Wiley & Sons, 1967.

Blalock uses a primarily sociological focus in an attempt to develop a systematic theory of minority-group relations, which he reduces in summary form to a list of 97 explicit theoretical propositions. Status consciousness and economic factors are discussed as being significant variables in different situations involving discrimination, leading usually to avoidance behavior. When the threat of competition is taken as the explanatory variable in discrimination, however, the discriminatory behavior is likely to entail more violence and direct injury to the minority. Blalock develops a power framework in which he conceives of race relations in terms of intergroup power contests involving four basic variables: (1) dominant-group resources, (2) dominant-group mobilization, (3) minority resources, and (4) minority mobilization. He notes specifically that without resources or power potential it is impossible to translate prejudice into effective discrimination, and that it is therefore fallacious to assume that theories of prejudice alone are sufficient to understand discrimination.—BM

26. Brim, Orville G., Jr. and Stanton Wheeler. Socialization After Childhood: Two Essays. New York, John Wiley and Sons, 1966. 113 pp.

The studies present a two-pronged approach focused on adult socialization. Both authors include a review of current literature and offer typologies to clarify research approaches.

Brim's essay examines individual personality responses to the socialization process. Consideration of conflict resolution, modes of deviance and control, and motivations for adult socialization (and resocialization) help place the individual within a social structure matrix. His concentration on self-concept is particularly useful for minority-oriented research.

The essay by Wheeler investigates socialization in large-scale bureaucratic organizations. Although the emphasis is on formal institutions, the theoretical framework applies to changes adults undergo in less structured acculturation. Wheeler's discussion of variables also raises questions about success and motivation in socialization processes.—PS

27. Buechley, Robert W. A Reproducible Method of Counting Persons of Spanish Surname, Journal of the American Statistical Association, LVI, No. 293 (March, 1961), 88-97.

One difficulty in establishing accurate statistics about the Spanish-surname population is the discrepancy between the proportion of the population represented by the researcher's sample and the proportion of the actual Spanish-surname group reported in Census data. Because of inaccurate or inadequate recording of Spanish surnames, researchers cannot always be positive their samples represent the total Spanish-surname population. The author proposes a method which, he believes, if adapted and expanded by the Bureau of the Census, would enable investigators to establish accurate statistical rates. Buechley developed a list of 306 of the most common Spanish-surnames in California and by statistical projection estimates the percentage of the total Spanish-surname population represented by persons having these names. Feeling intermarriage is an important indication of the cohesiveness of an ethnic group, Buechley drew his list from Spanish-surnamed women who married and bore children with Spanish surnames.—SD

28. Bullock, Paul. Employment Problems of the Mexican American, Industrial Relations, III (May, 1964), 37-50.

This is a survey of the employment status of the Mexican American compared to Negroes and Anglos. After a description of traditional Mexican culture and its hindrances to urban employment and social advance, the author turns to a statistical account of Mexican American labor. Bullock concludes that the Chicano is better off than the Negro and worse off than the Anglo in income and in employment. Despite a greater penetration into skilled and clerical positions, Chicanos do no better than Negroes in the high income professionals. The image of the Mexican American is that of a cheap, dependable laborer. Urban employers exploit them by taking advantage of language difficulties and lack of familiarity with their legal rights.—RM

29. Bullock, Paul and Robert Singleton. Some Problems in Minority-Group Education in the Los Angeles Public Schools, Journal of Negro Education, XXXII, No. 2 (Spring, 1963), 137-145.

School district zoning, dropout rates and transiency rates are considered in this study of Negro and Mexican American educational problems in Los Angeles. By encouraging "behavioral problems" to drop out or transfer and by failing to provide adequate counseling services, schools with large minority groups indirectly discriminate against their students. The authors call for increased public expenditures to improve the education of minority groups.—LH

30. Burma, John. The Civil Rights Situation of Mexican Americans and Spanish Americans, in Jitsuichi Masuoka and Preston Valien, Race Relations: Problems and Theory. Chapel Hill, University of North Carolina Press, 1961, 155-167.

This chapter surveys the status of Mexican Americans' and Hispanos' civil rights in the schools, politics, public facilities, economy, and social relations in the Southwest. In education, the author finds evidence of discrimination and segregation, but he believes it is declining. Burma expects slow progress in the political sphere as more Mexican Americans become politically active. In the other areas the author finds similar patterns; discrimination is present but gradually losing strength. Burma adopts Ruth Tuck's image of civil rights violations as a push with an elbow rather than a blow of the fist. It is therefore difficult to attack these violations directly. In the short run the author sees little change, but he feels many of the problems will be solved within twenty years.—RM

31. ——————. Interethnic Marriage in Los Angeles, 1948-1959, Social Forces, XLII (December, 1963), 156-165.

This study, based on marriage license records for Los Angeles County, focuses on marriages between whites and members of other racial groups: Negroes, Japanese, Chinese, Filipinos. The article presents data on intermarriage between Mexican Americans, classified as whites, and non-whites, but contains virtually nothing on marriages between Mexican Americans and Anglos.—RS

32. ——————————. Spanish-Speaking Groups in the United States. Durham, North Carolina, Duke University Press, 1954. 187 pp.

This is a sociological survey of the major Spanish-speaking groups in the United States. Mexican Americans are featured but the Hispanos of New Mexico, Filipinos and Puerto Ricans are also treated. Although occasionally lacking detailed descriptions, the author delineates the institutions of the Spanish-speaking: family, church, social structure and ethnic organizations. Burma also discusses prejudice, stock images, and acculturation. He includes an account of one aspect of traditional Hispano culture, the Penitente Brotherhood, an Indianized Christian fellowship combining Catholicism and indigenous religious forms.—RM

33. Busey, J. L. The Political Geography of Mexican Migration, Colorado Quarterly, II (Autumn, 1953), 181-190.

This essay attempts to suggest solutions to the problems of Mexican agricultural labor immigration. The first step would be recognition that the United States Southwest and the Mexican Northwest are part of a physical, climatic, and geographic unit which shares many cultural traits. The author wants the entire region to be developed by cooperative United States-Mexican government projects of internal improvements, land reclamation and irrigation. Busey feels this development would create a stronger Mexican economy enabling Mexican laborers to obtain good employment at home. The ensuing development would eliminate the need for low-salaried farm workers in the United States. Migration in the region would then be normal rather than a one-way mass movement.—RM

34. Bustamante, Charles J., and Patricia L. Bustamante. The Mexican-American and the United States. Mountain View, California: PATTY-LAR Publications, 1969. 60 pp.

This is a short intermediate level text dealing with historical background and contemporary issues pertaining to the Mexican American. The Bustamantes present a telescoped account of history which covers a time span from the beginnings of Spain, through the conquest of Mexico, the revolution and the establishment of the Mexican Republic, the Mexican American war, up to more recent history concerning the role of Mexican Americans through the depression and during the Second World War. In the final section of the publication, the authors discuss the problems of poverty, educational deprivation and discrimination in employment as they have emerged and as they now relate to Mexican Americans. The development of self-help organizations such as the CSO (Community Services Organization) is discussed, as well as some of the significant accomplishments they have brought about. Biographical sketches of effective leaders and their roles in these organizations are also included. Specifically, the role of Cesar Chavez, first as an organizer with the CSO and then as an organizer of farmworkers in the Delano area is outlined and presented as a prototype of leaders and organizers which are and will be involved in the "struggle for Mexican American rights and dignity."—BM

35. Cabrera, Y.A. A Study of American and Mexican-American Culture

Values and Their Significance in Education (Unpublished Ed.D. dissertation, University of Colorado, 1963), 359 pp.

This dissertation is an attempt to distinguish Mexican American culture value orientations from Anglo-American value orientations and to understand the nature of their conflicting differences and how they affect Mexican Americans in programs of education. The author believes that such a study could be used as a basis for planning curricula for Mexican Americans. He uses as a source of his information a review of the social science literature on cultural and ethnic value orientations, including works in psychology and education. He also reviews the literature on immigration to the United States, both immigration from Europe and from Mexico, and he points out several value assumptions that have been implicit in United States immigration policy. For Mexican American culture values the author relies heavily on a concept of a traditional folk culture and studies of rural life in Mexico, and he uses "a generalization applied to folk culture values considered to be held in common by persons of Mexican American or Spanish-speaking origin." Two conclusions central to his work are that needed changes in educational programs for Mexican American children are changes in emphasis rather than total curriculum revisions and also that there is a critical need for teachers with a sound understanding of American and Mexican culture values and with intensive training in the teaching of English as a foreign language. The appendix includes recommendations for an effective educational program for bilingual children and a basic oral vocabulary for Spanish-speaking children prior to the development of reading ability.—AP

36. Calderon, Carlos I. Put the Accent on Speech Errors, The Texas Outlook, XLIII (February, 1959), 26-28.

In this short article, the author is concerned with four mistakes in pronunciation of the English language commonly made by speakers whose native language is Spanish. The author provides specific suggestions and techniques for dealing with the following four common errors of pronunciation: (1) confusion of the b and v; (2) substitution of long u or oo sound for the sound of short u; (3) addition of e sound before the sp and st blends; (4) the addition of g before the w sound. The author believes that school teachers of bilingual students should attempt to correct these and other common speech errors because of the fact that children with pronunciation problems are often the objects of ridicule and also because there are obvious socioeconomic advantages in correct English pronunciation.—AP

37. California State Department of Education, California Plan for the Education of Migrant Children—Evaluation Report: 1968. Sacramento,California, 1969.

This report, written as required by the Federal government, is a general summary of the types of programs in California financed through Federal funds provided specifically to the state for the education of migrant children. Such programs include migrant teacher institutes, preschool programs, programs in English as a second language, nutritional and health activities, and programs which provide individual instruction to migrant children. The report provides a general description of each kind of program. It is evaluative only in the most general sense, citing only two case studies—and even here the results were inconclusive. The report also describes generally the interrelationships between the California Plan for Migrant Education and other Federal and State programs. It concludes with several recommendations, some of which include requests for more Federal funds, the lifting of the Federal limitation on the percentage of allocated funds which may be spent on program administrative costs, and the request for more lead-time from the government for the planning of programs.—AP

38. California State Department of Education, Nuevas Vistas—A Report of The Third Annual Conference of the California State Department of Education. Sacramento, California, 1970.

This is a report of a conference held in early 1969 on the education of Mexican Americans in California. It was initiated by the State Superintendent of Public Instruction and sponsored by the Mexican American Education Research Project. The report contains transcripts of several speeches delivered at the conference (including those of Eugene Gonzales, Manuel Guerra, and Ronald Reagan), progress reports on special educational projects and programs now under way in California, and reports of several workshops held at the conference. The report provides a summary of what the California State Department of Education takes to be its most significant and successful programs for the education of Mexican Americans.—AP

39. California State Department of Education, Racial and Ethnic Survey of California Public Schools. Part One: Distribution of Pupils, Fall, 1966. Part Two: Distribution of Employees, Fall, 1966. Sacramento, California, 1967.

These are reports of a survey made during the 1966-67 school year by the State Office of Compensatory Education. The reports contain data on the ethnic composition of pupils and personnel in California public schools. Information was collected on six racial and ethnic groups: (1) Spanish surname; (2) other white; (3) Negro; (4) Chinese, Japanese, and Korean; (5) American Indian; and (6) other nonwhite. The data were collected from school districts through county superintendents of schools, and they represent the student population in California public schools from the elementary through junior college levels. The information is broken down into ethnic composition according to size of school districts, grade levels, and by individual counties in California. It is the first comprehensive ethnic survey of California schools and all but six school districts are represented.—AP

40. California Department of Industrial Relations, Division of Fair Employment Practices. Californians of Spanish Surname. San Francisco, 1964. 54 pp.

This statistical survey compares the changing relationships of the Mexican American population with Anglos and nonwhites in numbers, employment, income and education. The data on changes are drawn from the 1950 and 1960 censuses. The Mexican Americans occupy a median position between Anglos and nonwhites in many of these categories, but their status is often only slightly more favorable than that of the nonwhites. The data focus on employment, vocations and income and yield some interesting information. For example, twice as many Mexican Americans were engaged in manufacturing as in farming.—RM

41. California Department of Industrial Relations, Division of Fair Employment Practices. Negroes and Mexican Americans in South and East Los Angeles. San Francisco, July, 1966. 39 pp.

This statistical survey is based on the special census of Los Angeles poverty areas after the Watts riot. The samples are too divergent in size and in percentages of ethnic groups surveyed to permit direct comparison between Negroes and Mexican Americans. However, the study shows that neither Negroes nor Mexican Americans shared a period of high general prosperity. Although their wages rose slightly and employment improved purchasing power declined. Erosion of family unity among Mexican Americans was indicated by the increasing percentages of married women living without their husbands.—RM

42. California Department of Justice, Division of Criminal Law and Enforcement, Guide to Community Relations for Peace Officers. n.p., March, 1958. 53 pp.

This pamphlet was prepared to educate law enforcement personnel in community and minority relations. It explores some common misunderstandings and erroneous ideas about minority groups and attempts basic explanations of the reasons for intergroup friction. The report also quotes a list of constitutional provisions relating to civil rights. A point-by-point rationale for concern with community relations and police image is presented. The bibliography of pertinent books, pamphlets, and audiovisual materials is also included.—PS

43. California. Mexicans in California: Report of Governor C.C. Young's Mexican Fact-Finding Committee. San Francisco, California, October 1930. 214 pp.

Although this report was officially the result of a select fact-finding committee, different portions were actually prepared by appropriate state departments. Material is organized for reference (e.g., agricultural and non-agricultural occupations are separate categories), and each topic is summarized. Sections of the report provide background on farm labor organization, including information on the cantaloupe pickers' strike in the Imperial Valley.—PS

44. California. Governor's Committee to Survey the Agricultural Resources of the San Joaquin Valley. Agricultural Labor in the San Joaquin Valley: Final Report and Recommendations. Sacramento, California, 1951. 402 pp.

This detailed state report covers many aspects of migratory farm labor problems. The report attempts to demonstrate the difficulties of reconciling the interests of the growers in an inexpensive, plentiful labor supply and the desires of the migrants for better working and living conditions.

The committee based their recommendations on research conducted by various state departments as well as on suggestions that emerged from a series of public hearings. In the conclusion, they recommended stabilization of the labor supply. Specific recommendations included strengthening controls over labor contractors, extension of unemployment insurance "if a feasible plan can be presented," regulations to upgrade housing standards and state assistance and intercountry cooperation in extending welfare benefits.—SD

45. California State Advisory Committee to the United States Commission on Civil Rights. Education and the Mexican-American Community in Los Angeles,n.p., April, 1968. 28 pp.

This report records the text of a hearing held in Los Angeles on educational facilities for Mexican Americans. Chicanos complained that the schools were inadequate for their needs and were unconcerned with Mexican American problems. The teachers were characterized as the rejects of the school system and criticized for being indifferent to their students and unable to speak Spanish. The school testing and placement facilities were labelled unfair since they were designed to test middle-class Anglo students and did not allow for cultural differences. Finally, it was alleged that local schools did not support special programs; while dependent on federal money to finance such programs, they made little effort to obtain these funds.—RM

46. Campa, Arthur L. Treasure of the Sangre de Cristos: Tales and Traditions of the Spanish Southwest. Norman, Oklahoma, University of Oklahoma Press, 1963. 210 pp.
This volume collects stories ranging in time from the Spanish explorations to the near-present. The tales recount legends of lost treasures and the men who searched for them. Recurring themes are discovery, tragedy, a dead man's map, and unsuccessful attempts to find the lost mine. Other folklore of New Mexico is interspersed with the stories of searches for gold.—RM

47. Cardenas, Leonard, Jr., Trends and Problems of Urbanization in the United States-Mexico Border Area, in Ellwyn R. Stoddard. Comparative U.S.-Mexico Border Studies, Border-State University Consortium for Latin America, Occasional Papers, No. 1, pp. 39-54.
The highest rate of population growth in Mexico is recorded in Mexico City, followed by the northern tier of states bordering the United States, specifically the urban centers next to the border itself. The 1950-1960 national population growth for Mexico was 34% whereas nine Mexican municipalities bordering the United States recorded an average population increase of 83% during the same time period. It is suggested that the attraction of these border municipalities to the migrant from the interior may be the common border with the United States and the possibility of economic improvement that it offers. The main problems which face governmental administration as a result of the constant influx of migrants into these areas are said to be housing, public services, and employment. Cardenas emphasizes the interdependence of the border cities, and states the fact that the problems of either side automatically become the shared problem of the other.—BM

48. Carlson, Hilding B. and Norman Henderson. The Intelligence of American Children of Mexican Parentage, Journal of Abnormal and Social Psychology, XLV (1950), 544-551.
This study contrasts intelligence scores of United States children of Mexican and non-Mexican parentage. The authors conclude that despite all controls devised, environmental factors still could have accounted for the relatively higher scores of the children of non-Mexican parentage. Parental background (rural-urban) and vocabulary (English-Spanish) were uncontrolled for the Mexican American children. Efforts were made, however, to control the effects of environment (rural-urban), total cultural context, amount and quality of the formal education of children and parents, inadequate diet, examiner prejudice, educational motivation, and variation due to the different age levels of the children.—LH

49. Carranza, Eliu. Pensamientos on los Chicanos: A Cultural Revolution. Berkeley, California, California Book Co., Ltd., 1969. 29 pp.
This is a series of essays setting forth the origins, reasons, and goals of the growing Chicano movement. Carranza advocates conscious rejection of the "shallow and hypocritical Anglo-white set of values" and a reevaluation of Mexican

American cultural precepts. His alternative is a New Humanism, with Chicanos engaging freedom and truth in their lives. Carranza says that this search for an honesty not found in Anglo society will encompass a re-thinking of accepted Mexican American traditions and creation of new educational forms based on individual respect.

In the concluding essay, the author makes a plea for communication among members of la raza. There should be unity without an accompanying loss of diversity of opinion.—PS

50. Carreno, Alberto Maria. Mexico Y Los Estados Unidos de America: Apuntaciones para la Historia del Acrecemiento Territorial de los Estados Unidos a Costa de Mexico Desde la Epoca Colonial hasta Nuestros Dias. Mexico, Editorial Jus S.A., 1962. 420 pp.

This is a brief history of how on a number of occasions, Mexico has lost various territories to the United States. The history begins with the acquisition by the United States of territories in dispute during the settlements of the boundary of the Louisiana Purchase, and moves on to the case of the Texas "Revolution" and the War with Mexico in 1846. Also included in this history is the case of the "Chamizal" which caused strained diplomatic relations between the two countries for many years.

More than just a historical narrative of the events surrounding the losses of territories to the United States, this work also contains material which deals with the protocol involved in the exchanges. Two cases in particular receive such coverage: the War of 1846 and the Chamizal dispute. In addition to using official government sources (especially Mexican), Carreno also relies on personal documents of the principal actors involved from both governments.—CV

51. Carter, Hugh and Bernice Doster. Residence and Occupation of Naturalized Americans from Mexico, United States Immigration and Naturalization Service Monthly Review, VIII (October, 1950), 47-53.

In this continuation of an earlier study of Mexicans naturalized in 1949, residence and occupation are considered. Half of the naturalized Mexicans lived in California and one-fourth settled in Texas; of these, 70% were living in metropolitan areas. The authors also concluded that naturalized Mexicans were generally more skilled than aliens.—LH

52. ————————. Social Characteristics of Naturalized Americans from Mexico: Age and Marital Status, United States Immigration and Naturalization Service Monthly Review, VIII (September, 1950), 35-39.

This is the first of three studies by the authors on recently naturalized Mexicans. The data for this study are based on a representative sample (20%) of those naturalized in 1949. The survey respondents were found to be younger than other aliens, having entered the United States as children rather than as young adults. There were more Mexican men than women entering the United States.—LH

53. Carter, Thomas P. Mexican Americans in School: A History of Educational Neglect. New York, College Entrance Examinations Board, 1970. 235 pp.

This study is intended as a resource text for educational researchers, teachers, administrators, and anyone else interested in the education of Mexican Americans. The author divides his study into six areas: (1) a history of problems and influences, (2) failure of the culture, (3) the default of the school, (4) Mexican

American reactions to school and community, (5) special school programs for Mexican American children, and (6) where to from here? In addition to reviewing most of the significant literature on the education of Mexican Americans, the present work is a substudy of the UCLA Mexican American Study Project and contains the author's interpretations of over 250 formal interviews that he conducted with school people and his comments on observations he made while visiting schools throughout the Southwest. A 180-item bibliography is included.—AP

54. ——————————. The Negative Self-Concept of Mexican-American Students, School and Society, XCVI (March 30, 1968), 217-219.

In this article the author challenges the assumption held by many educators who deal with Mexican-American children that the group contains a larger than normal percentage of individuals who view themselves negatively. His challenge is based on the results of an empirical study that he conducted in a school district in California with several junior high schools and one high school. The students in the schools were sixty-five percent Mexican American, and the parents of many of these were low-paid agricultural workers. Based on interviews with students, teachers, parents, and administrators and three sets of socio-psychological instruments designed to measure self-concept, Carter concluded that there was nothing to support the belief that Mexican American students saw themselves more negatively than Anglo students. This was in spite of the obvious fact that teachers and administrators believed them to be inferior and concluded that they saw themselves that way. The author suggests that, at least in the community he studied, the valid community for the Mexican American—the one that supports and maintains the individual and his self-concept—was his ethnic peer group or the adult Mexican American community or both. Carter also suggests that the too ready acceptance of such notions as the negative self-concept of Mexican Americans serves to protect educators from the in-depth examination of other problems relative to the success or failure of Mexican Americans in the schools.—AP

55. Casavantes, Edward J. A New Look at the Attributes of the Mexican-American. Albuquerque, New Mexico, Southwest Cooperative Education Laboratory, 1969. 15 pp.

Casavantes contends that studies of Mexican Americans confuse the effects of socioeconomic class and the effects of ethnicity in determining behavior. Many anthropologists are not describing Chicano culture, but rather the culture of poverty. He cites a study by Cohen and Hodges which compared the attitudes of lower-class Blacks, Anglos, and Chicanos and found no significant difference in their value systems. The value systems included emphasis on extended families, conservatism, non-innovation, anti-intellectualism, machismo, inability to postpone gratification, a dependence on physical force, and fatalism. Since 33% of the Mexican American population lives below poverty level, many of them share these values.

The author goes on to argue that this stereotype has been adopted by many Mexican Americans, especially militants, who believe that a Mexican American who adopts a middle-class style of life cannot be a true Chicano. Casavantes feels that this belief is a dysfunctional element in the Chicanos' attempt to demand their rights and better themselves. He stresses the differing life-styles of United States' Spanish-speaking groups and insists that they primarily share a tradition of Catholicism, the Spanish language, and a tendency toward dark eyes, hair and complexions. Chicanos should be free to adopt any life-style they choose without fear of losing their identities.—RM

56. Caskey, Owen L., ed. Guidance Needs of Mexican American Youth. Proceedings of the First Invitational Conference (November 10, 1967, Lubbock, Texas). Austin, Texas: Southwest Educational Development Laboratory, 1967. 87 pp.

This is a collection of the papers presented at the First Invitational Conference held in Lubbock, Texas, in 1967. The first part contains six major papers, the second part contains two reports on the educational and social factors which influence the Mexican American child, and the third part is a report of a symposium concerned with special problems and approaches in working with Mexican American children. The six papers of the first part are as follows:

Caskey, Owen L. "Guidance Needs of Mexican American Youth—An Introduction." (1-10)

Angel, Frank. "The Education of the Mexican American in the Southwest." (11-26)

Steglich, Winfred. "Sociocultural Characteristics of the Mexican American Student in the Southwest." (27-54)

Kirby, W.N. "The Mexican American Preschool Child." (55-62)

Webb, Doris J. "Counseling with Mexican American Children." (63-74)

Martinez, Mary. "The School Social Worker in the Mexican American Community." (75-87)—AP

57. Castañeda, Carlos E., trans. The Mexican Side of the Texan Revolution. Dallas, P.L. Turner Co., 1928. 378 pp.

Castañeda has collected diaries and depositions from Mexican leaders prominent in the Texas Revolution. The selections include accounts from Santa Ana, Martínez Caro, Filisola, Urrea, and Tornel y Mendivil. The translation and notes were prepared by an early Hispano scholar who concludes that these records prove Mexican dissension and personal envy played a more important role than Texan courage in causing Mexico's defeat.—RM

58. Castillo, Guadalupe, and Herminio Rios. Toward a True Chicano Bibliography: Mexican-American Newspapers: 1848-1942, El Grito, III (Summer, 1970), 17-24.

This listing of 193 Mexican American newspapers in publication between 1848 and 1942, in the states of Arizona, California, Colorado, New Mexico, and Texas, demonstrates the existence of a significant amount of recorded history relative to Mexican Americans. The authors suggest that these records represent a previously unrecognized but extremely important source of information concerning the political, economic, social, and artistic history of the Mexican American people, and they are presently working on an attempt to extend the bibliography to include all Mexican American newspapers published during the period from 1937 to 1970.—BM

59. Chala, John Elac. The Employment of Mexican Workers in U.S. Agriculture, 1900-1960; A Binational Economic Analysis. PhD. dissertation, University of California, Los Angeles, 1961.

This study is an economic analysis of Mexican agricultural workers in the United States, a situation viewed by the author as a case of international labor mobility on a binational basis. Chala identifies the political aspects of economic supply and demand for agricultural labor and subjects the data to an economic analysis which is presented in numerous tables. The origins and magnitude of Mexican migration to the United States are discussed. The author describes how the Mexicans who crossed the border for employment reasons have been affected by the changes in specific immigration policies dealing with Mexico. Mexican policy on immigration is also considered. The changing structure of American agriculture is examined, especially with respect to regional crop specialization, involving production techniques, and employment patterns. The labor force in agriculture is treated historically to emphasize the rising relative importance of Mexican workers in the 1950's, particularly in the west. The composition of the farm work force is considered in some detail. Finally, the employment of Mexican workers is related to agricultural policy.—LN

60. Chandler, Charles Ray. The Mexican American Protest Movement in Texas. Unpublished PhD dissertation, Department of Sociology, Tulane University, 1968.
According to the author, the purpose of this study is more to describe than to analyze the Mexican American protest movement of Texas up to 1967. Using an historical perspective, he begins with the founding of the League of United Latin American Citizens (LULAC) in 1929 and takes us through the formation of PASSO (Political Association of Spanish-Speaking Organizations) which resulted from the 1960 Viva Kennedy clubs. Although he mentions some of the newer "militant" organizations, the scope of his work does not actually enter into the period in which groups such as Mexican American Youth Organization (M.A.Y.O.) and La Raza Unida Party begin to take important roles in Chicano politics in Texas. Chandler sees the goals of the Mexican American movement prior to 1967 as generally consisting of the following basic three objectives: (1) the retention of Mexican culture, (2) the elimination of prejudice and discrimination against Mexican Americans, and (3) the improvement of employment, educational, health, and housing opportunities until they are equal to the level of those of the Anglo. He portrays the ideology of the movement as liberal reformist resorting to tactics of direct action. By extensive use of personal interviews, newspaper accounts, organizational files and as participant observer, he presents a descriptive analysis of a regional minority protest movement.—CV

61. Chavarria, Jesus. A Précis and a Tentative Bibliography on Chicano History, Aztlan I (Spring, 1970), 133-141.
This précis and tentative bibliography treats history as the discipline central to the concept of Chicano studies. In this article, the author presents a chronological outline of the history of the Chicano from his mesoamerican origins to the present, with a corresponding bibliography of the major works of significance to Chicano history.—AP

62. Chicano Coordinating Council on Higher Education, El Plan de Santa Barbara—A Chicano Plan for Higher Education. Oakland, California, La Causa Publications, 1969. 155 pp.
This is a plan for higher education drawn by a delegation of Chicano students, scholars, administrators, and community representatives who met in Santa Barbara, California in 1969. It contains sections on organizing and instituting Chicano Studies programs, position papers on recruitment and admissions, political action, campus organizing, and the relationship of the university to the Chicano

community. The appendix contains sample proposals for Chicano Studies programs at the junior college and college levels, with sample curricula and detailed course descriptions. The plan is prefaced by a manifesto emphasizing Chicano self-determination and the common struggle of all Chicanos in the dominant Anglo society.—AP

63. Christian, Jane and Chester Christian, Jr. Spanish Language and Culture in the Southwest, in Joshua A. Fishman, et al., Language Loyalty in the United States; the Maintenance and Perpetuation of Non-English Mother Tongues by American Ethnic and Religious Groups. The Hague, Morton and Co., 1966, pp. 280-317.

This article argues in favor of bilingual education for Spanish-speaking people in the Southwest. The authors contend that Mexican Americans often are not motivated to seek education because they find Anglo middle-class values—those inculcated in most United States schools—distasteful and alien. Anglo educators, the authors suggest, must realize that bilingual education oriented to the aspirations and interests of Mexican Americans would be the best way to eliminate the gap in education between Anglos and the Spanish-speaking. In addition, they argue, bilingual education would contribute to the vital diversity of United States society by preserving the Spanish language and "Hispanic" culture. The authors' discussion of "Hispanic" values draws on literary and linguistic sources from both Mexico and Spain.—RS

64. Christiansen, Ted and Gary Livermore. A Comparison of Anglo-American and Spanish-American Children on the WISC, The Journal of Social Psychology, LXXXI (June, 1970), 9-14.

This article is a report of a comparative study of groups of lower- and middle-class Anglo-American children and similar groups of Spanish American children, and their performance on the Wechsler Intelligence Scale for Children. The study examined both social class and ethnic origin as variables in the development of specific verbal and nonverbal factors of intelligence. Four groups of 23 thirteen- and fourteen-year-old students enrolled in regular public school classes were studied. The authors found that social class was a more important factor in differentiation among their subjects on WISC measures than was ethnic origin. They also found, however, that ethnic origin was a significant factor with respect to the subjects' performance on WISC measures of general intelligence, retention of verbal knowledge from previous experience, and ability to use verbal skills in new situations. They suggest that these lower scores of Spanish Americans might be attributed to the bilingual nature of the typical Spanish American home, where it is more difficult for these students to acquire many of the verbal skills needed in an Anglo culture.—AP

65. Citizens' Committee for the Defense of Mexican American Youth. The Sleepy Lagoon Case. Los Angeles, California, published by the Citizens' Committee, 1943. 24 pp.

In an internationally publicized court trial in 1942 in Los Angeles, 17 Chicanos were convicted for the murder of another young Mexican American in a gathering place known as the "Sleepy Lagoon." This pamphlet was published by the Citizens' Committee for the Defense of Mexican American Youth to arouse sympathy for the defendants and to raise money for the court fight which eventually reversed their convictions on the grounds of insubstantial evidence. The trial took place under the racial tensions that erupted in Los Angeles during World

War II, and the pamphlet was an attempt to counteract the sensational propaganda that had been circulated about the zoot suiter gangs of Mexican American youths.

The Committee appealed to wartime desires for unity with Latin America, and charged that the tensions had been created by Axis fifth column agents and their sympathizers to divide the Allies. The pamphlet includes quotes from speeches by Presidents Roosevelt and Camacho about the common heritage shared by Mexico and the United States, and examines police attitudes.—SD

66. Clark, Margaret. Health in the Mexican-American Culture. Berkeley, University of California Press, 1959. 239 pp.

This is an anthropological study conducted to improve public health agency service to Mexican Americans. It is based on research in the Sal si Puedes barrio in San Jose, California. The first section is a survey of Chicano community life: origins of the populace, education, literacy, employment, religious experience and family life. Clark then studies attitudes toward folk medicine and Anglo medical practices. The recommendations in the concluding sections focus primarily on the need to improve communications. Some barrio conditions create barriers to communication; residents who speak Spanish or are illiterate in both Spanish and English require Spanish speakers on agency staffs and non-technical medical instructions. Clark proposes that personnel who provide medical services to Chicanos study the Mexican American culture. The author also recommends financial assistance to help Chicanos pay for expensive treatments. Clark stresses the need for reconciling modern medical practice with folk beliefs and emphasizes the respect that should be accorded to herbal medicine. Finally, the author points out that the pragmatism of the Mexican American would enable him to accept Anglo medicine if its efficacy was demonstrated.—RM

67. Clark y Moreno, Joseph A. Bibliography of Bibliographies Relating to Mexican American Studies, El Grito, III (Summer, 1970), 25-31.

This bibliography consists of a listing of 89 bibliographies which deal both specifically and generally with Mexican American studies, and which draw upon works published from 1928 through 1970.—BM

68. Cleland, Robert G. The Cattle on a Thousand Hills: Southern California 1850-1870. San Marino, California, The Huntington Library, 1941. 315 pp.

This book is an economic and social narrative history of Southern California during the last days of the pastoral society. It deals mainly with the challenge to the California way of life posed by Anglo customs and the ultimate conversion of the great ranchos into farms and settlements. Beginning with a study of the 1784 land grants, the author traces the rancheros' careers through secularization, the United States' conquest and the rise and fall of the cattle boom of the 1850's. By the time the pastoral economy collapsed, most Californios had already been ruined and trade was controlled by Anglos.—RM

69. Coalson, George O. Mexican Contract Labor in American Agriculture, Southwestern Social Science Quarterly, XXXIII (December, 1952), 228-238.

Coalson discusses the bracero program from its inception in 1942 to 1951. The article focuses on the international agreements and the domestic legislation which regulated the program. The 1951 bill which was designed to implement previous agreements between the United States and Mexico receives particular attention.—RS

70. Cohen, Albert K. and Harold M. Hodges. Characteristics of the Lower Blue Collar Class, Social Problems, X (Spring, 1963), 303-333.

The authors studied characteristics of male heads of families in the lower-lower class. They conclude that Mexican American and Negro responses to value questions did not differ significantly from the responses of the Anglo participants. Since all interviewees were close to the border of the poverty line, the authors argued that the common attributes could be due to the respondents' similar economic status. Characteristics shared by the different groups included: preference for the traditional, fear of innovation, anti-intellectualism, male authoritarianism and a pervasive fatalism. This article attempts to counter theories which argue that traditional Mexican folk culture is the source of Chicano attributes.—RS

71. Coleman, James S., et al., Equality of Educational Opportunity. Washington, D.C.: U.S. Department of Health, Education, and Welfare, Office of Education, 1966.

This is an often-quoted and somewhat controversial 700-page study commissioned by the government as part of the Civil Rights Act of 1964. Although concerned primarily with Negro Americans, the commission also compiled data on four other minority groups, including Mexican Americans. The commission took as its goals the discovery of the extent of segregation of racial and ethnic groups in the public schools, the levels of equal educational opportunities, the measurement by standardized achievement tests of how much minority-group students learned, and the discovery of the possible relationship between students' achievement and the kinds of schools they attend. Included in the study is a massive collection of data on school conditions, student and teacher attitudes and backgrounds, levels of achievement by students in different kinds of schools, and the differences in achievement among students whose native language is not English.—AP

72. Colorado. Governor's Survey Committee on Migrant Labor.n.p., Denver, 1951. 72 pp.

The Committee examined: (1) the recruitment, availability and need for seasonal farm labor in Colorado and (2) the adequacy of state legislation protecting the housing, educational, health and welfare status of migrant workers. "Considerable evidence" was found that neither local workers nor outside agricultural laborers were fully utilized. The Committee recommended complete coordination of job offers and seekers through the Department of Employment Security. The sketchy outline of migrant living conditions which emerges is bleak: Colorado had no housing law which would enforce minimum sanitation standards; no health facilities were available except limited experimental programs; migrants were ineligible for welfare because of residency requirements and county welfare budgets were so limited they could not cover even "dire emergencies." Education for migrant children was found "theoretically available but practically non-existent" because even if a school had adequate physical facilities it did not have the staff and resources to provide a meaningful educational program. This brief report has interest because, in spite of political pressures and lack of funds, time and resources, the problems identified and the recommendations made appear repeatedly in studies of migrant workers.—SD

73. Cooke, W. Henry. The Segregation of Mexican-American School Children

in Southern California, School and Society, LXVII (June 5, 1948), 417-421.

This article begins with a review of the background of the segregation of Mexican Americans by school districts in California. The author cites several ways that school districts have traditionally gone about segregating their Mexican American pupils into separate schools. The major part of the article is a description of the conditions in Orange County, California, leading to a court suit in 1946 on behalf of Mexican American children against four Orange County school districts (Mendez, et al., vs. Westminster School District, et al.). The author carefully describes the Federal District Court decision in favor of the Mexican American children on the grounds that they were denied "equal protection of the laws." The author further describes the Court of Appeals opinion affirming the decision of the Federal District Court. He quotes the opinions of the judges in both cases, and discusses the impact of the final 1947 decisions making it illegal to segregate any ethnic group in California.—AP

74. Copp, Nelson Gage. Wetbacks and Braceros: Mexican Migrant Laborers and American Immigration Policy, 1930-1960. PhD dissertation, Boston University, 1963.

This study treats Mexican agricultural workers in relation to United States immigration history and policy. The author focuses his discussion on the development of federal government policy specifically designed to deal with Mexican agricultural workers. He surveys the social and economic conditions in Mexico and the United States during the period studied and indicates reasons for the migration of Mexican workers. He discusses the public hostility and discrimination toward Mexican workers (wetbacks and braceros) and American citizens of Mexican descent. The author expresses concern about the possible ethnic and cultural changes in the United States which may be effected by an immigration policy which allows a continuous sizeable influx of Mexicans.—LN

75. Córdova, Ignacio R. The Relationship of Acculturation, Achievement, and Alienation Among Spanish American Sixth Grade Students. Las Cruces, New Mexico, Educational Resources Information Center, New Mexico State University, February, 1969. 24 pp.

Viewing the school as the most important socializing force in United States society, Córdova examines the relationship between acculturation, achievement, teacher expectations and the alienation of Spanish American students. A study of 477 children from 16 schools indicates that low assimilation leads to low achievement and subsequently to negative self-concepts. These factors interact with poor teacher-pupil relationships to alienate Spanish American students, further limiting their achievement potential. The most alienated are students with high socioeconomic status and a high degree of acculturation. Acculturation does not equal increased achievement. In fact, "alienation is not bred by a lack of achievement, but rather by cultural conflicts, confusion, insecurity, and meaninglessness. Low achievement is only a symptom of alienation." Elimination of the language barrier, then, is not enough, the author argues. Psychological readiness of students is as important to learning as are technical skills. Córdova concludes that educators must radically alter the school system to permit biculturalism.—PS

76. Crawford, Fred R. The Forgotten Egg. Austin, Texas, State Department of Public Health, 1961. 43 pp.

This is a study of parents' awareness of possible mental health problems among their first grade school children. Spanish-speaking nurses conducted the survey in a middle-class Mexican American neighborhood in San Antonio. The researchers also wanted to learn the degree of Mexican American acceptance of the neighborhood clinic. They found that Mexican American families and Anglo teachers and nurses shared many of the same attitudes about child behavior patterns. The decrease in the treatment of mental problems by Mexican folk healers was not as great as the decline in the treatment of physical ailments by the curanderos. Compared to problem children, those without mental disorders came from more cohesive families with greater parental control and shared parental responsibilities. The survey also found that the local medical center was accepted and used by 75% of the inhabitants.—RM

77. Cue Canovas, Agustin. Los Estados Unidos y El Mexico Olvidado. Mexico D.F., 1970. 157 pp.
This is a history of the political lives of those Mexicans who found themselves in American territory after the Mexican War. It is a legal history of the loss of millions of acres of land by Spanish surname residents of New Mexico, Colorado, Utah, Arizona, California and Texas. The history begins with the signing of the Treaty of Guadalupe Hidalgo (1848) and the protocol involved in establishing the treaty as legal justification for what the author sees as a robbery of legally owned land by numerous breaches of the Treaty of 1848.
The author focuses on the loss of land by Mexican landholders in New Mexico and California and ends with a brief mention of the beginning stages of the Alianza movement in New Mexico. The appendix includes historical documents of land claims and indictment of land fraud.—CV

78. Daniels, Roger and Harry H.L. Kitano. American Racism: Exploration of the Nature of Prejudice. Englewood Cliffs, New Jersey: Prentice-Hall, 1970.
Daniels and Kitano employ a sociological perspective in an examination of patterns of racism in America, specifically in California, where prejudice has been directed toward Indians, Mexicans, Chinese, Japanese, Filipinos, and Negroes. Their view of race relations is explained as being based on the existence of a two-category system of stratification: white and nonwhite, in which all whites are viewed as superior to nonwhites. They analyze the structures and institutions that have been developed to maintain the two-category system, i.e. the beliefs, attitudes, organizations, and mechanisms such as the legal system, labor unions, mass media, educational systems, etc., which have supported distinctions between races. The underlying motivations of prejudice are explored, the groups and cultures against which prejudice is directed are systematically analyzed, and a history of racism in California is presented. Speculations concerning the future are also presented, outlining the possibilities either for rational solutions to the problem of prejudice, or for totalitarian, racist solutions.—BM

79. D'Antonio, William V. and William H. Form. Influentials in Two Border Cities: A Study in Community Decision-Making. Notre Dame, Indiana, University of Notre Dame Press, 1965. 273 pp.
This is a comparative study of decision-making and leadership in the twin border cities of El Paso, Texas and Ciudad Juárez, Chihuahua during the 1950's. The authors combine the two most common research methodologies in community power studies: they first identify the people who are reputed to have influence in

each city; then, they trace the process of decision-making on a number of important community issues to determine what role the reputed influentials and others actually played.

The authors found that in El Paso a pluralistic pattern of decision-making prevailed; those who were most influential in one issue area were not necessarily the most influential in others. Nonetheless, pluralism in El Paso seemed to operate only within a small, relatively cohesive community of leaders; the people who were most influential on each issue studied tended to be among the reputed influentials identified early in the book. These people were primarily either members of the business and professional community or current or former high political office holders. In Ciudad Juárez, contrary to El Paso, a cleavage existed between business and political leaders. Businessmen had influence on important community issues but they tended to be much less influential than political leaders. The latter, working with the resources of the official government party, the Partido Revolucionario Institucional, had strong support on the local level and close ties with national politicians.

The authors found that in El Paso the Mexican American population, largely unorganized and culturally unassimilated, had little impact on community decision-making. They do note, however, that with the development of Mexican American political clubs and other voluntary organizations in the 1960's the political impact of Mexican Americans seemed to be growing. They foresaw a continued development of pluralism in El Paso as the Mexican American population becomes less poor, better educated and better organized.—RS

80. ——————————, and Julian Samora. Occupational Stratification in Four Southwestern Communities: A Study of Ethnic Differential Employment in Hospitals, Social Forces, XLI (October, 1962), 17-25.

This attempt to measure the degree of assimilation of Spanish-surname people in the Southwest used occupational mobility in the field of health as an indicator. The authors analyzed the distribution of Spanish-surname personnel in the occupational hierarchies of ten hospitals in four cities: San Diego, Tucson, El Paso and Las Cruces, New Mexico. There tended to be proportionately more Spanish-surname people than Anglos in lower rank occupations, and proportionately fewer in higher rank positions. Nonetheless, the authors conclude that their findings do not entirely support the extremely pessimistic views of some researchers about the slow rate of assimilation of the Spanish-surname population into United States society. The authors feel that the rate of assimilation has increased in recent years and cite as important mechanisms of integration the economic and social impact of World War II, the increasing urbanization of the Spanish-surname population and the role of some Catholic institutions (for example, hospitals).—RS

81. Darcy, Nancy T. Bilingualism and the Measure of Intelligence: Review of a Decade of Research, The Journal of Genetic Psychology CIII (December, 1963), 259-282.

This article is a review of the significant literature on the relationship between bilingualism and the measurement of intelligence published during the decade 1953-1963. The author concentrates primarily on studies of Spanish-English and Welsh-English bilinguals. A section of the report is devoted to problems in research with bilingual subjects, such as divergent definitions of bilingualism, determining degrees of bilingualism, isolation of the bilingual influence from other environmental factors, and the relationship of language to conceptual thinking. The results of the studies that the author reviewed led her to conclude that bilingualism is not uniform as to kind and that a far greater amount of research is needed before one might be able to predict the influence of bilingualism on individuals of different races and in different environments. The author found that variables which might influence such studies, such as degree of bilingualism, socioeconomic status, and time limits on testing, were beginning to be taken into account by researchers during the decade under review. The author calls for more carefully controlled research, some of which should be longitudinal in nature. A 43-item bibliography is appended.—AP

82. De Hoyos, Arturo, Occupational and Educational Levels of Aspiration of Mexican-American Youth. (PhD dissertation, Michigan State University, 1961).

This is a study conducted by the author in Lansing, Michigan with 91 Mexican American teenage males. The author investigated the relationship between occupational and educational levels of aspiration to such factors as socioeconomic status and level of acculturation to American society. He made the general hypothesis that for the Mexican American youth of Lansing, Michigan, the levels of occupational and educational aspiration were positively correlated to their level of acculturation to the dominant society, and that these two variables in turn were also positively correlated to socioeconomic status. The author verified this hypothesis on the basis of the results of his investigation. The model that he used to determine levels of acculturation was based on three areas of behavior: language behavior, social participation, and orientation to certain achievement values. The author also found that the social experience of Mexican Americans in this area was quite different to that of Mexican Americans in the Southwest, especially with regard to school and residential segregation and employment opportunities.—AP

83. Demos, George D. Attitudes of Student Ethnic Groups on Issues Related to Education, California Journal of Educational Research, XI (November, 1960), 204-206.

This is a brief report of an investigation conducted by the author in an attempt to determine whether or not significant attitudinal differences toward eduation existed between Mexican American and Anglo-American pupils. The author's sample consisted of three groups of 105 secondary school students. The first group was broken down into three subgroups of randomly selected Mexican American students, 35 from the seventh-eighth grades, 35 from the ninth-tenth grades, and 35 from the eleventh-twelfth grades. The second group of 105 consisted of Anglo students similarly broken down into subgroups of 35. The third group consisted of 105 Anglo students matched with the Mexican American sample across age, sex, grade, social class, and IQ. A 29-item attitude scale was developed and administered using a 5-interval scale, and statistical methods of chi-square and analysis of variance were utilized to interpret the results. The author found that significant differences in attitudes toward education do exist between Mexican American and Anglo pupils. Even in comparing the matched groups, the author found significant differences in six areas. He also concluded that in almost every case the Anglo American students exhibited the more "desirable" attitudes. The author concludes with several recommendations for school practices, including suggestions on how to change the "undesirable" attitudes of Mexican American pupils.—AP

84. Derbyshire, Robert L. Adolescent Identity Crisis in Urban Mexican Americans in East Los Angeles, in Eugene B. Brody (ed.), Minority Group Adolescents in the United States. Baltimore, Maryland, Williams & Wilkins Co., 1968. pp. 73-110.

In this paper the author examines the effects of the simultaneous membership of young Mexican Americans in two minorities: a cultural minority and a social minority of adolescence; and he also investigates the influence of this dual membership upon identity crises. In the first part of his study, the author describes the socioeconomic conditions in East Los Angeles, and reviews the literature on minority status as a source of identity, identity crisis in adolescence, and the literature on sociocultural marginality as it relates to Mexican American adolescence. In the second part, Derbyshire discusses the results of an empirical study of adolescent Mexican Americans in East Los Angeles. In that study, he had made the following two hypotheses: (1) that adolescent identity crisis would be greater among young Mexican Americans who deny, reject, or are ambivalent toward Mexican American culture, and (2) that because of less incongruence between the sex role behavior of Mexican and Anglo females, Mexican American females would display significantly less identity conflict than would Mexican American males. On the basis of his analysis of a 34-page questionnaire administered to 89 adolescent Mexican Americans, the author was able to accept the first but forced to reject the second of his hypotheses. He also concluded that "Americanized" Mexican American youth are more vulnerable to deviant behavior, and that the forced acculturation of Mexican Americans by the dominant society may be dysfunctional for the adequate integration of dominant value orientations and behaviors. A 40-item bibliography is included.—AP

85. DeVos, George. Conflict, Dominance and Exploitation in Human Systems of Social Segregation, in Anthony deReuck and Julie Knight (eds.). Conflict in Society. London: J. & A. Churchill, 1966, pp. 60-81.

DeVos explains that there are two basic forms of exploitation practiced by dominant groups. One is the rationally goal-directed use of subordinates for the realization of one's own ambitions. The other form of exploitation he calls "expressive" exploitation and states that it arises from irrational and unconscious psychological processes which are a part of man's mental structure. It involves a biological and/or religious concept of unchangeable inferiority which sets apart one group from another, and as such justifies the maintenance of a fixed social order of dominance and subordination from birth to death. The elaborate caste structure of India, as an example of expressive exploitation, has its psychological equivalents in racist attitudes in America, where particular cultural or ethnic groups are considered to be biologically different or inferior to the majority of the society.

DeVos suggests that increased tension or insecurity among groups of individuals may result in culturally or institutionally available acts of scapegoating of members of subordinate groups in attempts to alleviate the tension. In connection with this, a psychological and sociological study by Bettelheim and Janowitz is cited as demonstrating that prejudice in individuals is inversely related to the strength of integration of the ego. Individuals, then, who manifest relatively weak integration of the ego, and who cannot well manage sources of intra-psychic tension, do not seem to have the ability to resolve inner conflicts without resorting to some form of projection, and are especially prone to continual recourse to such institutionalized scapegoating.—BM

86. ——————————. Minority Group Identity, in Joseph C. Finney (ed.). Culture Change, Mental Health, and Poverty. New York: Simon & Schuster, 1969, pp. 81-96.

This essay states that one of the general results of continuous social discrimination toward a subordinate minority group is the development of separate individual and collective patterns of social self-identity which are passed on and continued as subcultural patterns. These patterns of self-identity may include either retreat from contact with the majority, or the assumption of hostile and deviant roles in relation to the majority society, and they usually involve a degree of apathy and/or personal conflict which preclude the realization of inherent potential. DeVos suggests a general two-pronged approach aimed toward the development of programs to encourage the establishment of positive self-identity among minority groups:

1. Programs of intervening in early childhood to help lessen the psychological inculcation of a negative self-image and to help prevent the development of methods of cognitive integration which inhibit personal social learning.

2. Programs aimed at reducing negative sociological forces of disparagement and distantiation in relation to the minority group.—BM

87. Diaz-Guerrero, Rogelio. Neurosis and the Mexican Family Structure, American Journal of Psychiatry (December, 1955), pp. 411-417.

In this often cited article, the author describes what he takes to be the dominant family pattern in modern Mexico. The author believes that the Mexican family is founded upon two fundamental propositions: (1) the absolute and unquestioned supremacy of the father; and (2) the necessary and absolute self-sacrifice of the mother. These propositions derive from the sociocultural assumptions which are believed to underlie a great deal of role playing in the Mexican family. The author describes in detail the roles, expectations, and interpersonal relations of the individual members of the Mexican family. He then goes on to remark on the areas where neurotic difficulty would be expected and cites some evidence which seems to verify such expectations.—AP

88. Dickerson, Roy E. Some Suggestive Problems in the Americanization of Mexicans, The Pedagogical Seminary, XXVI (September, 1919), 288-297.

This article is one of the first to stress the use of American educational institutions as the chief agency for bringing about the assimilation of Mexican Americans. The author is concerned with the early failure of Mexican immigrants in the schools, and he cites several possible reasons for such failure. He bases his conclusions and suggestions on a study of teenage Mexican boys in Tucson, Arizona. Among the author's suggestions are the providing of a school curriculum adapted to the special needs of Mexican immigrants, more and better understanding of the culture from which they came, and a much more vigorous effort on the part of educators toward the assimilation of Mexican immigrants.—AP

89. Divine, Robert A. American Immigration Policy, 1924-1952. New Haven, Yale University Press, 1957. 220 pp.

Part of one chapter of this survey deals with the debate over Mexican immigration and the development of United States policy on the issue in the 1920's. A strong movement to extend the immigration restriction laws of 1924 to Mexico emerged in the late 1920's. Those who opposed Mexican immigration warned of the threat that Mexican labor might pose to United States workers; but their major objection to Mexicans, says Divine, was racist in nature. The restrictionists were opposed by certain economic interests in the Southwest who benefited from a supply of cheap labor. The State Department had concluded that good relations with the Latin American countries, particularly with Mexico, might be endangered if immigration quotas were applied to them. Primarily because of the opposition of the State Department and the President, a 1930 bill to restrict Mexican immigration did not pass Congress. Immigration from Mexico was restricted significantly, however, by an administrative directive the State Department issued in 1929 to discourage Congressional action. The directive, in effect, made it more difficult for Mexicans to obtain visas to enter the United States.—RS

90. Dobie, J. Frank, ed. Puro Mexicano. Austin, Texas Folklore Society, 1935. 261 pp.
Dobie collected Mexican folk tales of Spanish, Indian and recent Mexican origin. They represent a wide range of topics: animal lore, hero tales, magical occurrences, and Indian legends. The volume covers a time span from the Indian migration to the Americas to the present. The tales were collected by the Texas Folklore Society from Mexican informants and appear without accompanying analysis or classification. Of particular interest is a section of corridas (ballads) that deal with experiences of the Mexican immigrants to the United States. This collection shows cultural diversities among Mexicans and the wide compass of the Mexican experience.—RM

91. ——————. Tongues of the Monte. Garden City, New York, Doubleday, Doran and Co., Inc., 1935. 301 pp.
This is a collection of Mexican folk beliefs presented in the format of a wanderer's journey across northern Mexico. The central figure's love for and interest in the Mexican people, and his sharing of their experiences, exposes him to a great deal of folklore: sayings, magic formulas, foods, medicines, and legends. There is an emphasis on ghost stories and uncanny happenings.—RM

92. Dodson, Jack E. Minority Group Housing in Two Texas Cities, in Nathan Glazer and Davis McEntire, eds. Studies in Housing and Minority Groups, Berkeley, University of California Press, 1960.
The article contains a social description and comparison of Negroes and Mexican Americans in San Antonio, Texas and describes the Negroes' situation in Houston. Segregation against Mexican Americans is neither as rigid nor as formal as that directed against the Negro, but the Mexican American also suffers from de facto residential and school segregation. Mexican Americans with marks of high status are permitted everywhere. In San Antonio, however, the Chicano population lives in the city's worst housing. The author states that many Anglos' interpretation of Chicano culture allows them to believe that Mexican Americans prefer to live in inferior conditions; Chicanos' enthusiastic response to new housing made available to them attests differently. There is an account of the development of new housing within the financial reach of members of the minority population.—RM

93. Dorsey, Emmet E. The Political Role of Mexican-Americans, in Rose, Arnold M. and Caroline B. Rose (eds.). Minority Problems. New York: Harper & Row, 1965, pp. 202-204.
Organized effort by two organizations, the San Antonio teamsters union

(with a large local membership), and the Political Association of Spanish-speaking Organizations (PASO), conceived and guided the program through which the municipal government of Crystal City, Texas came under the control of the Mexican Americans of that city. Although 8,500 of the 10,000 residents of Crystal City are Mexican American, the Anglo minority had run the community since its founding in 1907. Under the new city government, community affairs appear to be proceeding in an orderly and constructive manner. A more equitable tax structure has been adopted and needed local improvements are being undertaken. The Anglos have reacted with hostility and resentment and are planning countermoves for the next election. They believe they are entitled to political control and feel that the new situation is "wrong." In the meantime, observes Dorsey, the city serves as an example of the power of the use of the franchise by underprivileged groups.—BM

94. Draper, Anne and Hal Draper. The Dirt on California: Agribusiness and the University. Berkeley, The Independent Socialist Clubs of America, 1968.

This pamphlet criticizes the orientation of agricultural research at the University of California. The authors allege that the University has consistently furthered and supported the interests of agribusiness: farm producers, food processors, and related manufacturing industries. The University, they argue, has funded virtually no research or services oriented to the interests of farm labor. Rather, it has concentrated almost entirely on the development of improved crops and farm technology and on disseminating information to the growers. Since the small family farm is no longer an important food producer, say the authors, government is in effect subsidizing research for one sector of big business.

The Drapers allege, in addition, that prominent University scholars and administrators, through written reports and spoken testimony, have tended to support the interests of agribusiness on controversial political matters. They cite University influence in the 1963-64 debate over the continuation of the bracero program and in subsequent attempts to persuade the California government to make "informal arrangements" to continue the program after its termination by Congress in 1964. The University, they say, again took the side of the growers in debates over legislation to regulate the hours and wages of agricultural workers.

The Drapers contend that after the bracero program ended there was an expansion of University research on the mechanization of agriculture. Finally, in a concluding argument, they allege that the University could have obtained greater profits from its crop developments and mechanical inventions if it had followed intelligent patent and licensing policies.—RS

95. Dunne, John Gregory. Delano: The Story of a Grape Strike. New York, Farrar, Straus and Giroux, 1967. 176 pp.

This is a journalistic account of César Chávez, the National Farm Workers of America Union and the Delano grape strike. Dunne records Chávez' past activities in labor and social organizations, particularly the Community Service Organization, and also draws portraits of the leaders of the growers. He recounts the difficulties faced by the Union: racial antipathies between the Chicano and Filipino members, the migratory nature of the workers, and the constant threat of mechanization to force the farm laborers out of work. Dunne was pessimistic about the ultimate success of the strike, believing that many local growers were not capable of handling massive wage increases.—RM

96. Duster, Troy. Violence and Civic Responsibility: Combinations of "Fear"

and "Right," in Raymond W. Mack, ed. Our Children's Burden: Studies of Desegregation in Nine American Communities. New York, Random House, 1968, pp. 3-39.

Shortly after the Watts riots, the burning of a Negro elementary school in Riverside, California precipitated that city's decision to integrate its schools. A member of the community, Duster relates the events leading up to Riverside's desegregation decision. Although the article focuses on Negro-Anglo relations, there are some comments about the effect of Black militancy on Mexican Americans in the community. Duster observes that Mexican Americans initially were jealous of extensive civil rights funding of Negro programs. He feels, however, that the Chicanos may be adopting a more aggressive stance foretelling solidarity with Black demands. Duster notes a phenomenon also recorded by scholars writing about other areas in the United States: although the median Mexican-American family income in Riverside was $1000 higher than that of Negroes, 50% of the Negro over-25 population had completed high school compared with only 18% of the Mexican American adult population.—SD

97. Dworkin, Anthony G. No Siesta Mañana: The Mexican American in Los Angeles, in Raymond W. Mack, ed. Our Children's Burden: Studies of Desegregation in Nine American Communities. New York, Random House, 1968, pp. 389-439.

Dworkin first gives a brief history of the Mexican Americans in Los Angeles and "data of discrimination" on income, employment and education. He then discusses traditional cultural traits which he feels have affected Mexican American educational participation. Conceptions of machismo and the extended family, for example, conflict with the Anglo (and largely female) dominated child-centered school system. Important factors that Dworkin discusses include the language barrier, teacher and counselor stereotypes of Mexican Americans, denial of cultural pluralism and segregation by grade assignments within de facto segregated schools. While much of the information is not new, the article effectively conveys the nature of the Mexican Americans' relationships with the school system and the scope of the problems they encounter.—SD

98. ——————. Stereotypes and Self-Images Held by Native-Born and Foreign-Born Mexican-Americans, Sociology and Social Research, XLIX (January, 1965), 214-224.

This is a report of a comparative study of the perceptions of Mexican Americans born in the United States as contrasted to those of Mexican Americans born in Mexico. The author compared both the stereotypes that the two groups of Mexican Americans held of Anglos and also the self-images that they held of themselves. The author used a free association interview method on 280 subjects, fifty of whom were college students, from the communities of East Los Angeles and San Gabriel, California. The author's findings strongly indicate that significantly more foreign-born subjects held favorable stereotypes and self-images than did the U.S.-born subjects. He attributed his findings to differences in the groups' definition of their present social situation, that is, whether they employed their prior socioeconomic situation or the socioeconomic situation of the dominant society as a standard of evaluation.—AP

99. Eaton, Joseph W. and Kenneth Polk. Measuring Delinquency: A Study of Probation Department Referrals. Pittsburgh, University of Pittsburgh Press, 1961.

88 pp.

This is a study of statistics on delinquency referrals to the Los Angeles County Probation Department during 1956. The book discusses the channels through which adolescents are referred to the Probation Department; the nature of the offenses committed; the "disposition" of the delinquents (the disciplinary or reform action taken toward them by the Probation Department); and the characteristics of adolescents referred to probation officials more than once. The statistics are analyzed in terms of several variables including age, sex, marital status of parents, geographical mobility and ethnic background. There are comparative data on rates of delinquency (defined as referral to the Probation Department) among Anglos, Negroes and Mexican Americans, and on differences in the Department's disposition of delinquents from these three groups. The study strongly criticizes many popular single-factor explanations of the causes of delinquency.—RS

100. Edmundson, Monro S. Los Manitos: A Study of Institutional Values. New Orleans, Middle American Research Institute, Tulane University, 1957. 68 pp.

This is an anthropological report on the social structure and values of the Hispanos of northern New Mexico. It concludes that their cultural traits are those of a "traditional" society; there is an emphasis on age seniority, segregation of the sexes, extended family units, and political and economic systems that place power in the hands of patróns. Edmundson traces cultural characteristics to childhood when a strong father teaches submission; a Freudian analysis of sexual relationships concludes that male dominance meets the culturally induced needs of both sexes. Hispano training, in the author's view, adjusts the bulk of the population to limited aspirations, fatalism and apathy. Edmundson's analysis equates "American" culture with middle-class norms, which he sets up in opposition to the Hispano value system. He clearly implies the superiority of "American" values, and does not see the relationship of poverty to the Hispano values. By analogy, he expands the "traditional" Hispano cultural traits into every aspect of Chicano existence; even the location of their dwellings show, in his view, a passive outlook.—RM

101. Educational Resources Information Center.

ERIC is a federally-funded system of nineteen clearinghouses located across the United States designed to gather, analyze, store and disseminate information about current educational research. Each clearinghouse concentrates on a particular educational area, but all of them maintain complete files including the work of the other locations. Documents available in the ERIC system may be purchased in hard copy or microfiche form.

ERIC clearinghouses contain quantities of material on Mexican Americans, much of which is unpublished or not usually available. Most of the entries are about education, but specialized linguistic, sociological, psychological, and economic studies are not uncommon. The files are especially helpful in locating such things as working papers, conference speeches, and political statements.

Further information may be obtained through the United States Department of Health, Education and Welfare, Office of Education, Bureau of Research, Educational Resources Information Center, Washington, D.C.—PS

102. Educational Testing Service. Research on the Disadvantaged: An Annotated List of Relevant ETS Studies, 1951-1969. Princeton, New Jersey: Educational Testing Service, 1969.

This list consists of reports of 79 ETS research studies completed during the period from 1951 through August of 1969, and also of 21 studies in progress at the time of publication. Four general types of investigations are included:

1. Investigations of the educational, personal, and social characteristics of the disadvantaged.

2. Studies of other populations in which socioeconomic status or minority group performance is a variable.

3. Studies dealing with theoretical and methodological developments relating to the analysis of data concerning the disadvantaged.

4. Surveys and analyses of literature and theory of importance to research on the disadvantaged.

None of the studies listed deals specifically with Mexican Americans. They are concerned more generally with the "disadvantaged" as referring to socioeconomic status, social class, etc. Several of the studies, however, do contain material and information which could be relevant to research dealing with Mexican Americans.—BM

103. Ellis, John M. Mortality Differentials for a Spanish-Surname Population Group, Southwestern Social Science Quarterly, XXXIX (March, 1959), 314-321.

The author studied data on mortality rates in the Anglo and Spanish-surname populations of Houston, Texas for the years 1949-1951. Ellis found that the mortality rates of Spanish-surname males compared favorably with those of Anglo males. The death rates of Spanish-surname females, however, were somewhat lower than those of Latin males but substantially higher than those of Anglo females in almost all age groups. The author suggests that certain cultural attitudes among the Spanish-surname population may account for this difference in female mortality rates. Feminine modesty, fatalism and the belief that it is a woman's duty to remain close to the home and the family are factors which might deter many Latin women from seeking medical assistance or submitting to hospitalization.—RS

104. Estes, Dwain M. and David W. Darling, eds. Improving Educational Opportunities of the Mexican-American. Proceedings of the First Texas Conference for the Mexican-American. Austin, Texas: Southwest Educational Development Laboratory, 1967.

This is a report of the first such Texas Conference held in April of 1967. The report contains the eleven papers presented at the conference and also a description of several special programs for Spanish-speaking children then under way in Texas. Some of the more relevant papers are annotated separately in this bibliography.

Lamanna, Richard A. and Julian Samora, "Recent Trends in Educational Status of Mexican-Americans in Texas."

Gomez, Severo, "The Meaning and Implications of Bilingualism for Texas Schools."

Andersson, Theodore, "The Concept of Bilingualism.".

Manuel, H.T., "The Spanish-Speaking Child in Texas Schools."—AP

105. Evans, Francis B. A Study of Sociocultural Characteristics of Mexican-American and Anglo Junior High School Students and the Relation of These Characteristics to Achievement. Ed.D. dissertation, New Mexico State University, 1969.

This dissertation is based on a study of 126 junior high school students, 87 of whom were Mexican American. Basing his findings that Mexican American students, regardless of the amount of English spoken in the home, when compared to Anglo students, (1) came from families of much lower socioeconomic status, (2) had fatalistic, present-time orientations, (3) had lower self-concepts of ability, (4) had a passive, accepting attitude toward life, (5) had a high striving orientation, (6) experienced less democratic parental independence training practices, and (7) had high religious social distance. In relating these characteristics to achievement, the author found a significant and positive correlation with (1) high self-concept of ability, (2) democratic parental independence training practices, (3) activistic, future-time orientation, and (4) low religious social distance. Some of these findings conflict with other studies, and the dissertation includes a useful review of the literature, an extensive bibliography, and a discussion of whether the findings might be characteristic of the culture of poverty in general, rather than specific to Mexican Americans alone.—AP

106. Fabrega, Horacio, John D. Swartz, and Carole Ann Wallace. Ethnic Differences in Psychopathology—II. Specific Differences with Emphasis on a Mexican American Group, Journal of Psychiatric Research, VI (1968), 221-235.
This is a report of a comparative study of a group of Mexican American schizophrenic patients with a similar group of Negro schizophrenics and also an Anglo group. Each group was matched across variables of age, sex, I.Q. estimate, number of previous psychiatric hospitalizations, and education. The authors hypothesized that there would be significant differences between the Mexican American group and the other two groups on the basis of previous studies of Mexican American cultural patterns indicating a greater tolerance of deviant psychotic behavior in the family and community. On the basis of this information, the authors made several predictions, including the hypothesis that psychopathology among the Mexican American sample would be more severe, since it was likely that only the more critical patients were hospitalized. The authors found, in fact, that the Mexican American patients were more chronic, regressed, and disorganized, and the authors provide several possible explanations for their findings.—AP

107. Fabrega, Horacio Jr., and Carole Ann Wallace. Value Identification and Psychiatric Disability: An Analysis Involving Americans of Mexican Descent, Behavioral Science, 13 (1968), 362-371.
This study is based on data collected from a research project conducted among two groups of Mexican Americans living in border areas of South Texas: (1) a group of psychiatric outpatients, and (2) a group of nonpatients. The authors report that the nonpatient group showed significantly higher measures of stability, economic self-sufficiency, and social competence. Scalogram analysis indicated that the nonpatients took either a very traditional or a very nontraditional posture, whereas patients seemed to follow both traditional and nontraditional patterns to a moderate extent, with very few persons having commitments at either extreme. The possibility is suggested that well-defined and exclusive types of orientations enable greater psychological organization and improved social performance by allowing individuals to act within a framework of fewer basic premises. Psychological consistency is maintained, according to the authors, by exclusive reliance on either Mexican or Anglo choices in many different contexts, and as a result productivity is increased. On the other hand, anxiety resulting from cognitive inconsistency between reliance on combined Mexican and Anglo traits may interfere with adequate work performance and satisfactory interpersonal relationships.—BM

108. Fallows, Marjorie. The Mexican-American Laborers: A Different Drummer? Massachusetts Review, VIII (Winter, 1967), 166-176.

This article argues that even though some Mexican Americans have become more militant they have not given up their traditional values. Fallows claims that Chicanos are still suspicious of organizers and organizations. César Chávez has succeeded because he fulfills the traditional role of patrón, a man who handles contacts with outsiders and arranges community activities. The author believes that without Chávez the entire union movement would collapse. The original National Farm Workers of America operated as a welfare cooperative, and the author makes a distinction between the institutional patrón role of the union and the personal patrón role of Chávez. Fallows believes that Anglos have made greater attitude changes than Chicanos. Emerging values, the author says, permit Anglos to accept other cultures and encourage them to participate in minority group improvement efforts.—RM

109. Finney, Joseph C. (ed.). Culture Change, Mental Health, and Poverty. New York: Simon and Schuster, 1969.

This volume consists of a collection of essays and discussions resulting from a conference on ethnopsychology and cross-cultural psychiatry held in 1965 at the University of Kentucky and participated in by psychiatrists, psychologists, anthropologists, and economists. The rationale of the conference, as reflected in this particular book, involved the premise that a combination of approaches is essential in the attempt to overcome the crippling effects of discrimination and poverty on individual personalities and on the social system as a whole.

Specific questions under discussion at the conference were concerned with: (1) the possibility of judging objectively whether a way of life is malfunctioning and unsatisfactory to a particular group; (2) the circumstances, if any, under which there is a right or duty to intervene in an attempt to change a group of people and their way of life; (3) the extent to which the attempt to bring about change (if the need for it is indicated) should be directed primarily toward persons or institutions.—BM

110. Fisher, Lloyd H. The Harvest Labor Market in California. Cambridge, Massachusetts, Harvard University Press, 1953. 148 pp.

This book is an economic and social study of the California agricultural labor market. It emphasizes the theory of the market and the role of government and employers associations in the system of labor contracting and wage fixing. The author points out that recognition of the need for reform of the seasonal farm labor market is not new. He compares the recommendations of the 1951 President's Commission on Migratory Labor with the suggestions of a similar California committee appointed in 1950. Fisher then analyzes the role of competing private power groups by comparing their influence on these two federal and state reports. The author feels that there is a need for reform but suggests that two serious obstacles are the Herculean size of the task and the laborers' lack of political power. Fisher has little faith that legislation, government policies, or administrative programs will fundamentally alter the farm labor market. He believes that the best hope of improving the lot of the farm worker is agricultural mechanization and the transfer of seasonal laborers to industrial jobs.—RM

111. Fishman, Joshua A., et al. Language Loyalty in the United States; the

Maintenance and Perpetuation of Non-English Mother Tongues by American Ethnic and Religious Groups. The Hague, Morton and Co., 1966, pp. 280-317.

The essays in this book focus on the problem of perpetuating the languages and cultures that immigrants brought to the United States. One of the articles in the work is annotated separately: Christian, Jane and Chester Christian, Jr. "Spanish Language and Culture in the Southwest." Some of the other articles—for instance, those on the ethnic group press, foreign language broadcasting, and the history of non-English groups—also contain information about the Mexican Americans.—RS

112. Flores, Solomon H. The Nature and Effectiveness of Bilingual Education Programs for the Spanish-Speaking Child in the United States. (PhD dissertation, Ohio State University, 1969).

This dissertation consists of an attempt to identify the operational models and strategies presently being used in bilingual education programs with the purpose of synthesizing the know-how of existing programs in such a way that educators might have at their disposal the fruits of available knowledge in the field. To this end the author investigated in depth five bilingual education programs, three with Mexican Americans in Texas, one with Cubans in Florida, and one with Puerto Ricans in New York. The author reviews the literature on bilingual education, sets criteria for establishing the best possible bilingual education program for Spanish-speaking students, and then examines the five on-going programs in the light of these criteria, making recommendations and offering guidelines for future bilingual programs.—AP

113. Fogel, Walter. Education and Income of Mexican Americans in the Southwest. Mexican-American Study Project Advance Report 1. Los Angeles, Division of Research, Graduate School of Business, University of California, 1965. 28 pp.

This report studies the relation between educational attainment and income among Anglos, Spanish-surname people, Negroes and Orientals in the Southwest. The study is based on census data. The authors found that educational attainment (measured by the number of years of schooling) and income had a strong positive correlation among all groups. The median income of Anglos was higher than those of the other groups at all levels of schooling. The median earnings of the Spanish-surnamed, however, also tended to be greater than those of Negroes and Orientals when education was held constant. Educational attainment seems to have a greater effect on the income of the Spanish-surnamed than it does on the earnings of Negroes and Orientals. The authors believe that this result suggests that Spanish-surname persons face less discrimination in the labor market than do people in these other minority groups.

The study also notes that an increase in the median educational level of a group may not have an effect on its median income for several years. They point out, for instance, that employment shifts from manual to non-manual jobs tend to require a substantial jump of several years in schooling, not merely a small increase. In addition, income level depends on post-school experience as well as education.—RS

114. ——————. Job Gains of Mexican-American Men, Monthly Labor Review, XCI (October, 1968), 22-37.

This survey, based on census data from 1930 to 1960, compares occupational shifts among Mexican Americans and the rest of the population. While the general population was shifting from agricultural to non-agricultural jobs, Mexican Americans lagged behind and were not able to make comparable occupational gains. The delay resulted from Mexican American occupational preferences, lack of industrial qualifications and discrimination by employers. Although more gradually than the general population, Mexican Americans did make gains by entering non-farm occupations. The most rapid movement in this direction occurred in California and Colorado during the 1940's as a result of the growth of war industries. After the war, Anglo migration to the West filled the jobs created by economic growth and slowed down Mexican American job gains.—RM

115. ——————. Mexican Americans in Southwest Labor Markets. Mexican American Study Project Advance Report 10. Los Angeles, Division of Research, Graduate School of Business, University of California, 1967. 198 pp.

Fogel presents an analysis of the Mexican American occupational status in the Southwest. He makes comparisons between states and ethnic groups and notes differences in the Mexican American situation across time and among generations. The discrimination which limits Mexican Americans to jobs in small, marginal firms is reflected in their low incomes; even when Chicanos penetrate job classifications held by Anglos their earnings tend to be lower. However, relative to educational attainment, Mexican Americans' incomes are the highest of any disadvantaged minority in the Southwest. Fogel notes that there is great variation among the states. Declining farm employment in Colorado and New Mexico forces migration to cities whose slow economic growth creates few high paying jobs. In Southern Texas Mexican Americans and Negroes are forced to compete for many of the same jobs, and the effects of a low economic growth rate are aggravated by racial discrimination. Mexican Americans have benefited from California's industrial expansion, but Fogel feels frustration of high Chicano expectations may lead to bitterness and confrontation. Time comparisons reveal that Chicanos made more gains than Blacks in the 1950's, but their advance was not as great as that of the Negroes in the 1940's. Second generation Chicanos made substantial advances over the low first generation position, but Fogel feels the small gains made by the third and succeeding generations are discouraging. Finally, Fogel discusses concern over Chicano-Black job competition and notes that the lowering of job barriers has tended to benefit both groups equally.—SD

116. Forbes, Jack D. Education of the Culturally Different: A Multi-Cultural Approach. Berkeley, Far West Laboratory for Educational Research and Development, 1968. 35 pp.

Forbes argues that many Anglo educators use the term "cultural deprivation" to escape blame for the poor school performance of minority group children. Instead, educators shift the burden of failure onto the children, whom they see coming not from a different culture but from a cultural vacuum. Using schools to force cultural homogeneity and assimilation of Anglo values creates minority group withdrawal, hostility and alienation. In his discussion of the need for a multi-cultural approach and a redefinition of the function of the school, Forbes deals with the importance of school-community relations and good teacher-child and teacher-parent rapport. This essay is intended in part as a philosophical introduction to the author's handbooks on the education of Mexican Americans and Afro-Americans in the Far West. There is a brief bibliographic section.—SD

117. ——————. Mexican-Americans: A Handbook for Educators.

Berkeley, Far West Laboratory for Educational Research and Development, 1967. 34 pp.

This is a concise manual treating Mexican American culture with respect to educational programs. The author's suggestions for the practical application of bilingual programs in the school routine are directed to teachers and administrators.—PS

118. ——————. Race and Color in Mexican-American Problems, Journal of Human Relations, XVI (1968), 55-68.

After outlining the history of Anglo color prejudice against Mexican Americans from Richard Henry Dana to the present, the author concludes that Anglos have always favored lighter skinned, more "Castilian" Mexican Americans. Forbes feels that anti-Indian prejudice damages Chicano self-esteem and hinders social mobility. He believes that the Mexican American future cannot be satisfactory until the race problem is solved; prejudice against Chicanos will not disappear until prejudice against Negroes and Indians does. Further, the feeling of inferiority engendered in Mexican Americans must be eradicated before they can organize politically with Indians and Blacks.—RM

119. Francis, E. K. Multiple Intergroup Relations in the Upper Rio Grande Region, American Sociological Review, XXI (1956), 84-87.

This is a historical sketch of relations between Hispanos and Anglos in New Mexico. The author argues that the institutional framework of a society—the pattern of political, economic and social power distribution—is more important than cultural factors in conditioning relations between and within ethnic groups. In New Mexico, he notes, relations between Hispanos and Anglos have changed considerably as the institutional framework of the society has evolved. The shift of political power to Anglos following the Mexican American war, the large-scale immigration of Anglos to New Mexico a generation later, and the important changes in social and economic institutions since the late nineteenth century have all affected relations between Hispanos and Anglos.—RS

120. Galarza, Ernesto. Merchants of Labor: The Mexican Bracero Story. San Jose, California, The Rosicrucian Press, 1964. 259 pp.

This is a study of the bracero in California. An introductory chapter traces the antecedents of the bracero program from 1880 to 1942. The rest of the book covers the period from World War II to the present. In 1942 the United States, concerned with wartime manpower shortages and increased demands for agricultural products, entered into an agreement with Mexico to manage and promote the seasonal importation of Mexican agricultural workers into the Southwestern states. By 1960 the "temporary" war-time agreement, formalized by Congressional action in 1951, was still in effect. The work discusses the government's administration of the bracero program, the treatment of braceros by their employers in commercial agriculture and the effects of the bracero system on domestic labor and on the agricultural labor movement in California. Galarza concludes that the bracero program had a profoundly adverse effect on the wages and conditions of domestic labor, and helped commercial agriculture in California hold the line against the organized labor movement for twenty years. He also feels that government agencies created to administer the program soon evolved into active collaborators of agribusinessmen, encouraging collusion in determining wage and hiring policies and discouraging the workers' efforts to unionize. The author notes the failure of national labor organizations to provide strong backing for the movement to unionize agricultural workers in California.—RS

121. ——————————. Spiders in the House and Workers in the Field. Notre Dame, Indiana. University of Notre Dame Press, 1970. 306 pp.

This is a case study of the legal process. The author presents a documented historical and critical study of nine legal suits for defamation which resulted from the National Farm Workers Union's attempt to achieve union recognition from DiGiorgio Corporation, the largest firm in agribusiness at that time; during the 1947 Strike near Arvin, California. The showing (publication) of the movie "Poverty in the Valley of Plenty" and literary reviews of the movie, were the basis for liability in nine civil suits. The Nixon-Morton-Steed Report, however, released by members of Congress on the Arvin Labor Strike, played a concurrently decisive role. Galarza inquires into the multiple uses of the report: judicial, juridical, legislative, inquisitional, publicitarian, constitutional, and prophetic.

The prolonged legal confrontation between union organizers and the DiGiorgio Corporation provides the setting for Galarza's portrayal of the interlockings of the DiGiorgio Corporation with agribusiness, the influence of agribusiness on public policy, the industry's connections with governmental agencies, Mexico-United States Diplomacy, and the union's campaign against the alien contract labor system.

Galarza bases his study on government documents, legal documents, law reports, depositions, books, magazines and newspapers, as well as his personal experience as a party to most of the legal suits in question and as a union organizer and director of education and research for the National Farm Workers Union.—LGN

123. —————————— Strangers in Our Fields. Washington, D.C., United States Section, Joint United States-Mexico Trade Union Committee, 1956. 80 pp.

This book attempts to determine the degree to which the bracero actually benefited from the contractual, legal and civil rights guaranteed him by the governments of the United States and Mexico. It was written for the United States Section of the Joint United States-Mexico Trade Union Committee, which represented the AFL-CIO and other major unions. The author concludes that exploitation of the braceros by their employers was the rule, not the exception.

Galarza bases his study on data gathered from extensive interviews with braceros in Southwestern Arizona and California in 1955. He attempted to check statements made by the braceros concerning wages, deductions and rates of pay against paycheck stubs and other documentary evidence. But the difficulties of getting this type of material and of obtaining data from employers caused him to rely primarily on the evidence gathered from the braceros themselves. Despite this understandable limitation, Galarza demonstrates that there were widespread violations of the rights guaranteed braceros by law.—RS

124. ——————————, Herman Gallegos and Julian Samora, Mexican-Americans in the Southwest. Santa Barbara: McNally & Loftin, 1969. 90 pp.

This small book attempts to present a comprehensive and up-to-date overview of the Mexican Americans in the Southwest. It is a report of the results of a two year study made by the authors during which they traveled throughout the United States and parts of Mexico. The report contains information on population distribution, immigration, current economic and employment profiles, and the political organization of Mexican Americans in the sixties.—AP

125. Gamio, Manuel. Forjando patria. Mexico City, Editorial Porrua, S.A., Second edition, 1960 (First edition, 1916). 206 pp.
This book is an expression of a movement to revalorize the cultural contribution of the Indian to Mexico. To become a truly unified nation and culture, said Gamio, Mexico had to cease pretending that it was purely European. It had to realize that its nationality lay in the fusion of the "iron" of the Spanish with the "bronze" of the Indian. Each of these cultural traditions, said Gamio, was of equal importance and relevance to the new nation which had to be forged. Gamio urged Mexicans to undertake a comprehensive program of self-study. He emphasized particularly the need for historical and anthropological knowledge about Indian culture and society, which had long been neglected or denigrated.
Gamio was primarily concerned with the creation of a unified nation out of disparate cultural, geographic and ethnic elements. No style of artistic expression or way of life, he thought, was inherently better than any other. Hence, a people should not strive to adopt another culture, but should develop its own to the fullest.—RS

126. ——————————. Mexican Immigration to the United States. Chicago, University of Chicago Press, 1930. 196 pp.
This study treats the different economic and social forces tending to produce immigration from Mexico. Gamio also deals with the reception of the immigrants in the United States in terms of wages, prejudice, and acceptance. Low pay and scarce employment in Mexico provided the impetus for migration, and agricultural employers in search of cheap labor controlled the stream of migrants once it reached the United States. Gamio gives a basically economic interpretation of the movement. He believes that little cultural alteration takes place in the immigrant; the Mexican continues to value Mexican institutions and desires to return home eventually.—RM

127. ——————————. The Mexican Immigrant, His Life Story, Autobiographic Documents Collected by Manuel Gamio. Chicago, University of Chicago Press, 1931. 288 pp.
These are the collected statements of 57 immigrants from Mexico during the 1920's, telling why they left Mexico and how they lived in the United States. The most important reasons found for immigration were the disruption of life in Mexico by the Revolution of 1910 and simple curiosity. These documents demonstrate a strong loyalty to Mexico, a hope to return eventually, indifference to the Catholic religion, violently mixed feelings toward America, and often a distrust of American-born people with Spanish or Mexican backgrounds.—RM

128. —————————— Número, procedencia y distribución geográfica de los immigrantes mexicanos en los Estados Unidos. Mexico City, Talleres Gráficos Editorial y "Diario Oficial," 1930. 20 pp.
This is an analysis of statistics on Mexican migration to and from the United States between 1910 and 1928 and a study of the geographic origin and distribution of temporary Mexican migrants in the United States between 1920 and

1928. Gamio derives his data on population movements from the Department of Migration of the Mexican government. This agency kept a record of the number of Mexicans who returned to their homeland each year as well as of those who left it. Although Gamio admits there is no way of estimating the number of Mexicans who entered the United States illegally, he feels that it is safe to conclude, from the data on official crossings, that the great majority of Mexican migrants were temporary, or seasonal. Part of this temporary migration, he notes, was clearly related to political events and fluctuations in economic conditions in Mexico. There was no foundation, he argues, to the fear that a large number of people was moving permanently from Mexico to the United States.

In order to obtain data on the geographic origin and the subsequent distribution of Mexican migrants to the United States, Gamio studied all money orders sent by Mexicans from this country to their homeland during the months of January and July, 1920 to 1928. He thus expanded a previous study based on more limited but similar data which he reported in his Mexican Immigration to the United States (1930). He found that the three contiguous states of Guanajuato, Michoacán and Jalisco in the central-western part of Mexico provided nearly 57% of the migrants to the United States. No other state furnished above 7%. California, Texas and Illinois received over 60% of the total number of migrants.—RS

129. Gans, Herbert J. The Urban Villagers. New York, The Free Press, 1962. 335 pp.

Gans' ethnography of Italian-Americans attempts to discern whether ethnicity or class is a more relevant concept for understanding a slum-dweller's way of life. His decision, bolstered by an extensive review of working- and lower-class studies, is that behavior patterns result from social and economic situations, with variation according to ethnic group membership.

The responses people make to particular combinations of opportunities and deprivations are subcultures. In defining the working-class subculture said to describe West Enders, Gans introduces some subtleties. Class subcultures are identified by "focal concerns," not by quantifiable socioeconomic data. Family structure is the most important of these concerns, followed by self-concept, the nature of relationships with non-family persons, and attitudes toward education and work. Thus, the extensive value changes necessary for movement between subcultures explains the recent United States trend toward rigid class stratification: increased earning power is not the only component of upward mobility. People may acquire material comforts without altering their life-style substantially. Those who do change cultures experience severe psychological and emotional stress.

Gans' proposition overtly questions the wisdom of using middle-class values in solving the problems of low-income populations. The author concludes his study with challenges to the "planners and caretakers," the professionals charged with treating slum-dwellers and urban redevelopment.—PS

130. Garretson, O.K. A Study of the Causes of Retardation Among Mexican Children in a Small School System in Arizona, Journal of Educational Psychology, XIX (January, 1928), 31-40.

This article is mainly of historical interest. It was written at a time when there was increasing interest and public pressure to place some limitations on immigration to the United States, and the rationale that individuals of certain racial or ethnic groups were inherently inferior in mental ability was commonly advanced in support of such restrictions. In this study, the author investigates the possible causes of retardation of Mexican school children in one small school system. On the basis of his data, he eliminates irregular attendance, transience, and language difficulties as significant factors. Then, on the basis of three types of intelligence tests he administered, he concludes that Mexican children are, in fact, inferior in native intellectual ability—as compared to their average Anglo counterparts—and that this inferior mental ability is the principal factor governing retardation of the Mexican child.—AP

131. Garth, Thomas R. and Harper D. Johnson. The Intelligence and Achievement of Mexican Children in the United States. Journal of Abnormal and Social Psychology, XXIX (1934), 222-229.
In this early study, the author attempts to measure the influence of educational achievement upon intelligence scores of Spanish-speaking children. The author's sample was 683 "Mexican" children from El Paso, Texas, and rural New Mexico. All were of low socioeconomic status, enrolled in public schools, and between the ages of six and eighteen. The author's analysis of his data from intelligence and achievement tests indicated (1) that there was a high correlation between achievement and intelligence test scores, (2) that the "Mexican" child was more like the "white American" child in intelligence and achievement at the early ages but rapidly became dissimilar with age, and (3) that the influence of achievement on intelligence was about four times greater than that of school grade placement.—AP

132. Gazaway, Rena. Portrait of a Rural Village, in Joseph C. Finney (ed.). Culture Change, Mental Health, and Poverty. New York: Simon & Schuster, 1969, pp. 42-57.
In this article, the author points out that poverty is not merely an economic problem and that no real solution can ignore the culture and value differences that exist. Perhaps the reason government programs have failed to ease conditions of poverty, Gazaway explains, is that they have neglected to take into consideration the social and psychological effects of poverty on an individual's sense of personal identity. Particular difficulties incident to the solution of problems involving poverty are enumerated, and the need for the development of specific and concrete methods or programs to combat conditions of deprivation is stressed.—BM

133. Gil, Mario. Nuestros Buenos Vecinos. Mexico, Editorial Azteca S.A., 1964. 306 pp.
This is a history of what the author sees as a relationship of Imperialism between Mexico and the United States. He studies the concept of Manifest Destiny and illustrates its political and social ramifications for both countries. He studies the problems of those Mexicans who after the War of 1846 remained in the United States—the Chicanos, and attempts to document his charges of imperialism on the part of the United States. He not only covers the conflicts between the United States and Mexico which have resulted in vast losses of territory for Mexico but also deals with cases of intervention such as the punitive expedition of Pershing.—CV

134. Glazer, Nathan and Daniel P. Moynihan. Beyond the Melting Pot. Cambridge, Massachusetts, M.I.T. Press, 1963. 315 pp.
This is a sociological ethnic group account based on the concept of continuing cultural pluralism. The central point of the study is that the melting pot did not work, at least in New York City, where ethnic groups continue to maintain

religious, social and political identity. Some of the ethnic groups in New York (Irish, Italians and Jews) have been able to play vital, complete roles in United States politics, science and arts without losing ethnic identity. The work does not deal directly with Mexican Americans.—RM

135. Goldkind, Victor. Factors in the Differential Acculturation of Mexicans in a Michigan City. Unpublished doctoral dissertation, Michigan State University, 1963. 270 pp.

The author hypothesizes that numerous demographic characteristics influence Mexican American acculturation into Anglo society. The results are mixed, with several factors—occupational position, racial appearance, and religious affiliation—less significantly related to acculturation than predicted. The majority of the results confirmed logical expectations: fluency in English, grade of school completed, extent of agricultural experience, for example, were all significantly related to acculturation. In all, thirty demographic characteristics were tested against twenty-four measures of acculturation.

The study attempts to measure in detail the difficult concept of acculturation (seen as occurring in four dimensions: position in the occupational structure, activity in voluntary organizations, contact with Anglos and retention of ethnic cultural traits). The research was conducted in East Lansing, Michigan. There is a discussion of the difficulties of drawing a true random sample of Mexican Americans.—SD

136. Goldschmidt, Walter. As You Sow. New York, Harcourt, Brace, 1947. 288 pp.

The author describes social structure and behavior in California farm communities, predicating a rigid two-class stratification based on the industrial character of agriculture. Goldschmidt discusses social controls and conflicts between classes and ethnic groups and makes consistent references to economic motivations of local behavior.—PS

137. Gomez-Q., Juan. Research Notes on the Twentieth Century, Aztlan, I (Spring, 1970), 115-132.

These notes are divided into three major sections. Section one contains notes on periodization. The author chronologically divides the twentieth century experience of the Mexican American into five major periods: (1) the First Steps (1900-1920); (2) Assimilation and Struggle (1920-1940); (3) the Period of the War (1940-1945); (4) the Post-War Surgence (1945-1965); and (5) La Reconquista—the Movement (1965-1970). The author discusses briefly the significant events that mark each period. In section two of these notes are comments on the agricultural strikes of the 1930's. The author discusses the uniqueness and significance of the strikes and the patterns that they took. Section three is devoted to a review of the Plan de San Diego. The Plan de San Diego (1915) was the principal document of a revolutionary and irredentist movement of Mexicans and Mexican Americans whose principal aim was to reclaim the Southwest from the United States through armed overthrow. Gomez discusses the discovery of the Plan by Anglos in Texas in early 1915, their subsequent reaction and retaliation, the growth of the irredentist movement throughout the year 1915, and the eventual forced migration of over half the population of the Lower Rio Grande Valley. The author compares the ideology of the Plan de San Diego with that of more contemporary plans, and he sees it as an important historical document from which much can be learned. A translated copy of the Plan is included, along with a bibliography.—AP

138. González, Nancie L. The Spanish American of New Mexico: A Distinctive Heritage. Mexican American Study Project Advance Report 9. Los Angeles, Division of Research, Graduate School of Business, University of California, 1967. 132 pp.

The author examines the history of the Hispanos in New Mexico and discusses such topics as la raza, social class status, and their cultural traditions.

The United States' conquest of the area in 1846 brought substantial changes in Hispano life due to the opening of new settlements and the growth of opportunities for wage labor in agriculture, ranching and industry. Gonzáles observes that, in spite of post-World War II prosperity, the Hispanos as a class have been increasingly dispossessed of their land, rights and cultural heritage. The author points out that the recently urbanized majority of Hispanos face the same barriers of language and culture as do Mexican Americans. González feels that Hispano members of the middle economic class have combated discrimination by adopting either the Anglo way of life or militant identification and sympathy with Mexican American demands. The author observes there is some evidence that Hispanos in New Mexico are more successful than Mexican Americans in other Southwestern states, but have more difficulty than Anglos in attaining the symbols of upper class status.—SD

139. Goodman, Mary Ellen and Alma Beman. Child's Eye View of Life in an Urban Barrio, in Spanish Speaking People in the United States; Proceedings of the 1968 Annual Spring Meeting of the American Ethnological Society, June Helm, ed. Seattle, Distributed by the University of Washington Press, 1968, pp. 84-103.

This is a sociological survey of the values of children in a Houston, Texas barrio. The authors feel that the children are happy and tranquil primarily because of family solidarity. The children perceive physical and social disruption in barrio life due, for example, to freeway construction and Negro in-migration. They attributed these changes to external forces, not the barrio's lack of power and resources. School and television are the main outside influences on the children, but they ignore the glamor roles offered. The children aspire primarily to familiar, local work roles, although they desire better jobs than those held by their adult relatives. The study finds growing ethnic pride and hope in the barrio and maintains that life styles and values of the barrio children are conducive to modest success.—RM

140. Gordon, Milton M. Assimilation in American Life: The Role of Race, Religion, and National Origin. New York, Oxford University Press, 1964. 265 pp.

This book is a summary of theoretical works on assimilation, acculturation, and amalgamation. It traces in a historical context the evolution of the theories of "Anglo-conformity," "the melting pot" and cultural pluralism.

Basing his conclusions partly on interviews with leaders of organizations dealing with intergroup relations, Gordon stresses that the ethnic group is a large subsociety with social classes and a network of primary groups and institutions. He proposes a combination of ethnicity and class ("ethclass") as a functional concept for analysis of United States intergroup relations. Gordon feels that even though most immigrants have been culturally assimilated into the mainstream of United States life, their social contacts have continued to center around their original ethnic group.—PS

141. Grambs, Jean Dresden. Intergroup Education: Methods and Materials, Englewood Cliffs, New Jersey, Prentice-Hall, Inc., 1968. 199 pp.

This book provides a perceptive discussion of developments in the field of intergroup education, an assessment of methods and materials for teacher use and a bibliography. In her analysis of the current theories and problems of intergroup education, Grambs points out that the need of white suburban schools for such intercultural programs is as great as the need of the city ghetto schools. The author also explores the roles that teachers and others in the school system often play in resisting the introduction of intergroup education. The 110 page annotated bibliography covers a myriad of materials: general background and theoretical works, fiction, text and film resources for elementary and secondary students, bibliographies and journals.—SD

142. Grebler, Leo. Mexican Immigration to the United States: The Record and its Implications. Mexican-American Study Project Advance Report 2. Los Angeles, Division of Research, Graduate School of Business, University of California, 1966. 106 pp.

This general survey of Mexican immigration to the United States focuses on temporary migrations (of braceros, green-carders, and others) as well as on permanent population movements. The book includes: an analysis of the features of Mexican immigration which make it different from earlier, European migratory currents to the United States; a historical and statistical review of Mexican immigration; and an analysis of the economic factors in both Mexico and the United States which have influenced the movement of people across the border. Grebler also studies the immigrants themselves—their demographic and social characteristics, their geographic origins in Mexico, their distribution in the United States, and the characteristics which distinguish them from the general population of Mexico. An appendix, written by Ronald Wyse, surveys in historical perspective the United States immigration and nationality laws that have applied to Mexicans. Numerous statistical tables are included. The work is both descriptive and analytical.—RS

143. ——————. The Schooling Gap: Signs of Progress. Mexican-American Study Project Advance Report 7. Los Angeles, Division of Research, Graduate School of Business, University of California, 1967. 48 pp.

This is an analysis of 1960 census data on educational attainment among Anglos, Negroes and Spanish-surname people in the American Southwest. For all three groups the author studied: schooling records of adults and of the younger generation; contrasts in median educational levels between urban and rural areas and between states, regions and various cities of the Southwest; and statistics on school enrollment. He devotes a final chapter to the differences in educational attainment (measured by the number of years of schooling) between native- and foreign-born Spanish-surname people. The study notes evidence of improvement in the educational achievement of Spanish-surname persons. Between 1950 and 1960 the schooling gap between the Spanish-surname and the Anglo populations decreased. In addition, in 1960 the median educational attainment of the younger generation of Spanish-surname people and of the native-born was markedly greater than the educational level of those over 25 years of age and of the foreign-born. Nonetheless, the gap between school-age Spanish-surname children and Anglos remained great. The lag was evident in the relatively late entry of Spanish-surname children into formal education, the increasing differentials in school enrollment between the two groups in the more advanced grades, and the low proportion of Spanish-surname young persons who graduated from high school or college. In addition, the author found great state and local variations in the educational differences between Anglos and the Spanish-surnamed.—RS

144. ——————, Joan W. Moore and Ralph C. Guzman. The Mexican-American People: The Nation's Second Largest Minority. New York: The Free Press, 1970. 777 pp.

This volume, representing the culmination of more than four years of research, uses an interdisciplinary approach in an attempt to present an integrated and multi-faceted portrait of the Mexican American minority in relation to the dominant American society. The authors utilize data obtained from such diverse sources as census material, household interview surveys, informal interviews, direct observation, and published and unpublished literature concerning the Mexican American people, in order to develop a comprehensive analysis of interrelationships between historical antecedents, economic and educational conditions, social class and family structure, cultural values, religious and ethical norms, and political participation and effectiveness. The conclusions of the work stress the internal diversity of the Mexican American minority, their growing potential for assimilation and participation in the larger society, and the great need for the creation of conditions in which Mexican Americans can develop their individual abilities without hindrance, and in which they are free to make alternative choices involving their cultural identity.—BM

145. Greer, Scott. Last Man In: Racial Access to Union Power. Glencoe, Illinois, The Free Press, 1959. 189 pp.

This survey focuses on Los Angeles industrial operative and one-job unions with heavy Negro and Mexican American membership. In those unions, Greer concluded that race has little to do with the role the union member plays in the association but that race greatly affects the occupation the worker enters. Negroes and Mexican Americans are usually the dominant blocs in locals of unions of low-prestige workers, so their representatives are elected to office. Chicanos and Blacks who are upwardly mobile into occupations where they are in the minority of union membership have little chance for election. The author believes that Mexican Americans have a tendency to cling to the old patrón system, are hard to organize, and are less involved in plant meetings and other union activities than the average union member.—RM

146. ——————. The Participation of Ethnic Minorities in the Labor Unions of Los Angeles County. Unpublished PhD dissertation, University of California, Los Angeles, 1952.

This study involves a description and an analysis of the access of ethnic minority groups to membership in labor unions and their subsequent opportunities for attaining positions of union leadership. It also deals indirectly with the analytic problem of determining the extent to which the unions constitute an independent variable which influences ethnic relations within the general society. Greer analyzes the membership and leadership structure of various selected union organizations and develops a typology which he considers capable of being utilized not only as a framework for analysis within the scope of the present dissertation, but also as a heuristic instrument for analysis in future research concerning participation and internal control in labor unions.—BM

147. —————————. Situational Pressures and the Functional Role of the Ethnic Labor Leader, Social Forces, XXXII (October, 1953), 41-45.

Greer's discussion is based on the premise that all labor leaders face a "protest versus accommodation" dilemma; they must fight for demands in order to keep membership support while simultaneously reaching accommodations with the company management. The pressures are intensified for Mexican American and Negro leaders who must in addition gain advances for members of their minority while retaining Anglo leadership support.—SD

148. Griffith, Beatrice. American Me. Boston, Houghton Mifflin Co., 1948. 309 pp.

Griffith combines stories written by Chicano youth with her own sociological analysis in a description of urban Mexican American life. This presentation moves from behavior which Anglo society considers "problematic" ("The Smoke") through the cultural bases of life-style ("The Fire") to a concluding section on goals and aspirations ("The Phoenix"). The semi-fictional narratives "tell it like it was."

Many of the examples provide a panorama of wartime life in California urban barrios. The glossary includes information and definitions of pachuco and barrio slang.—PS

149. Guerra, Manuel H. The Retention of Mexican American Students in Higher Education with Special Reference to Bicultural and Bilingual Problems. Long Beach, California: California State College, Long Beach, May, 1969. 27 pp.

In this monograph, presented at the Conference on Increasing Opportunities for Mexican American Students in Higher Education held in Long Beach, California in May of 1969, the author examines the current status of the Mexican American student in higher education. Of primary concern in this monograph are the traditional admissions standards and testing instruments used by colleges and universities. The author finds that such concepts as "academic standards" and "admissions standards" have not taken into account the values and opinions of the minority community for at least three reasons: (1) such standards have intellectually discriminated against minority peoples whom white Americans have traditionally regarded with historic contempt, disrespect or suspicion, (2) most administrators, though well-intentioned, have a gross ignorance of minority problems and a reputation of recorded misjudgments with regard to minority education, and (3) both administrations and faculties are committed to a status quo point of view, making any necessary innovative change with regard to minority education difficult if not impossible. The author suggests that new criteria of admissions be found that will bring more disadvantaged Americans to the learning process, perhaps even giving some credit to students for their bicultural and bilingual talents.

The author sees two central problems in keeping Mexican Americans in higher education: financial capability and academic scholarship. Regarding the first, such ideas as the raising of tuition and the awarding of financial scholarships to more affluent students regardless of need can be fatal to Mexican American students whose economic situations are already acute. With regard to the problems of academic scholarship, the author makes several suggestions for the revision of much of the public school curriculum to meet the special needs of bicultural and bilingual Mexican American students.—AP

150. ——————. Why Juanito Doesn't Read, CTA Journal (October, 1965), pp. 17-19.

In this short article, the author points out some of the difficulties that the young bilingual Mexican American child faces in learning to read in the schools. While there are linguistic, environmental, and emotional factors which hinder his reading achievement, the author believes that psychocultural reasons predominate, aided by a lack of sympathy throughout society, indifference of teachers, and continuous prejudice on the playground. The author points out that there have been few empirical studies by competent linguists on the problems of bilingualism faced by Mexican American children, and also that two trends have dominated sociological studies. Sociologists have tended to combine the problems of minority groups, treating them as a single phenomenon, and have relied on an "acculturation" model that may no longer be adequate as a tool of explanation. Guerra suggests that future investigators of Mexican Americans should speak Spanish proficiently and understand the customs, attitudes, and inclinations of the Mexican American.—AP

151. Gutierrez, Jose Angel. La Raza and Revolution: The Empirical Conditions of Revolution in Four South Texas Counties. Unpublished thesis for the M.A. degree, St. Mary's University, San Antonio, Texas, August, 1968.

In this study, the phenomenon of revolution is defined as a form of social change achieved through the use of violence. Gutierrez attempts to elaborate on the prerequisite empirical conditions of revolution and then to apply these conditions to the situation of the Mexican American people of South Texas. He contends that recent developments in the Mexican American movement have brought about a sense of group identity, solidarity, and a desire for change, and that the primary psychological, economic, and political conditions for revolution exist at the present time among the Mexican Americans.—BM

152. Guzmán, Ralph. The Hand of Esau; Words Change, Practices Remain in Racial Covenants, Frontier, VII, No. 8 (June, 1956), 7, 16.

This is a brief description of housing discrimination against one Mexican family in Lynwood, California, a Los Angeles suburb. The author is concerned with Mexican Americans whose difficulties are as great as the problems of those who receive publicity and become causes célèbres; the difficulties encountered by one family who would have gone unnoticed are described here.—LH

153. ——————. How El Centro Did It, Frontier, VII, No. 4 (February, 1956), 13, 16.

The author relates the story of a successful court battle against the school segregation of Mexican Americans and Negroes in the El Centro school district. The National Association for the Advancement of Colored People and the Alianza-Hispano-Americana worked together to win the case, which Mr. Guzmán describes on the basis of personal participation.—LH

154. ——————. Politics and Policies of the Mexican-American Community, in Eugene P. Dvorin and Arthur I. Misner, eds. California Politics and Policies. Palo Alto, California, Addison-Wesley, 1966, pp. 350-384.

This chapter in a work about various California ethnic and interest groups in politics gives a history of Mexican American political action groups. Guzmán begins with a sketch of the Chicano's social history in California, his current economic position, his heritage of Mexican loyalty and his strife with Anglos. The author deals with politics stressing the recent nature of much of the Chicano activism; there was little activity before World War II. Pre-war groups such as the Order of the Sons of America and the League of United Latin American Citizens (LULAC) sought the goal of assimilation into Anglo culture. The Community Service Organization first organized Chicano grassroots democracy and moved into Anglo political fields. The members of the World War II veteran group, the American GI Forum, were mainly Democratic partisans, interested in defense against prejudice. Recent political organizations in California are associated with the liberal wing of the Democratic party, especially the Political Association of Spanish-Speaking Organizations which is identified with the Kennedy family in politics.—RM

155. Haber, Alan, Louis A. Ferman and Joyce L. Kornbluh. Poverty in America: A Book of Readings, Ann Arbor, University of Michigan Press, 1968 rev. ed. 651 pp.

This collection deals with the nature of poverty in contemporary United States industrial society and the methods of coping with economic inequality. It undertakes a causal analysis of relevant institutional processes, rather than reiterating already well-documented descriptions of poverty.

The book emphasizes political and economic facets, and gives secondary attention to psychology, social structure, cultural values, education, and activist movements. Outstanding articles by Martin Deutsch, Herbert Gans, Michael Harrington, Arthur Pearl, and Frank Riessman, and Raymond F. Clapp are reprinted.—PS

156. Hadley, Eleanor M. A Central Analysis of the Wetback Problem, Law and Contemporary Problems, XXI (1956), 334-357.

This analysis of the "wetback" problem from 1944 to 1954 is based on testimony from congressional hearings, government statistics, and newspaper articles. The author looks at the problem from the standpoint of national immigration policy and labor and agricultural problems.—LH

157. Hall, Edward T. The Manpower Potential in Our Ethnic Groups. Washington, D.C.: United States Department of Labor, Manpower Administration, 1967. 24 pp.

Hall suggests that all peoples have particular culturally produced talents, many of which can be translated into skills which would be useful to contemporary American life. In support of this theory, examples are presented of specific types of skills demonstrated by American Indians, Eskimos, Mexican Americans, and Negroes, and of instances in which these skills have been adapted and usefully employed within the economy.

It is admitted that technically very little is known about skills as they relate to ethnic affiliation, and the author suggests that, in order to overcome this inadequacy, there exists a very real need for large-scale experimentation using pilot projects which are designed to identify and develop the inherent skills of America's ethnic groups. The information thus gained would not only make it possible for members of deprived ethnic groups to become creative participants in the national culture and provide manpower in needed areas, but might also serve as a basis for meeting and dealing with some of the complex problems facing us in our cities. Hall states that the growth of the cities has been much too rapid, and that we should begin taking jobs to the people—to Indian reservations, to the deep south, to

Appalachia, etc. In this way the skills, capabilities, and potentials of our ethnic groups could be matched to our national needs without the destruction of ethnic dignity or basic way of life, and without the necessity of uprooting homes and communities.—BM

158. Handman, Max Sylvius. Economic Reasons for the Coming of the Mexican Immigrant, American Journal of Sociology, XXXV (January, 1930), 601-611.

Handman studied the economic conditions in the American Southwest which helped create and sustain the large-scale immigration of Mexican laborers after World War I. He placed particular emphasis on the increase in the demand for agricultural workers in the Southwest. The expansion of the truck-gardening industry (resulting, in part, from higher standards of living and improved technology in the canning industry) and the growth of cotton production in Texas were most important in increasing this demand. These types of agriculture lacked mechanization and were highly labor intensive. In cotton, the demand for workers was particularly acute because of the substantial migration of Negroes from rural to urban areas during the 1920's. The expanded demand for agricultural products, in addition to aggravating the need for labor, inflated land values in many areas of the Southwest, and increased the desire of landowners to minimize labor costs. These and other pull factors, in combination with the willingness of Mexicans to migrate after the disruption of their traditional rural society during the Revolution of 1910-1917, resulted in the large post-war inflow of Mexican labor.

The author concludes that the coming of the Mexican to Southwestern agriculture was economically inevitable and desirable. He regarded as shameful, however, the exploitation of this foreign labor force, and noted with alarm the economic threat which the Mexican worker posed to the American laborer.—RS

159. Harrigan, Joan. Materiales Tocante Los Latinos. Colorado: Colorado Department of Education, October, 1967.

This bibliography is the result of an attempt to compile a multi-purpose list of materials relating to the Spanish-surnamed citizen. The compilers suggest that the bibliography is designed to serve the needs of such diverse groups as general public library patrons, school students, and professional individuals. The work includes, among other things, a section listing general reading materials for young people from preschool to high school ages, and also a section listing dual language editions and separate Spanish and English editions of children's books.—BM

160. Heathman, James E. and Cecilia J. Martínez. Mexican American Education—A Selected Bibliography. Las Cruces, New Mexico, Educational Resources Information Center, Clearinghouse on Rural Education and Small Schools, New Mexico State University, 1969. 56 pp.

This bibliography lists many research findings and developments about the education of Mexican Americans. It is especially strong on bilingualism and includes teacher guides and program evaluations as well as more general social science studies. There is a subject index.—SD

161. Heller, Celia S. Mexican American Youth: Forgotten Youth at the Crossroads. New York, Random House, 1966. 113 pp.

This study concludes that there are ambitious and mobility oriented Mexican American youths who share ideals of getting ahead, although often on a reduced scale, with their Anglo peers. However, the Chicanos have greater handicaps in reaching their goals. The author argues that prejudice and lack of relevant education hold back Chicanos, but she also stresses that traditional Mexican American culture hampers successful achievement. The author feels that large families, few achievement models, lack of emphasis on achievement in family instruction, the machismo ideal and group loyalties all tend to keep the Chicano young people from advancing economically. In some data comparisons the author takes into account the fact that she is judging the performances of poor Mexican Americans against those of middle-class Anglos. The book leans heavily on older works, some of which present the stock image of Mexican American traditional culture stressing machismo, fatalism and humility.—RM

162. Heller Committee for Research in Social Economics and Constantine Panunzio. How Mexicans Earn and Live: A Study of the Incomes and Expenditures of One Hundred Mexican Families in San Diego, California. University of California Publications in Economics, XIII, No. 1 (Berkeley, University of California Press, 1933), 106 pp.
This study examined the yearly expenditures of a group of low-income Mexican American wage earners and small tradesmen in San Diego. Data are included on specific occupations, amount and source of incomes, and number of family members. There is detailed information on expenditure items, ranging from food, clothing and housing to leisure activities, automobiles and medical care.
The authors found that although food accounted for 33% ($500) of the total family expenditure, the amount was "insufficient to provide a minimum standard diet." They concluded that with the exception of diet, the Mexican Americans had adopted the United States standard of living "to a large extent," and offered as examples "the clothing worn, the good housing conditions, and the fact that 30% of the average budget went for items other than the 'necessities' of food, clothing and shelter."
The authors also compared the Mexican Americans' spending patterns with those reported in previous studies of six other United States working class groups. They found that the Mexican Americans emphasized spending on new secondary wants—automobiles, radios, and movies—at the expense of food, housing and savings. The authors also noted that although housing conditions were more crowded than those of all other groups except the New York tenement dwellers, the Mexican Americans benefited from growing public sanitation facilities. The authors observed that the low level of insurance and savings may have been accounted for by the ever-present possibility of returning to Mexico.—SD

163. Hendrick, Irving G. The Development of a School Integration Plan in Riverside, California: A History and Perspective. The Riverside School Study, a joint project of the Riverside Unified School District and the University of California, Riverside. State McAteer Project Number M7-14. 264 pp.
This is a historical narrative of the events leading up to adoption in October of 1965 of a comprehensive plan to integrate the schools of Riverside, California. Riverside was the first school system in a city of over 100,000 people to develop and implement a full scale racial balance plan. In his historical narrative, the author includes a brief history of the city since its founding, the movements of its minority groups, and the significant social and educational developments leading to a condition in the early 1960's of severe racial imbalance in three of the city's elementary schools. The author chronicles the activities of all of the significant groups involved—the city, the school board, and Black and Mexican American

community groups—which led to an eventual boycott of the schools. An evaluation of the implementation of the integration plan is also included.—AP

164. Hernández, Deluvina. Mexican American Challenge to a Sacred Cow. University of California, Los Angeles, Mexican American Cultural Center, March, 1970. 61 pp.

This monograph is a critical review and analysis of two recent UCLA Graduate School of Education research studies on the Mexican American. The two studies are Audrey J. Schwartz, Comparative Values and Achievement of Mexican American and Anglo Pupils (1969) and C. Wayne Gordon, Audrey J. Schwartz, et al., Educational Achievement and Aspirations of Mexican-American Youth in a Metropolitan Context (1968). The sacred cow under attack in this case is social science research, specifically social science research on the Mexican American. The author criticizes the two UCLA studies on several grounds, the primary ones being research bias, an inadequate and inappropriate theoretical framework, and sophistry and irrationality. The author states that the researchers were biased by their expectations which were based on an academically perpetuated but false stereotype, and that the motivation for their studies involved a conflict of interests and an ignorance and insensitivity to the observed subcultural group. The theoretical framework was inadequate in its reliance on a stereotype which fails to distinguish between behavior which indicates cultural values and behavior which is a response to a social stimulus. The author does not limit her challenge to the two UCLA studies alone, and she has much critical comment on contemporary social science research in general.—AP

165. Hernandez, Luis F. The Culturally Disadvantaged Mexican-American Student, Journal of Secondary Education, XLII, Part I (February, 1967) and Part II (March, 1967), 59-65, 123-128.

This article is directed toward teachers and administrators and attempts to give them some understanding of the special situation of Mexican American students in the schools In Part I, the author discusses the shortcomings of the public schools and their personnel. He sees a lack of understanding and cross-cultural experience on the part of teachers, an inadequate training in handling the special problems of bilingual students, and an inability to be empathetic with the students and problems of the Mexican American community. The author discusses the agrarian folk-culture background of many Mexican Americans, differences in Mexican American and Anglo values, and problems of identity, self-image, language, and achievement. While the author is sensitive to the common stereotype of the Mexican American and he differentiates eight major groups of Mexican Americans in the Southwest, he discusses in a general way Mexican Americans and their negative self-image, their patriarchal family, and their concept of machismo.

Part II of the article is concerned primarily with the problems that the Mexican American faces in getting out of the barrio, or Mexican American community, the problems of social and economic advancement in Anglo society, and the impact of the Anglo's rejection of the Mexican American. It is the author's thesis that what most hinders the Mexican American in social and economic advancement is not language difficulty but rather a negative self-image and a lack of self-confidence.—AP

166. ——————. Teaching English to the Culturally Disadvantaged

Mexican-American Student, English Journal, LXII (January, 1968), 87-92.

This article was written primarily for the benefit of English teachers who have large numbers of Mexican American students in their classrooms. The author discriminates between four types of Mexican American students the English teacher is likely to face in the classroom, and he analyzes these groups to further understanding of the distinct type of teaching situation relevant to each group. The author also includes some information on non-standard usage and pronunciation common among Mexican Americans, stressing that only those pronunciation errors that lead to spelling errors should receive focus. Comments and suggestions are also made on possible reading and writing programs, and on the kind of special information that the teacher should have on each Mexican American student.—AP

167. Herr, Selma E. Effect of Pre-First Grade Training Upon Reading Readiness and Reading Achievement Among Spanish-American Children, Journal of Educational Psychology, XXXVII, No. 2 (February, 1946), 87-102.

In order to measure the effect of a year of pre-first grade training upon the reading ability of Spanish-speaking children, two groups of five-year-olds in New Mexico were selected for testing in 1940. The experimental group, which received preschool training, read much better than the control group in the first grade. The author encouraged the development of pre-school programs for Spanish American children.—LH

168. Hiestand, Dale L. Economic Growth and Employment Opportunities for Minorities. New York, Columbia University Press, 1964. 127 pp.

In this work the author concludes that specific economic variables are not as important to the growth or decline of minority group employment as are non-econoimic forces, such as changed attitudes and behavior of the majority group toward the minorities. The study is based on census data, and emphasizes geographical and technological considerations relevant to minority labor problems. In some geographical regions there is little opportunity for employment. The increased technical specialization required in newly automated industries eliminates minorities because of their lack of training. There is no direct reference to Mexican Americans.—RM

169. Higham, John. Strangers in the Land: Patterns of American Nativism, 1860-1925. New York, Atheneum, 1955. 330 pp.

This account traces American xenophobia to fears: Americans feared that immigrants would inundate the Anglo-Saxon race with "inferior" bloods, that Roman Catholics would intrigue to overthrow the government and the Protestant religions, and that the alien political beliefs held by many immigrants would cause rebellion and anarchy. The book does not mention Mexican Americans.—RM

170. Hishiki, Patricia. The Self Concepts of Sixth Grade Girls of Mexican-American Descent, California Journal of Educational Research, XX (March, 1969), 56-62.

This article reports the results of a comparative study of seventy Caucasian sixth grade girls in Georgia and sixty-five Mexican American sixth grade girls in East Los Angeles. The author's conclusions about self-concept and scholastic characteristics are based on scores on four measuring instruments, a Self Concept Scale, a Child Self-Description Scale, the Lorge-Thorndike Intelligence Test, and the Stanford Achievement Test. Her findings show that a significant difference exists between the self-concepts of the Georgia group and those of the Mexican American girls. The mean concept scores for both self and ideal self were significantly higher for the Georgia group. The author also found a significant and positive correlation between scores on the Self Concept Scale and scores on the Lorge-Thorndike Intelligence Test for both groups, but greater correlation for the Mexican American group.—AP

171. Holmes, Jack E. Politics in New Mexico. Albuquerque, University of New Mexico Press, 1967. 335 pp.

This is a comprehensive history of political behavior in New Mexico. The author sees the history as a unique case of ethnic pluralism. He feels that social, cultural and economic factors, all of which are central to the substantial Hispanic vote, determine election outcomes. Holmes treats such factors as the intensity of campaign efforts in specific areas, the influence of factions, and long-term trends in the important independent vote. Histories of charismatic and influential individuals are interwoven with discussions of critical issues. Assertions about behavior on all levels of political organization (county, state, national) are documented with tables and graphs.

Holmes differentiates between areas in which Spanish American voters hold a majority and those in which they constitute a minority. In the former, intragroup divisions occur along standard two-party lines; in the latter, Spanish Americans form an ethnic block. Traditional examinations of Spanish American political behavior base their conclusions on sociological concepts of family structure, church control, and patrón systems. Holmes explains their political behavior in terms of historical involvement in stable, competitive party politics and institutions.—PS

172. Honigmann, John J. Middle Class Values and Cross-cultural Understanding, in Joseph C. Finney (ed.). Culture Change, Mental Health, and Poverty. New York: Simon & Schuster, 1969, pp. 1-19.

In this article, Honigmann is particularly concerned with the possibility that the standards social psychiatry uses to evaluate personality disorder and the factors which precede it are bound up in the culture of middle-class America. He also expresses doubt as to the efficacy of the standards and methods of social psychiatry in obtaining useful knowledge bearing on the human condition in the culture of poverty. When social psychiatrists operate exclusively from the limited cultural perspective of their own social class, he states, the results are likely to include serious misconstructions and distortions. Rather than imposing too much of themselves and their own culture onto that way of life they are seeking to understand, and even to change, anthropologists and social psychologists should make greater use of the structure inherent in the data they observe and allow change and planning in a specific culture to be emergent and self-directed.—BM

173. Horgan, Paul. Great River: The Rio Grande in North American History. 2 vols. New York, Rinehart, 1954. Vol. I, 440 pp.; Vol. II, 492 pp.

This Pulitzer prize-winning work is a narrative history of the lands along the Rio Grande, with special emphasis placed on Texas. The first volume deals with the indigenous Indian populations and tells the story of the Spanish exploration and settlement of the area. The second volume treats Mexico and the United States, especially the Anglo in-migration and the resulting social and sometimes physical clashes. The detailed coverage ends with the victory of the United States in the

Mexican War, although Horgan describes incidents up to the Zimmermann Affair in World War I. This is a study of events, explorations, battles, and empire building, not a social analysis.—RM

174. Hudson, Wilson M., ed. The Healer of Los Olmos and Other Mexican Lore. Dallas, Southern Methodist University Press, 1951. 139 pp.

This book consists primarily of two collections of stories: one by Ruth Dodson, "Don Pedrito Jaramillo: The Curandero of Los Olmos," and the other by Soledad Pérez, "Mexican Folklore from Austin." Dodson recounts stories about the miraculous cures of a famous folk healer of the late 19th century, a figure still venerated by many Mexican Americans of South Texas. Pérez presents Mexican American folk tales and discusses some common folk illnesses and remedies; she also attempts to classify some of her stories by theme and to trace their derivations.—RS

175. Humphrey, Norman D. The Changing Structure of the Detroit Mexican Family: An Index of Acculturation, American Sociological Review, IX (December, 1944), 622-626.

According to this study, the structure of the first generation Mexican American family in Detroit had undergone two basic changes that provided a good index of the process of acculturation. The status of the father had declined from what it had been in Mexico, and the status of the children had increased. The eldest son, in particular, had acquired a new role—that of a mentor, trained in American ways, to his siblings—and a new prestige within the family. The status of the mother had tended not to change, although in certain cases the more acculturated woman had reversed the family roles and had become superordinate to her husband.

The author bases his analysis on data from interviews with Mexican Americans in Detroit but does not indicate the size of his sample or make his methodology explicit.—RS

176. ——————. The Detroit Mexican Immigrant and Naturalization, Social Forces, XXII (1943-44), 322-325.

The observations in this article are examples of early impressions of the problems encountered by Mexican Americans. The article is primarily an editing of random conversations.—LH

177. ——————. Employment Patterns of Mexicans in Detroit, Monthly Labor Review, LXI (1946), 913-923.

Although no attempt at statistical analysis is made in this description of patterns of employment in Detroit from 1920 to 1938, the information on Mexican Americans provides a historical perspective. Over 50 case records from the Detroit Department of Public Welfare were used as the basis for descriptions of agricultural (sugar-beet), railroad, and factory (packing-house, fertilizer plant, and automobile) labor. The problems encountered in adjusting to industrial work are emphasized.—LH

178. Hutchinson, E.P. Immigrants and Their Children, 1850-1950. New York, John Wiley and Sons, Inc., 1956. 278 pp.

Hutchinson prepared an analysis of census data on first and second immigrant generations in the United States. The book covers the changing composition and geographic distribution of the foreign stock from 1920 to 1950, complementing the earlier work by Niles Carpenter, Immigrants and their Children, 1920. The volume also studies the occupational distribution of the foreign white stock, 1870 to 1950. Hutchinson has data on the occupational and geographic distribution of Mexican Americans and Spanish-surname people in the Southwest. Other types of census data (for instance, on natality, sex ratios, education or family size) are not included.—RS

179. Hyman, Herbert H. Political Socialization. New York, The Free Press, 1959. 136 pp.

In this summary work, the author explicitly limits his model of political socialization to the "processes of learning that most members of a society or of a subgroup experience, in contrast with learning that is idiosyncratic in character." Hyman explores the cognitive sets underlying political behavior along three dimensions: political participation, political orientation, and a democratic or authoritarian tendency. The presentation of age and sex differences in child socialization culminates in an examination of generational variations. The family is traditionally named as the major socializing agent.

In addition to outlining a systematic framework for investigation, the author reviews many major works relating to politics and psychology. Tangential references are footnoted.—PS

180. Inter-Agency Committee on Mexican-American Affairs. The Mexican American: A New Focus on Opportunity. Washington, D.C., 1968. 32 pp.

This report contains testimony presented before members of the United States Cabinet by men and women, usually Mexican American, considered experts or influential in the fields of education, politics, social service, agriculture and labor relations. Sections of the book focus on different aspects of governmental-Chicano interaction. The presentations offer short statements about the problems faced by Mexican Americans in almost every social field and recommend programs to meet them.—RM

181. Inter-Agency Committee on Mexican American Affairs. The Mexican American, A New Focus on Opportunity: A Guide to Materials Relating to Persons of Mexican Heritage in the United States. [Washington, D.C.] March, 1969. 144 pp.

This bibliography gives extensive coverage to books, journal articles, unpublished materials including dissertations, and other bibliographies. The organization of the section on periodical literature makes the volume less useful than it might be; articles are listed alphabetically by journal rather than by author. Other features, however, expand the appeal of the work: there are annotations of selected audiovisual materials and listings of currently published periodicals of interest to the Mexican American community, and United States producers or distributors of Spanish audiovisual aids.—RS

182. Jaco, E. Gartley. Mental Health of the Spanish-American in Texas, in Marvin K. Opler, ed., Culture and Mental Health. New York, The Macmillan Company, 1959, pp. 467-488.

Jaco attempts to determine the incidence of severe mental illness among Anglos, the Spanish-surnamed, and nonwhites. He analyzed the statistics on all patients treated for major psychoses (for instance, schizophrenia) by public and private mental health facilities in Texas during 1951-52. He found that, relative to population, there were three times as many cases of severe mental illness reported among Anglos as among the Spanish-surnamed. Jaco states that the Spanish-surnamed have health attitudes different from those of Anglos, and that these attitudes may keep some people with mental illness from going to a physician. He argues, however, that he has greatly reduced the effect of these cultural factors on his data by analyzing only the statistics on the most severe of mental illnesses. People with major psychoses, he asserts, would almost always have to seek the aid of a doctor. Jaco thus argues that the statistics on the reported cases of severe mental illness among Anglos and the Spanish-surnamed reflect fairly well the relative incidence of these illnesses within the two groups. He suggests that the Spanish-surname population has a lower incidence of major psychoses than does the Anglo because it is a "warm, supportive and a reasonably secure subcultural group."—RS

183. Jenkinson, Michael. Tijerina: Land Grant Conflict in New Mexico. Albuquerque, Paisano Press, 1968. 103 pp.

This is not so much an account of a man's life as it is a meshing of the events of his life into the account of a historical land struggle. It is a journalistic history of the events of June 1967 of Tierra Amarilla, New Mexico. A concise undocumented history of the conflict between claimants of land grants and the United States government is presented as background for the emergence of the Alianza de Pueblos Mercedes movement in Northern New Mexico.—CV

184. Jensen, Arthur R. Learning Abilities in Mexican-American and Anglo-American Children, California Journal of Eduational Research, XII, No. 4 (September, 1961), 147-159.

In contrast to standard intelligence tests, the tests devised in this experiment did not depend on language facility or familiarity with Anglo culture. The subjects were bilingual Mexican Americans and Anglos from monolingual English speaking families in grades four to six in Contra Costa County, California public schools. The students were first classified by IQ score as measured by the California Test of Mental Maturity; they were then given a battery of non-verbal and manual tests. Mexican Americans classified as low IQ performed much better on the language-independent tests than did low IQ Anglo children; high IQ children of both groups performed equally well on the second set of tests. The author concluded that the standard IQ test did not measure the abilities of Mexican Americans accurately and that such tests should not be used as the basis for putting Mexican Americans in slow-learners' classes.—LH

185. Jessor, Richard and Theodore D. Graves, Robert C. Hanson, Shirley L. Jessor. Society, Personality and Deviant Behavior: A Study of a Tri-Ethnic Community. New York, Holt, Rinehart and Winston, Inc., 1968. 421 pp.

This research project tested a theory to account for the different rates of deviant behavior (primarily, alcohol use) found among Anglos, Mexican Americans and Indians in a small Colorado community. The researchers postulated that deviancy is one among many possible behavioral adaptations; the choice of deviancy or conformity results from complex personality and sociocultural pressures and controls. Anglos, who contributed least to community deviance rates, had the strongest social controls and the greatest access to opportunity (thus the "least pressure to adopt...illegitimate...means" to achieve goals). Mexican American access to opportunity was as low as, if not lower than, that of the Indians, but Indians exhibited more pervasive anomie and weaker social controls. The Mexican

American deviance rate, while intermediate between the two other groups, was close to that of the Anglos, leading the authors to suggest that social controls may play a more important role than pressures in influencing the occurrence of deviance.

The book focuses on the rigorous development of the theory and its methodological implementation; one interested in Mexican Americans can, however, obtain ethnic comparisons from the data. One particular finding, for example, suggests that the traditional terms "future oriented" and "past oriented" are not as accurate as the concept of extended and restricted time perspectives. There is evidence of a generational change, since, contrary to the adult population, the difference between the time perspectives of Anglo and Mexican American high school students was not significant. Important ethnic comparisons also emerge from other testing measures, such as alienation, delay of gratification, and social norms.

This study complements the concept of a "culture of poverty" cutting across ethnic or regional lines. The authors suggest that differing deviance rates are explained not by ethnic identity but by differing social-psychological status; "place Anglos in the situation of Indians, and deviance rates should increase markedly."—SD

186. Johnson, Dale L., and Melvin P. Sikes, Rorschach and TAT Responses of Negro, Mexican-American, and Anglo Psychiatric Patients, Journal of Projective Techniques and Personality Assessment, XXIX (March, 1965), 183-188.

This is a report of a study of three groups of 25 Negro, Mexican American, and Anglo psychiatric patients in a veterans hospital in Houston, Texas. The study was designed to explore personality differences between members of these subcultures through the use of Rorschach and Thematic Apperception Test projective techniques. The subjects were fairly matched across age, sex, educational level, and occupational level. An analysis of the resulting data indicated several statistically significant differences, among them: (1) distinct differences on the Rorschach on measures of hostility; (2) differences indicated by the TAT between Mexican Americans and the other Negro and Anglo groups in themes of family unity, and more specifically in father-son and mother-son relationships. The authors suggest that these results possibly demonstrate the persistence of Mexican American cultural values regarding family interpersonal relationships.—AP

187. Jones, Lamar B. Mexican-American Labor Problems in Texas. PhD dissertation, University of Texas, Department of Economics, 1965.

This study charts the interrelation between technological change and structural unemployment of Mexican-American workers in the Texas border area. The author analyzes the manpower problems of this regional labor force historically, in order to determine the causal factors that have been operative in producing a persistent pocket of poverty, unemployment, and underemployment in the agricultural sector of the economy. The study demonstrates that the pressures of continued in-migration of alien commuters and "wetbacks" and the progress of agricultural mechanization have acted to reinforce one another, producing a surplus labor force that is largely prevented from seeking other occupational outlets. In Texas, this problem is illustrated most clearly by the decline in Mexican Americans employed as farm laborers. In 1960, the total figures for all Mexican Americans employed as farm laborers (citizens, aliens, commuters) was 261,000. Of these, 40% or 104,000 were braceros working under Public Law 78. Anticipating the end of the bracero program, Texas corporate agriculturalists intensified their efforts toward further mechanization, resulting in a decline to only 17,700 braceros employed by 1963. Looking toward means of relocating this surplus labor force created by structural imbalances, the author recommends the improvement of educational and technical training for Mexican Americans and the unionization of Mexican Americans to protect their interest while not damaging either Mexican nationals or the domestic Anglo-American market. The author is convinced that these major problems in reallocating Mexican American laborers can be resolved to the benefit of all sectors of the population.—MLB

188. Juárez, Rumaldo Z. Educational Status Orientations of Mexican American and Anglo American Youth in Selected Low-Income Counties of Texas, Washington, D.C., United States Department of Agriculture, 1968. 137 pp.

This documented report challenges Talcott Parson's assertion that Mexican Americans have a low status orientation. Research findings on Mexican American and Anglo high school sophomores in Texas indicate that both groups have high educational aspirations, although Anglo youth are more certain about attaining their desired educational status. Social class as a variable is found to influence expectation more than it does aspiration, suggesting a strong awareness of reality among poor youth.

The author presents a model supporting Robert Merton's hypothesis of a culturally shared universal value orientation. He makes analytical distinctions and provides a statement of research techniques. All materials used in the study are included in an appendix.—PS

189. Kaplan, Bert (ed.). Studying Personality Cross-Culturally. Evanston, Illinois: Row, Peterson, 1961.

This book consists of a collection of works dealing with theory and research in the specialized field of culture and personality. The authors represent the perspectives of the disciplines of anthropology, history, psychiatry, psychoanalysis, psychology, and sociology. The studies include a historical development of the main issues of culture-personality study, theoretical presentations on the role of personality and motivational processes as they affect the functioning of a society, the place of linguistics in cross-cultural personality development, and discussions of projective techniques and psychiatric interviewing.—BM

190. Karno, Marvin and Robert B. Edgerton. Perception of Mental Illness in a Mexican-American Community. Archives of General Psychiatry, XX (February, 1969), 233-238.

This is an introductory report to a forthcoming series of papers that will present the findings of more than five years of collaborative research on mental illness among Mexican Americans in East Los Angeles. The central issue in this report is the discrepancy between the reported low incidence of mental illness among Mexican Americans and the authors' hypothesis that the true incidence of mental illness is much higher. After a review of some of the literature indicating a low incidence of mental illness, the authors report on their own data collected through comprehensive and testing of 444 adult Mexican Americans in two areas of East Los Angeles. A preliminary analysis of their data has led them to make the following three tentative conclusions: (1) the underutilization of psychiatric facilities by Mexican Americans is not due to the fact that they share a cultural tradition which causes them to perceive mental illness in significantly different ways than do Anglos; (2) the low incidence of Mexican Americans in psychiatric treatment facilities does not reflect a lower incidence of mental illness than that found in other ethnic groups; and (3) the underrepresentation of Mexican Americans in psychiatric treatment facilities is due to a complex of social and cultural factors. A 28-item bibliography is included.—AP

191. Kearns, B.J.R. Childrearing Practices Among Selected Culturally Deprived Minorities, The Journal of Genetic Psychology, CXVI (June, 1970), 149-155.

This is a study of differences in childrearing practices among three distinct cultural groups in Tucson, Arizona. The author based her study on comprehensive formal interviews with 50 Anglo, 50 Mexican American, and 50 Papago Indian mothers in Tucson. The data, which were collected on an adapted form of the interview schedule developed by Sears, Maccoby, and Levin, provided the author with information indicating the existence of significant differences in the childrearing practices of the three groups. Kearns believes that these findings suggest that many early childhood education programs need to be reexamined.—AP

192. Kerchoff, Alan C. Anomie and Achievement Motivation: A Study of Personality Development Within Cultural Disorganization, Social Forces, 37 (March, 1959), 196-202.

The main theme of this article is that the development of the need for achievement must take place in a social setting in which there are stable norms. Populations in which a stable normative structure is lacking will not produce individuals with high levels of need for achievement. It is also suggested that those who are least successful in defining a consistent self-image in relation to the major population segment will be least likely to develop high levels of need for achievement.—BM

193. Keston, M.J. and C. A. Jimine. A Study of the Performance on English and Spanish Editions of the Stanford-Binet Intelligence Test by Spanish-American Children, Journal of Genetic Psychology, LXXXV (1954), 263-269.

The authors compared the performance of bilingual children on English and Spanish versions of the Stanford-Binet Intelligence Test. Fifty Spanish-surnamed children in the fourth grade of five Albuquerque, New Mexico schools were administered tests by a bilingual examiner. Because the test depended on education and school achievement, bilingual children performed better in the language in which they had formal instruction—English. However, the English version was not a completely fair measure because of the children's language difficulties. The Spanish translation was not suited to the children's cultural background because once they entered school their formal use of Spanish deteriorated.—LH

194. Kibbe, Pauline R. The Economic Plight of Mexicans, in Edward C. McDonagh and Eugene S. Richards. Ethnic Relations in the United States. New York, Appleton-Century Crofts, Inc., 1953, pp. 189-200.

This account criticizes the promotion of wetback migration by Anglo agriculturalists and its effect on Mexican American economic problems in Texas. The author states that the Immigration Service and the Governor of Texas secretly cooperated with the growers.—RM

195. ——————. Latin Americans in Texas. Albuquerque, University of New Mexico Press, 1946. 279 pp.

This book is an introductory survey about the inequities borne by the Mexican American in Texas. Kibbe points out the adverse effect that discrimination in Texas has on Inter-American relations. The opening sections recount the course of hemispheric relations and summarize Mexican history. The body of the work then describes the nature and scope of domestic Texan problems: education, housing, sanitation, health, employment in industry and agriculture, social and civil inequities. Solutions to these problems are suggested as the author details the current (1943-46) efforts of local and state agencies. Kibbe calls attention to past abuses, for example, the procurement of state school aid with enrollment statistics inflated by listing Mexican American children; no subsequent attempt was made by officials to insure attendance of the children in the schools. Kibbe seems optimistic that once committees make studies and legislation is passed, the problems mentioned will be well on the way to eradication.—SD

196. Kiev, Ari. Curanderismo: Mexican-American Folk Psychiatry. New York, The Free Press, 1968. 192 pp.

Kiev studies the folk healing practices of Mexican Americans using his own discipline of psychiatry as well as anthropological methods. He concludes that curanderismo (Mexican American folk medicine) provides successful therapy, especially for minor mental disturbances, because it fits the needs and beliefs of a non-assimilated minority. Members of the minority group, Kiev feels, would not accept modern psychiatry because it is depersonalized and does not recognize the validity of folk ailments such as susto (fright) and mal ojo (the evil eye). The curanderos are within the Indian-Catholic folk traditions of Mexico and yet are alert to the stresses affecting a population caught between two cultures. For this reason, Kiev feels that the curanderos play an important role in reconciling Mexican Americans to their transitional cultural status.

Although the curandero's treatment primarily follows a traditional format, it does take into account current environmental conditions. Kiev feels that for Mexican Americans curanderismo is superior in some cases to modern United States practice because it is related to, rather than isolated from, the patients' institutional environment and belief systems. However, curanderismo is helpless when faced with mental disorders of organic origin. Also, major psychoses can be aggravated by certain aspects of curanderismo therapy, such as the forced acceptance of a strong father figure (the curandero) and the transference of guilt to a mythical witch (bruja).—RM

197. Kluckhohn, Florence R. The Spanish-Americans of Atrisco in Florence R. Kluckhohn and Fred L. Strodtbeck, eds. Variations in Value Orientations. Evanston, Illinois, Row, Peterson, 1961, pp. 175-258.

The study sets out to investigate Hispanos' lack of assimilation and the continuing friction between the Atrisqueños and neighboring Anglo communities. Culture and personality differences explain the history of political and economic interactions between the ethnic groups. Hispanos are traditionally characterized as passively existing, "Subjugated-to-Nature, and Present-oriented people" and Anglos as active, "Mastery-over-Nature, and a Future-oriented group." Theoretical bases for personality evaluations are reviewed in an introductory chapter, but the specific methodology used to study the community is not discussed.

The author presents Atrisco as a cohesive community originally organized about the central principles of family solidarity and elder-brother dominance, but now seeking to cope with the decline of patrón and hermano mayor traditions.

Data on economic transactions and family budgets supplement participant-observation techniques. Original data from 1936 and a re-study of the community in 1951 add a time dimensionto the article. Discussion of intracommunity political activity is detailed, although decision-making is usually explained by adherence to or deviance from the modal personality of Hispanos described above.—PS

198. Knowlton, Clark S. Patrón-Peón Pattern among the Spanish-Americans of New Mexico. Social Forces, XLI (October, 1962), 12-17.

Knowlton studied the disintegration of the patrón-peón system among the Hispanos of New Mexico. Since the Depression, particularly in the years following World War II, the traditional leaders of Hispano society—large landholders, village merchants and political leaders—have lost their positions of economic and social dominance to Anglo competitors. The Anglo leaders, however, have not assumed the social role played by the patrón in Spanish-speaking society. As a result, says the author, a vacuum has developed in the social organization of Hispanos. Traditional patterns of decision-making, financing and coordinating community activities, mediating conflict between members of the group, and caring for the poor and the weak have disintegrated with the decline of the patrón and have not been replaced. The relative scarcity of economic, political and cultural leaders within the Hispano community has increased the stresses of acculturation and made it more difficult for the Spanish-speaking people of New Mexico to articulate their needs and to act effectively in politics.—RS

199. ————————. The Spanish Americans in New Mexico, Sociology and Social Research, XLV (July, 1961), 448-454.

This is an overview of the kinds of social and cultural changes which are affecting the Hispanos of New Mexico. It is an introduction to the problems associated with rapid acculturation and to the areas of needed research.—LH

200. Krassowski, Witold. Naturalization and Assimilation—Proneness of California Immigrant Populations: A Statistical Study. PhD dissertation, University of California at Los Angeles, 1963.

This study analyzes the speed of naturalization of immigrant groups in California in terms of several different variables. The findings indicate that immigrants of high occupational status tend to naturalize far more rapidly than immigrants of low occupational status, and that more recent immigrants have naturalized much more quickly than those who arrived in the nineteen-twenties or thirties. The statistics also showed, contrary to the hypotheses first posited by Krassowski, that there is an inverse relation between the degree of cultural similarity with the new normative society and the speed of naturalization, and also that those immigrants who are under the influence of a coethnic milieu tend to naturalize significantly faster than those who are not.—BM

201. LaBrucherie, Roger A. Aliens in the Fields: The Green Card Commuter Under the Immigration and Naturalization Laws, Stanford Law Review, XXI, No. 6 (June, 1969), 1750-1776.

This article traces the legal status of commuters since 1921 and outlines the inconsistencies of agency enforcement of the statutes. The author then reviews the conflicting claims for and against continuing the "green card" program; he opts for a compromise between the economic needs of the border towns and the Mexican commuters and the pressures of domestic unemployment and labor unions. Two current plans for phasing out the program—the Ruttenberg-Scammon proposal and the Kennedy bill—are reviewed.—SD

202. Lamana, Richard, and Julian Samora. Recent Trends in Educational Status of Mexican-Americans in Texas, in Dwain M. Estes and David Darling, eds. Proceedings of the First Texas Conference for the Mexican American. San Antonio, Texas: Southwest Educational Development Laboratory, 1967. pp. 20-41.

This article is based on an analysis of the 1950 and 1960 census figures for Texas, and it is an attempt to make clear the significance of the changes that took place in the educational status of Mexican Americans over the ten year period. The article presents an interpretation of what the statistics mean for Mexican Americans, both in an absolute sense and also in relation to the educational status of the total population. Some of the findings included: (1) while the median level of education for Mexican Americans increased from 3.6 to 4.8 years of schooling over the ten year period, this increase of 1.2 years was lower than that of the total population over the same period; (2) the educational status of Mexican Americans in Texas is clearly the poorest in the Southwest; (3) the best educated Mexican Americans are becoming more geographically segregated from the least educated; (4) the greatest increase in educational status for Mexican Americans has been in areas where the percentage of Mexican Americans in the community is the smallest; and (5) the relative educational status of Mexican Americans in Texas remains unchanged at best.—AP

203. Landes, Ruth. Culture in American Education—Anthropological Approaches to Minority and Dominant Groups in the Schools. New York: John Wiley & Sons, Inc., 1965. 330 pp.

In this book the author attempts to specify some of the contributions that anthropologists and the study of anthropology can make to the field of education, and, in particular, to the training and retraining of teachers who work in multi-cultural schools. The context of the book is the author's personal description of her work in an experimental project at Claremont College in Southern California. The project was one designed to give teachers and social workers some anthropological insights that would be helpful in their work with minority-group individuals. What the author has to say about Mexican Americans seems to be based on a static traditional-culture paradigm, rather than being realistically descriptive of Mexican Americans as they exist today.—AP

204. —————————. Latin-Americans of the Southwest. New York, McGraw-Hill, 1965. 100 pp.

This is an introductory work which touches many aspects of Mexican American and Hispano life in the United States. Beginning with current economic discrimination and demographic statistics, Landes gives backgrounds for these conditions by discussing Spanish exploration and settlement in the United States, Mexican history and the history of Anglo-Mexican rivalries. The author then describes, in anthropological terms, Mexican American culture and beliefs and concludes with an account of the development of Mexican American leadership and the problems of Mexican identity in an Anglo culture. The book is based largely on secondary literature.—RM

205. Landolt, Robert G. The Mexican-American Workers of San Antonio.

Unpublished PhD dissertation, University of Texas, 1965.

This is a study of the labor problems faced by the Mexican American in Texas focusing on the city of San Antonio. Done in 1962 and 1963, the study utilizes detailed employment data and related information gathered from executives of thirty-one selected private firms and government agencies as well as membership data of major labor union locals. In a historical context the roles of politics, education, housing, health and other social factors are examined. The author demonstrates that proper utilization of Mexican American labor has not occurred due to San Antonio's economic dependency on the military, Kelly Air Force Base, as its main industry, thus providing little impetus to economic development of those industrial sectors likely to provide employment for Mexican Americans. After considering all facets of this difficult problem, the author makes the following policy recommendations: (1) that public officials cease the use of public policies that tend to play off various segments of the city against one another to the detriment of Mexican Americans, i.e., using Mexican Americans as strikebreakers in an attempt to thwart the creation of responsible labor unions; (2) that the Mexican American community put forward its most talented and responsible citizens as community spokesman; (3) that the Anglo sector of the community as a whole strive to lessen prejudice and to break down social barriers discriminating against Mexican American citizens; and (4) that San Antonio seek to diversify its industrial base for a more balanced economic development.—MLB

206. Lane, John Hart. Voluntary Associations Among Mexican Americans in San Antonio, Texas: Organizational and Leadership Characteristics. Unpublished PhD dissertation, University of Texas, at Austin.

In this study the author attempts to analyze the ethnic voluntary associations among Mexican Americans in San Antonio, Texas, with respect to such considerations as the kinds of organizations which exist, the ways in which they vary, the characteristics of the elected leadership, the degree of participation in voluntary associations by the adult Mexican American population, and the extent of similarity with the position of the Negro American. Lane identifies certain factors which tend to promote the development and support of organizations. These factors include a favorable sociopolitical environment, a relatively high socioeconomic status, and a richness of organizational life. Urbanization and leadership capabilities are also discussed as factors which tend to promote the building and sustenance of voluntary associations.—BM

207. Lasker, Gabriel W. and F.G. Evans. Age, Environment and Migration: Further Anthropomorphic Findings on Migrant and Non-Migrant Mexicans, American Journal of Physical Anthropology, XIX (1961), 203-211.

The effects of age, environment and migration on the body dimensions of over 250 adults in Uruapan, Mexico are treated in this detailed study. Informative tables illuminate the differences between United States born and native Mexicans' body dimensions. Although age was found to be the most significant factor, environment and migration did affect body dimensions.—LH

208. Lázaro Salinas, José. La emigración de braceros. Mexico, n.p., 1955. 190 pp.

This is a study of the bracero program. Salinas discusses major aspects of the bracero controversy and refutes the argument that any failure of the ejidal land reform causes bracero emigration. Instead, he attributes bracerismo to deeper causes such as the natural poverty of Mexico's agricultural lands. Second, he urges a new concord with the United States to perpetuate and improve the system. Third, he proposes the institutionalization of safeguards by the Mexican government. In particular, abuses in the regional recruitment and channeling process require attention. The author illustrates the complexities and unfairness of the system with vivid case histories. The study is based on statistics and two years of personal investigation including interviews.—SD

209. Lemert, Edwin M. and Judy Rosberg. The Administration of Justice to Minority Groups in Los Angeles County. University of California Publications in Culture and Society, II, No. 1 (Berkeley, University of California Press, 1948). 27 pp.

This study compared the sentences meted out by the courts to a sample of Anglos, Negroes, Mexican Americans, Jews and members of certain other minority groups who had been convicted of committing felonies. The statistical data for the analysis were gathered from the Superior Court records of Los Angeles County for 1938. The study also examined the attitudes of probation officers toward Mexican Americans and Negroes, since these officials wielded the greatest influence in determining the length of sentences. The authors based this part of their work on an interpretive reading of reports of the Los Angeles County Probation Department for 1938 and other years.

The authors concluded that the data supported their original hypothesis: that probation officers and judges responded to certain types of deviation on the part of Negroes and Mexican Americans as manifestations of a minority group—Anglo power struggle. For the same deviation harsher sentences were often given to Negroes and Mexican Americans than to Anglos. The study questions the conclusion that higher rates of arrest and conviction for felonies among Mexican Americans and Negroes than among Anglos necessarily indicates a greater propensity toward criminal behavior among these minority groups.—RS

210. Letwin, Leon. Some Perspectives on Minority Access to Legal Education, Experiment Innovation, II (May, 1969), 1-24.

In this article, the author presents an overview of the many aspects of the problem of increasing the access of minority-group individuals to the law schools. He first cites the statistics showing the extremely low number of Mexican Americans and Negroes in California's law schools, and argues for increased access. Letwin then examines the traditional admissions standards of law schools, and questions whether or not the traditional criteria are completely valid, giving several desirable qualities of prospective students that the criteria do not measure or show. The author believes that increased numbers of minority students in the law schools will not only help to alleviate an acute need of minority lawyers, but that their presence in the law schools will have a strong and beneficial impact on the character of the law school itself, perhaps even serving to thwart an increasing disenchantment with the American legal system by minority groups. A large part of this article consists of a description of the problems encountered during the course of a special summer institute at UCLA for incoming minority students who had been accepted to law schools in California. The author, a law professor who directed the program, evaluates the program's effectiveness and discusses such problems as the recruitment of minority students and necessary financial aid.—AP

211. Levine, Harry. Bilingualism: Its Effect on Emotional and Social

Development, Journal of Secondary Education, XLIV (February, 1969), 69-73.

This article is a review of some of the pertinent literature concerned with the relationship between bilingualism and social and emotional adjustment. The author points out that while there has been a large amount of research on some aspects of bilingualism—such as its influence on intelligence quotients and how to teach bilingual children—little has been written on its effects on the social and emotional adjustment of those who are bilingual. The author also points out that the case of the Spanish-speaking bilingual in the Southwest does not exactly parallel other cases of bilinguals in the United States, because of the proximity of the Southwest to Mexico and the continuous inflow of Spanish-speaking immigrants. A 15-item bibliography is appended.—AP

212. Lewis, Hilda P. and Edward R. Lewis. Written Language Performance of Sixth-Grade Children of Low Socio-Economic Status from Bilingual and from Monolingual Backgrounds, Journal of Experimental Education, XXXIII, No. 3 (Spring, 1965), 237-242.

In comparing the written language performances of monolingual, Chinese bilingual and Spanish bilingual children, the authors found only a slight relationship between bilingual background and written language performance. Sixth-grade children of similar IQ's from racially and ethnically mixed low socioeconomic neighborhoods in a California city were used as subjects. Measurements of written language performance included verbal output, range of vocabulary, accuracy of spelling, grammatical correctness, quality of sentence structure and effectiveness of expression. Although most of the conclusions concerned the Chinese bilingual group, several tables of data collected in this experiment contain information on bilingualism among the Spanish-speaking.—LH

213. Lewis, Oscar. The Culture of Poverty, Scientific American, CCXV, No. 4 (October, 1966), 19-25.

In this article, Lewis sets forth the conceptual boundaries of his "culture of poverty" theory. Lewis' theory focuses on the family and community, rather than on individual personality. Basic to this controversial idea is the distinction between poverty (limited resources, low technology) and the culture of poverty (a design for living adapted to special demands of Western society). Although a slum neighborhood may have discernible esprit de corps, its low level of organization makes it a marginal subculture in a class-stratified, capitalist society.

The culture of poverty is most often found in colonial societies among "the people who come from the lower strata of a rapidly changing society and who are already partially alienated from it." It contains, then, a certain potential for protest or revolt against the established order. Such involvement in a movement (political or religious) destroys the core of a culture of poverty because it creates a sense of solidarity with larger groups.

In viewing the culture of poverty as an entire style of life and set of values the author attempts to describe a phenomenon on its own terms and to eliminate negative connotations of such attributes as "present-time orientation," or what might appear to outsiders to be "instability." The approach is designed for cross-cultural comparisons, suggesting that what is often seen as an ethnic or national characteristic is really a widespread example of adaptation to situation and necessity.—PS

214. Lipshultz, Robert J. American Attitudes Toward Mexican Immigration,

1924-1952, M.A. thesis, Department of History, University of Texas, Austin, 1962.

Relying on periodicals, congressional hearings, senate investigations and other public documents, the author investigates American attitudes toward Mexican immigration from 1924 to 1952. The author's main thesis is that American attitudes towards Mexican immigration can best be viewed as a function of two interrelated processes: (1) The clash of economic interest between the corporate agriculturalists on the one hand and a diverse coalition composed of small farmers and various organizations representing the American industrial and agricultural working class on the other; (2) The long term growth and stability of the agricultural sector of the total economy and the consequent fluctuations and the demand for cheap labor in the southwest. The author concludes that American attitudes have changed through three distinct time periods according to which of the two antagonistic economic interests is predominant and to the instability of the economic system. The first period from 1924-1935 was marked by the dominance of corporate interest resulting in a policy of unlimited immigration in order to fill the need of a cheap labor force. The second coincides with the end of the depression and World War II. This was a time of conflict between restrictionist policies of the AFL and small farmer interest and rapid expansion of agricultural market in response to wartime needs. In the third period, the conflict continued, but with the increasing consolidation of restrictionist forces which articulated a racial ideology to justify and rationalize the exclusion of Mexicans on the grounds of anti-American values and cultural standards.—MLB

215. Loomis, Charles P. El Cerrito, New Mexico: A Changing Village, New Mexico Historical Review, XXXIII (January, 1958), 53-75.

In this essay Loomis recounts the changes he found upon revisiting a Hispano village he had previously studied. He discovered that between 1950 and 1958 approximately three-fourths of the population had moved away, in many instances to Pueblo, Colorado. The old Hispano culture was incapable of meeting the inhabitants' needs and most residents had lost their hope for the future. Their belief in their way of life was declining in the face of increased social linkage with the outside world, which occurred through contacts created by the Rural Electrification Administration, radio and improved transportation. The median age level was higher, family authority was breaking down and the young were abandoning the village and the Hispano culture.—RM

216. Lopez, Enrique Hank. Back to Bachimba, Horizon, IX, No. 1 (Winter, 1967), 80-83.

Lopez describes his reactions as a Mexican American who feels at home neither in the United States nor in Bachimba, his paternal home in the Mexican state of Chihuahua.—LH

217. Lopez, Richard Emilio. Anxiety, Acculturation and the Urban Chicano. Berkeley, California: California Book Co., 1970. 41 pp.

This study explores the relationship between acculturation and anxiety in a sample of Mexican American college students. In the introduction to the study, Lopez cites and briefly discusses a number of works dealing with the concepts of acculturation and anxiety, and with recent research on Mexican Americans. He hypothesizes that Mexican American college freshmen who were moderately acculturated into Anglo culture would be more anxious than Mexican American freshmen who were either high or low in acculturation, and that highly-acculturated

Mexican American freshmen would be more anxious than Mexican American freshmen low in acculturation. The results of the investigation did not support either of the hypotheses and it was suggested that this might be due to the fact that the Chicano freshmen sampled were not representative of the general Mexican American population.—BM

218. Lopez, Ronald W. The El Monte Berry Strike of 1933, Aztlan, I (Spring, 1970), 101-114.
In 1933, there were 37 agricultural strikes in California, affecting some 50,000 workers and 65 percent of the state's entire crop value. This paper is a case study of one of the more important strikes, which is pointed out by the author as being one of many organized attempts by the Mexican American community to rectify some of the injustices against them. The strike in El Monte, California was one of the biggest and most publicized of the strikes. The author attempts to evaluate the influence of the significant parties involved in the strike: the Communist Party, the Cannery and Agricultural Workers Industrial Union (C&AWIU), the workers, the Mexican Consulate, the U.S. Department of Labor, an ex-president of Mexico, Plutarco Calles, and the Los Angeles Chamber of Commerce. He describes the significant events of the strike and its eventual outcome. The formation of a nationally oriented union of Mexican American workers in 1933 is seen as a forerunner of the more contemporary organization of the grape workers in California.—AP

219. Lorenz, James D., Jr. The Application of Cost-Utility Analysis to the Practice of Law: A Special Case Study of California Farm Workers, Kansas Law Review, Symposium on Legal Problems of the Poor, XV (1967), 409-451.
Lorenz proposes establishing a theory to weigh the social costs of directed change against the offsetting social benefits. As a beginning step in establishing a working model, Lorenz establishes the ramifications of alternative legal approaches to the problems faced by migrant agricultural workers in California. He sets the context for these legal problems by describing the basic economic, social and cultural situation of the farm workers. The legal issues are then presented in great detail; Lorenz covers housing, debtors' rights and remedies, welfare, employment, government services and treatment in such areas as education, voting rights and due process.—SD

220. Lowry, Edith E. They Starve That We May Eat. New York, Council of Women for Home Missions and Missionary Education Movement, 1938. 70 pp.
This book written under the sponsorship of the Council of Women for Home Missions and Missionary Education Movement is an appeal for betterment of the plight of the migrant farm worker. The history and working and living conditions of migrant labor is traced; the activities of the Home Missions (later the Migrant Ministry of the National Council of Churches) in providing public health nurses and day care centers are described. The author calls for comprehensive federal, state and county action, while retaining the conviction that churches can play a special role in galvanizing the conscience of communities about their migrant population. There is a foreword by Henry Wallace (as Secretary of Agriculture) and some photographs from the Farm Security Administration.—SD

221. Mack, Raymond W., ed. Our Children's Burden—Studies of Desegregation in Nine American Communities. New York, Random House, 1968.

461 pp.

Two chapters in this book have been annotated; see Duster, Troy. Violence and Civic Responsibility: Combinations of 'Fear' and 'Right' " and Dworkin, Anthony G. "No Siesta Mañana: The Mexican American in Los Angeles."

222. Madsen, William. The Alcoholic Agringado, American Anthropologist, LXVI (April, 1964), 355-361.

This is a study of the psychological stresses on agringados—Mexican Americans who have consciously rejected their culture and have adopted many of the outward patterns of Anglo life. The author also discusses some of the ways in which these partially acculturated people resolve or escape these stresses. Madsen argues, on the basis of his own observations and of those of police and probation officials, that alcoholism is sometimes one of these means of escape. He discusses the conflicting values of Mexican American and Anglo society, the attitudes toward liquor among both groups, and the factors which might lead the agringado toward alcoholism. He notes finally that public and private therapy for alcoholism usually fails with Mexican Americans since it is generally oriented toward helping Anglos. He suggests that therapists should understand Mexican American culture and the problems of value conflict.—RS

223. —————————. Mexican-Americans of South Texas. San Francisco, Holt Rinehart and Winston, 1964. 112 pp.

This anthropological study is based on field research conducted from 1957 to 1961 in four communities in Hidalgo County, South Texas, the county in which the city of McAllen is located. The communities studied range from a "rural-folk society" of Mexican Americans to a "bicultural urban center." The main concern of the book is to provide an understanding of some of the psychological and social stresses which the acculturation process places on Mexican Americans. The volume includes many case histories to illustrate generalizations. The organization of the work is topical, with chapters on the class structure of Mexican American society, the family, religion, education, and politics. Beliefs about the causes of illness and the role of the folk healer (curandero) in Mexican American society are topics which receive special attention. The author, whose study was financed by the Hogg Foundation for Mental Health at the University of Texas, emphasizes the contribution of the curandero as folk psychotherapist in cushioning the psychological shocks of acculturation.

Madsen criticizes the well-meaning Anglo who denigrates Mexican American values as inferior to his own—for example, the physician who ridicules the folk medicine of Mexican Americans, the social worker and the teacher who advocate the suppression of the Spanish language and the inculcation of Anglo values. Madsen argues that the solution to the problems of acculturation rests, in part, on "a two-way process of education among the Anglo and Latin populations."—RS

224. Maloney, Thomas. Factionalism and Futility: A Case Study of Political and Economic Reform in New Mexico, Spanish-Speaking People in the United States; Proceedings of the 1968 Annual Spring Meeting of the American Ethnological Society. Seattle, Distributed by the University of Washington Press, 1968, pp.154-161.

This is an account of how political reform benefiting the Hispanos of northern New Mexico is being frustrated by Hispano factions that fight mostly for political spoils. Maloney concludes that the Hispanos have no unity; the only recent unifying force is Reies Tijerina's land grant movement. The author rejects, however, the idea that the personalism and factionalism can be explained in terms of machismo or other attributes of Spanish culture, and maintains rather that any demographically similar community would develop similar political traits.—RM

225. Manuel, H.T. Recruiting and Training Teachers for Spanish-Speaking Children in the Southwest, School and Society, XCVI (March 30, 1968), 211-214.
In this short article, the author discusses both the problem of teacher recruitment and the special needs of the Spanish-speaking child. Given the teachers, the author contends that there is no great problem in getting them to teach the Spanish-speaking, that is, no special incentives are required. It is primarily a problem of training and retraining. To this end, teachers are required who can deal with classes with larger than normal percentages of educationally retarded children. In addition, teachers wherever possible should be bilingual and aware of the cultural background of their students. With regard to the special needs of the Spanish-speaking child, the author suggests that the schools can in part meet these needs by extending formal education downward with special preschool programs, the revision of elementary curriculum materials made necessary as a result of preschool programs, and the teaching of both Spanish and English through all levels of elementary school.—AP

226. Manuel, Hershel T. Spanish-Speaking Children of the Southwest. Austin, University of Texas Press, 1965. 195 pp.
This is a survey of the problems faced by Spanish-speaking children in getting an education: culture conflict, prejudice, language problems, poverty, and the migratory nature of some of the population. With an emphasis on Texas, Manuel presents a case based on school and census statistics, fleshed out by the inclusion of autobiographical material on the experiences faced by Mexican American children in the course of their educations. The author includes a chapter on the literature about Mexican American education, and reviews various educational controversies. Manuel writes from an assimilationist point of view.—RM

227. Marden, Charles F., and Gladys Meyer. Minorities in American Society. (3rd ed.). New York: American Book Co., 1968. 486 pp.
This volume consists of a description and analysis of dominant-minority relations in the United States. Each numerically significant minority group, including the Mexican American, is considered in relation to the dominant group, primarily within a framework which follows the order of the establishment of dominance, the maintenance of dominance, and the decline of dominance. Generally speaking, emphasis is placed on an elaboration of the pluralistic rather than the integrationist theory of assimilation. A sociological perspective is employed in the consideration of dominant-minority relationships, and the current situation is discussed in terms of problem areas and social policy.—BM

228. Martinez, Juan R. Mexican Emigration to the United States, 1910-1930, PhD dissertation, University of California, Berkeley, 1957.
Beginning with a discussion of the historical background of the American Southwest since 1848, the author pursues the parallel task of delineating developments in both the Mexican and American economies which resulted in the creation of a large ethnic and cultural minority in the United States. Concentrating on the time of the Mexican Revolution until the great depression, this study traces the effects of immigration both in terms of American immigration policy and

Mexican emigration policy toward its nationals. Basically the situation is described in terms of a surplus labor force escaping Mexican underdevelopment for work in the industrial cities of America as well as in the agricultural sector. As a result of this push-pull process Mexicans were dispersed throughout many of the states. Contrary to popular belief, this dispersion was so great that by 1927 Mexicans constituted 75 to 90% of the hand workers in Ohio, Michigan, Minnesota, and North Dakota, and by 1932 a quarter of a million Mexicans were employed in the railway system. From his research, the author concludes that Mexican emigration to the United States was a function of dislocation within the Mexican economy and fluctuated according to the cyclical pattern of American economic growth in the 1920's and 1930's.—MLB

229. Mason, Evelyn P. Cross-validation Study of Personality Characteristics of Junior High Students from American Indian, Mexican, and Caucasian Ethnic Backgrounds, The Journal of Social Psychology, LXXVII (February, 1969), 15-24.

This study reports on an analysis of the results of the California Psychological Inventory administered to 22 American Indian, nine Mexican American, and 16 Caucasian 13- and 14-year-old boys and girls in northwest Washington state. The author's previous study (1966) indicated that the Mexican American male responded more positively than the Caucasian or Indian to the scales of social responsibility, tolerance, and intellectual efficiency. The present study did not support the previous results, and in this study the Caucasian sample had the highest scores on the same scales. The author discusses several other significant ethnic differences that the results of her study indicated.—AP

230. Massa Gil, Beatriz. Bibliografia Sobre Migracion de Trabajadores Mexicano a Los Estados Unidos. Mexico D.F., Biblioteca del Banco de Mexico, 1959. 122 pp.

This bibliography of American sources includes entries from government documents, journal and magazine articles as well as newspaper stories and editorials on the subjects of immigration bracero laborers, labor contracts between the countries of Mexico and the United States; the volume includes material published in the period of 1950 to 1958. The author is presently completing the sequel to this work which will cover material published between 1959 and 1970.—CV

231. Materials for Mexican-American Studies Program in Harbor College Library. 17 pp.

This is a relatively short bibliography, wider in scope than in depth. It lists materials in the areas of philosophy, social sciences, languages, science, applied science, fine arts, literature, travel, biography, history, and fiction. The materials are arranged in each area strictly according to shelflist number, rather than alphabetically.—BM

232. Matthiessen, Peter. Organizer: Profile of César Chávez, The New Yorker, Part 1 (June 21, 1969), 42 ff., Part 2 (June 28, 1969), 43 ff.

This article describes César Chávez' entrance into social action and his subsequent training as a community organizer with Saul Alinsky's Community Services Organization (C.S.O.). Through informal interviews, the author elicits many personal notes about Chávez, such as his thoughts during his fast to dramatize the grape boycott and his conversations with the late Senator Robert Kennedy. The emergent human portrait includes a discussion of Chávez' wife and family and their reactions to his demanding career. Chávez, the man, is then placed in a larger perspective with a brief summation of farm labor history in California's San Joaquin Valley. To round out the picture, the reporter also covers growers' reactions and attitudes and reports conversations with strikebreakers about why they continue to cross picket lines.—PS

233. ——————————. Sal Si Puedes—César Chávez and the New American Revolution. New York, Random House, 1969. 372 pp.

This is a journalistic account of the California grape strike by the United Farm Workers Organizing Committee and its leader, César Chávez, covering the period from the early Sixties to late 1969. The author records his experiences as an observer of the strike in its many aspects, interviewing farm workers in the fields, growers, boycott leaders, and union officials, in an attempt to get at the varying personalities and motives of the central individuals involved in the strike. A large part of the narrative is the author's personal description of the background and daily activities of César Chávez—his meetings with fellow workers, negotiating sessions with growers, meetings with senators, his long hunger fasts, and his interactions with those closest to him, his family and fellow organizers.—AP

234. Mayeske, George W. Educational Achievement Among Mexican-Americans—A Special Report from the Educational Opportunities Survey. Technical Note 22, Department of Health, Education and Welfare, National Center for Educational Statistics, Washington, D.C., January, 1969. 9 pp.

A survey of 5% of the nation's schools (grades 1, 3, 6, 9, 12) was conducted to determine the extent of racial and ethnic segregation, the degree of equal educational opportunity, the amount of racial and ethnic group differences on standard achievement tests, and the relationships between the kinds of schools attended and achievement test performance. Although no specific description of research technique is included, approximately 20% of the difference in Mexican American children's achievement is attributable to the kinds of schools attended. Teacher attitude and ability is generally of little consequence, but it becomes more important in the higher grades. Although student motivation is important at all levels, a key aspect is confidence that one can control the environment through individual efforts. Variations in school characteristics had little effect on these attitudes.—PS

235. McDonagh, Edward C. Attitudes Towards Ethnic Farm Workers in Coachella Valley, Sociology and Social Research, XL (September, 1955), 10-18.

This statistical study of the attitudes of ranchers and high school students was based on a questionnaire which asked for reactions to Filipinos, Chicanos and Negroes as well as to Mexican nationals who had entered the United States both legally and illegally. Five stereotypes—"ambition, honesty, hard-working, law-abiding and morality"—were checked.—LH

236. McEntire, Davis. Residence and Race. Final and Comprehensive Report to the Commission on Race and Housing. Berkeley, University of California Press, 1960. 409 pp.

This is a study of the residential patterns of minorities, the characteristics and quality of minority housing, and discrimination in the building and real estate industries. The work also analyzes the role that government has played in federal housing projects, urban renewal and legislation against discrimination. The author uses a variety of sources, including census material, reports of federal, state and local agencies, and interviews with brokers, builders and mortgage lenders. The data are presented in a comparative context.—RS

237. McKinnon, William and Richard Centers. Authoritarianism and Urban Stratification, American Journal of Sociology, LXI (May, 1956), 610-620.

The authors try to measure the degree of authoritarianism or equalitarianism among individuals of various social classes. An authoritarian-equalitarian scale was used in interviews among ethnic and social cross-sections of the population of Los Angeles County. The authors found a greater percentage of authoritarians in the working class than in the middle class. Authoritarianism was related inversely to education, occupation and other stratification variables. The Mexican American and Negro populations had a greater percentage of authoritarians than did the Anglo population. The authors attributed these differences to the lower social and educational levels of the two minority groups.

The questions used to measure the degree of authoritarianism or equalitarianism (for example, whether or not people can be trusted, whether or not the most important thing a child should learn is obedience to his parents, whether or not women should stay out of politics) were designed for an Anglo population.—RS

238. McWilliams, Carey. Factories in the Fields. Boston, Little, Brown and Co., 1939. 325 pp.

This is a work on California agriculture and agricultural workers before World War II. McWilliams' analysis is made in terms of a capitalist-worker conflict. His central thesis is that land in California was monopolized from the beginning by a few men through fraudulent Spanish grants, illegal speculation in state and federal land grants, and force. California agriculture was always dominated by single crop concentrations—wheat, fruit, cotton, etc.—that were organized like factories for efficiency. Agriculture was also based on the exploitation of a series of minority group immigrants as a cheap labor force. Running as common threads in these factories in the fields system were repression of ethnic union organization by force and the gradual organization and rationalization of both crop production and marketing and the farm labor supply. The author concludes with an account of unionization attempts and suggests the conditions advantageous and disadvantageous to union formation.—RM

239. ——————. Ill Fares the Land: Migrants and Migratory Labor in the United States. Boston, Little, Brown and Co., 1942. 390 pp.

This book discusses the subject of migrant labor. The analysis is expressed in terms of capitalist-proletariat conflict. In covering the different geographical regions where migrants were employed, the survey discusses the ethnic group involved, physical conditions and racial strife. After a brief agricultural history of each region, McWilliams concentrates on delineating the area's social conflicts. Although Mexican Americans do not occupy a central position in the book, their status in each region is treated and the chapter on Texas focuses on them.—RM

240. ——————. The Mexicans in America. New York, Teachers College Press, 1968. 31 pp.

This is an overview of the history and current situation of Mexican Americans. It discusses most of the questions usually encountered when dealing with the problems of Mexican American and Anglo culture.—RM

241. ——————. North From Mexico: The Spanish Speaking People of the United States. New York, J.P. Lippincott Co., 1961 edition, 304 pp.
This book, which originally appeared in 1948, is an interpretive history of the peoples who moved north from Mexico to the regions now part of the United States. The survey extends from the Spanish explorations down to the end of World War II and covers the entire Southwest; there is a slight emphasis on Southern California. The central theme is Anglo-Chicano relationships and the strife that frequently followed their initial contacts. McWilliams stresses the exploitation and prejudice faced by the Mexican Americans and their frequent rebellions against subordinate status.—RM

242. ——————. Southern California Country. New York, Duell, Sloan and Pearce, 1946. 378 pp.
This is a narrative history of Southern California and a source of stories about the cults, personalities, and values that give the region its unique qualities. It studies the Californios and their relations with Anglos and Indians; McWilliams' analyses are made in terms of class divisions. McWilliams also treats the growth of the romantic legends about the Californios, including Helen Hunt Jackson, John McGroarty's "Mission Play," and tourism based on "Spanish charm." There is also a short section on the Mexican American in Southern California in the 1940's.—RM

243. Mead, Margaret (ed.). Studies of Whole Cultures: The Spanish Americans of New Mexico, U.S.A. in her Cultural Patterns and Technical Change. New York: New American Library, 1955, pp. 151-177.
This discussion of the culture of New Mexico's Spanish Americans is based primarily on observation and interpretation, and is presented within the context of a general survey concerning the introduction of technical change in developing areas and the possible effects of such change on the mental health of the areas' inhabitants. Specific values and attitudes are outlined as being characteristic of the Spanish Americans, and the varying effects of Anglo contact upon individuals and communities are described. It is stated that those who do begin to move into the larger society and to identify with groups other than family and community are primarily the young people. Because of the difficulties and anxieties attendant on seeking an Anglo adjustment, however, such changes in youth are relatively temporary, and basic traditional patterns of training, family life, and kinship responsibility appear to the author to be readopted later in life, thus maintaining the culture in a condition of relatively little change.—BM

244. Mendes, Richard H.P. Bibliography on Community Organization. Washington, D.C.; President's Committee on Juvenile Delinquency and Youth Crime; June 1965. 98 pp.
This bibliography contains materials on the techniques, theory and empirical foundations of community organization, as well as a section devoted specifically to citizen participation in voluntary democratic associations.—PS

245. Merton, Robert K. Social Theory and Social Structure. (Enlarged edition). New York: The Free Press, 1968. 702 pp.
This work systematically outlines the foundations of functional sociology, dealing with studies in theoretical sociology, social and cultural structure, the

sociology of knowledge and mass communications, and in the sociology of science. In the section concerning social and cultural structure, Merton attempts to discover how some social structures exert a definite pressure upon certain persons in the society to engage in nonconformist rather than conformist conduct. Deviant behavior is seen as a symptom of dissociation between culturally prescribed aspirations and socially structured avenues for reaching these aspirations. In other words, when there is a disjunction between the goals and means phases of the social structure, anomie may result. In America, for example, a heavy emphasis is placed on wealth as a basic symbol of success, but there is no corresponding emphasis upon the legitimate means for achieving this goal. Merton states that five types of adaptation can be made to this type of situation: conformity, innovation, ritualism, retreatism, or rebellion, depending on the individual degree of rejection or acceptance of cultural goals and institutionalized means.—BM

246. Mexican-American Education. Special Report. Department of Health, Education and Welfare, Office of Education, Washington, D.C. 1968. 31 pp.

The Mexican American Affairs Unit of the Office of Education undertook a field survey to acquire first-hand acquaintance with regional and local problems and to locate available resources and match them to needs. Travels and meetings through Arizona, California, New Mexico, Colorado, and Texas revealed a lack of coordination among all government levels and a lack of creativity in the schools. Early childhood education, teacher training, bilingual education, and programs for adult and vocational education were major areas of concern in all states, with some variance regarding priority. The report contains specific recommendations for improving the state of education for Mexican Americans and closes with a summary of federal programs which might help.—PS

247. Mexican-American Study Project. Division of Research, Graduate School of Business, University of California, Los Angeles. See Grebler, Leo, et al. The Mexican American.

248. Mexican-American Study Project Revised Bibliography. With a Bibliographical Essay by Ralph Guzmán. Advance Report 3. Los Angeles, Division of Research, Graduate School of Business, University of California, 1967. 99 pp.

This is an extensive listing of books, journal articles and bibliographies as well as doctoral and masters' dissertations and other unpublished material. A bibliographical essay by Ralph Guzmán introduces the volume and discusses the major scholarly works on Mexican Americans since the 1920's.—BM

249. Mexican-Americans: A Selective Guide to Materials in the UCSB Library. University of California at Santa Barbara, California, 1969.

This bibliography, primarily sociological in emphasis, contains a list of approximately 500 books, articles, and government publications available in the UCSB library, which deal with the Mexican American minority in the United States. The materials are arranged in separate sections and are ordered alphabetically according to author or title. Two brief sections concerning curriculum materials and current Mexican American newspapers complete the bibliography.—BM

250. Mexican-American History: A Critical Selective Bibliography. Mexican-American Historical Society, Santa Barbara, California, 1969. 20 pp.

This bibliography is a short selective list of books compiled for the use of teachers of Mexican American history. It consists of a listing of materials concerning the history of the North American Indian, the history of Spain, the history of Mexico, and a final section listing books and journal articles specifically dealing with Mexican American history.—BM

251. Mexico. Ministerio de Relaciones Exteriores. La Proteccion de Mexicanos en los Estados Unidos, by Ernesto Hidalgo. Mexico, 1940. 72 pp.

This pamphlet offers some examples of Mexican opinion about the emigration of Mexicans to the United States and the treatment they received there. Hidalgo was the author of a legislative bill to provide legal aid for Mexicans in the United States, and he wrote this booklet to point out the large number of emigrants and the Mexican government's obligation to look after their recurring needs. In 1926, Hidalgo spoke about the "interminable and painful caravan of Mexicans [who go to the United States] to enrich with their sweat the lands that through bitter irony ought to be returned to us." The concluding section contains comments from various Mexican consuls about the program; their reactions include many examples of abuses suffered by Mexicans in the United States.—SD

252. Meyers, Frederic. Employment and Relative Earnings of Spanish-Name Persons in Texas Industries, Southern Economic Journal, XIX (April, 1953), 494-507.

This is an "exploratory" study of earnings and employment pattern differences between Spanish-surname and non-Spanish-surname employees. It is based on employer reports to the Texas Employment Commission. Although most of the hypotheses tested did not yield statistically significant results, the study does have information on the place of Spanish-surname people in Texas industries.—LH

253. Mintz, Sidney W. and Eric R. Wolf. An Analysis of Ritual Co-Parenthood (Compadrazgo), Southwestern Journal of Anthropology, VI, No. 4 (Winter, 1950), 341-368.

The first part of this article describes the historical antecedents of compadrazgo, a complex system of godparentage usually formalized at Catholic baptisms in Latin America. The pervasive compadre mechanism is portrayed as a hardy survivor of traditional social-kinship affiliations in the face of industrial development and increasing impersonalization. The authors analyzed compadrazgo in five "modern communities with Latin American culture," including the Indian village of Pascua, Arizona. Although regarded by participants with some reverence, this flexible alliance also serves to solidify or advance an individual's economic position. Mintz and Wolf find that the degree of economic diversity in a community determines the shape of different varieties of compadrazgo.

The authors' finding that rapid social change may also increase the number of compadre relationships suggests an interesting parallel to current revivals of the custom among Mexican Americans. Godparentage specifies social-familial relationships which promise security through alliances in a threatening environment.—PS

254. Mittelbach, Frank G. and Grace Marshall. The Burden of Poverty. Mexican-American Study Project Advance Report 5, Division of Research, Graduate School of Business, University of California, Los Angeles, 1966. 48 pp.

This study of poverty in the Southwestern United States is based on data from the 1960 census. The focus is on the Spanish-surname population, but the Anglo and nonwhite groups are also studied. Defining the poverty line as a family income of $3,000, the authors analyze the incidence of poverty among each group in every Southwestern state and in urban and rural areas. They find that, while census data on median incomes indicate that there was some improvement during the 1950's in the welfare of the Spanish-surname population relative to that of the Anglo, the gap between the two in 1960 was still great. The incidence of poverty among Spanish-surname families in the Southwest, while less than that among nonwhites, was more than twice as high as that among Anglos. The authors note that while poverty was widespread in the rural sectors of the Spanish-surname population, a majority of the poor in this group lived in urban areas. The incidence of broken homes (measured by the percentage of heads of families who were female) was, surprisingly, somewhat greater in the Spanish-surname population (both total and poor) than among Anglos; poverty among Spanish-surname people was aggravated by a high birth rate and relatively large families. By emphasizing that several factors correlate with low family income—for instance, old age, a broken family, farm employment, a low level of education—the study points to the need for a variety of approaches in the fight against poverty.—RS

255. Mittelbach, Frank G. and Joan W. Moore. Ethnic Endogamy—the Case of Mexican Americans, American Journal of Sociology, LXXIV (July, 1968), 50-62.
Sex and generational differences, occupational status and age at the time of marriage are considered in this study of Mexican American marriage patterns. The article focuses on exogamy rates among three generations of Mexican Americans in Los Angeles. Using marriage licenses, the authors examined 7,492 cases in which one or both spouses had a Spanish surname. Exogamy was more prevalent among high-status individuals, women, young men, and those furthest removed from immigrant status. The study concludes with a brief discussion of assimilation.—LH

256. Mittelbach, Frank G., Joan W. Moore and Ronald McDaniel. Intermarriage of Mexican-Americans. Mexican-American Study Project Advance Report 6. Division of Research. Graduate School of Business, University of California, Los Angeles, 1966, 47 pp.
The authors try to measure the degree of assimilation of Mexican Americans into Anglo society, using the extent of intermarriage between the two groups as an indicator. The work is based on data from Los Angeles County marriage licenses for 1963. Two earlier articles on intermarriage in Los Angeles—those of Panunzio (1942) and of Burma (1963)—and other works on marriage patterns in the urban Southwest provide the study with an excellent comparative framework. The authors find that although the majority of Mexican Americans in Los Angeles (about 75%) still tend to marry within their ethnic group, the proportion marrying outside the group has increased since the 1930's. They note, in addition, that marriage patterns vary according to generation, sex, social status and age. The incidence of out-marriage increases with each succeeding generation. Within the ethnic group, first generation Mexican Americans (those born in Mexico) tend to marry other immigrant Mexican Americans and second and third generation persons tend to choose mates who are also native-born Mexican Americans of their generation. The incidence of out-marriage is greater among women than among men within each generation, and varies directly with social status. Finally, those who marry outside the group tend to be younger than those who marry within it. The

authors conclude that the Mexican American population is gradually being assimilated into Anglo society.—RS

257. Montiel, Miguel. The Social Science Myth of the Mexican American Family, El Grito, III (Summer, 1970), 56-63.

In this article, the author is critical of many studies on the Mexican American family which he sees as lacking both methodological sophistication and empirical verification. In particular, the author is critical of the dominance of a psychoanalytic interpretation of the concept of machismo and the central role that this interpretation has had in explanations of both the Mexican and the Mexican American family. The author looks first at the influence of this interpretation on two Mexican thinkers (Ramos and Paz), and then illustrates his criticism of work in the social sciences by briefly looking at three examples of studies of the Mexican family, those by Bermudez, Diaz-Guerrero, and G. M. Gilbert. Montiel also briefly reviews some of the literature on the Mexican American family.—AP

258. Moore, Joan W. Colonialism: The Case of the Mexican American, Social Problems, XVII (Spring, 1970), 463-472.

In this essay, the author offers an analysis that discards the concepts of "assimilation" and "acculturation" that have traditionally served as explanatory models for the political behavior of most immigrant groups to the United States, as in many ways inapplicable to the Mexican Americans of the Southwest. Instead, she offers the paradigm of colonialism as more suitable to explain groups who entered American society not as volunteer immigrants but through some form of involuntary relationship. The author then specifies three distinct types of colonialism in three regions of the Southwest: "classic colonialism" in New Mexico, "conflict colonialism" in Texas, and "economic colonialism" in California. These models are then applied to explain a traditional stereotype—the supposed low degree of formal voluntary organization among Mexican Americans and their subsequent lack of participation in political activity. The author concludes by saying that the present militant Chicano movement itself has emphasized the paradigm of colonialism as a way of transcending the enormous disparity in Mexican American experience.—AP

259. —————————. Mexican-Americans: Problems and Prospects. Institute for Research on Poverty, University of Wisconsin, Madison, University of Wisconsin Press, November, 1966, 58 pp.

This is an introduction to the current situation of the Mexican American population, with a strong statistical base from the census of 1960 and the data collected by the Mexican American Study Project at the University of California at Los Angeles. After delineating the educational, economic, employment and social position of the Chicanos vis-a-vis the Anglo and nonwhite populations, the author discusses urban problems, lack of public services, and the social pathology associated with poverty. Moore criticizes the academic literature which describes Mexican Americans in terms of a traditional Spanish culture, arguing that these interpretations are based on studies of a declining portion of the Chicano population. The author warns that this approach may be adopted by Anglos and by Mexican American leaders who are looking for a strong cultural identity and seize a simplistic one at the expense of the great diversity existing among Mexican Americans. Moore concludes with a review of policies adopted by Mexican Americans and by Anglo governing bodies and adds some personal recommendations.—RM

260. ——————. Political and Ethical Problems in a Large-Scale Study of a Minority Population, in Gideon Sjoberg, ed. Ethics, Politics and Social Research. Cambridge, Massachusetts, Schenckman Publishing Company, Inc., 1967, pp. 225-244.

The problems encountered in setting up the Mexican-American Study Project at the University of California at Los Angeles are presented in this article by one of the original staff members. They faced the common dilemma of selecting representative samples and achieving breadth of scope with limited funds. The author discusses the difficulties of community participation in research and the conflicts between scholarly interests and the aims of local groups. In addition to raising general ethical and methodological questions, the work gives background information on the Study Project Reports, all of which are annotated in this bibliography.—PS

261. ——————. Social Class, Assimilation and Acculturation, in Spanish Speaking People in the United States; Proceedings of the 1968 Annual Spring Meeting of the American Ethnological Society. Seattle, distributed by the University of Washington Press, 1968, pp. 19-33.

This is a sociological survey comparing samples of the Mexican American populations of Los Angeles and San Antonio for assimilation, acculturation, and social mobility. Moore takes an intermediate position between the ethnic pluralism argued by Milton Gordon and the complete assimilation advocated by Lloyd Warner, and follows Alex Simirenko's division of second-generation ethnic immigrants into the conservative "colonists," loyal to the ethnic community, and the "frontiersmen," who leave the community both spatially and emotionally. Moore concludes that the greater and more diverse job opportunities in Los Angeles and its more heterogeneous population result in more mobility than in San Antonio, especially in terms of income. The "frontiersmen," more destructive of ethnic exclusiveness and traditionalism, are more assimilated, so there is a fairly high rate of third-generation intermarriage and more upward mobility in terms of job prestige and income. However, the colonial areas will persist, because of the ethnic exclusiveness of those who choose to remain there and because the communities function as receiving areas for newcomers.—RM

262. Moore, Joan W. and Frank G. Mittelbach, with the assistance of Ronald McDaniel. Residential Segregation in the Urban Southwest; a Comparative Study. Mexican-American Study Project Advance Report 4, Division of Research, Graduate School of Business, University of California, Los Angeles, 1966.

This study used data from the 1960 census to derive indices of residential segregation for thirty-five cities in the American Southwest. The authors found that the degree of segregation of Spanish-surname people from Anglos was generally high, but in all cases was exceeded by that of Negroes from Anglos. Spanish-surname persons were generally more segregated from Negroes than from Anglos, but in nine cities the opposite was true. Beyond these similarities, the degree and pattern of segregation varied considerably from city to city.

In an attempt to explain these variations the authors studied a wide range of cultural, economic and social factors, using the statistical method of multiple regression analysis. They found that the intensity of the three types of segregation (Negroes from Anglos, the Spanish-surnamed from Anglos, and the

Spanish-surnamed from Negroes) varied directly with the size of the city. The degree of segregation of Negroes and of the Spanish-surnamed from Anglos was positively correlated with the proportion of large households—which the authors interpret as an indicator of the lack of acculturation—within the minority groups. It was also associated with income differences—lower incomes within the minority groups than among Anglos—but was not related to low minority income as such.

The authors also found that the intensity of segregation of both Negroes and the Spanish-surnamed from Anglos varied directly with the proportion of Blacks in the non-Anglo population. Apparently, say the authors, when Blacks form a high percentage of the non-Anglo population, Anglos tend to consider the Spanish-surnamed as "Negroes"—at least when buying and selling a house; when Negroes, on the other hand, are less visible, Anglos might be said to discriminate more finely between the two minority groups, and be less concerned about residential integration with either of them.

The authors also found that the pattern of segregation of Negroes from the Spanish-surnamed was not significantly related to the percentage of Blacks in the non-Anglo population, nor was it associated with income differences between the two groups. They note, finally, that other variables for which they were unable to devise adequate measures—for instance, "the taste for discrimination" within the Anglo population—may also be very important in explaining residential segregation.—RS

263. Moore, Truman. The Slaves We Rent. New York, Random House, 1965. 171 pp.

The author presents a description and analysis of farm labor conditions throughout the United States. The study includes historical material on origins of the migrant streams and development of transitory labor practices. Moore's discussion of various attempts to alleviate unsatisfactory conditions in fields and labor camps covers the activities of all major organizations and of local efforts. The author then recommends union organizing and inclusion of agricultural workers under protective federal labor laws. The work concludes with a section explaining the dilemma of small growers and outlining the impact of agribusiness consolidation on migrant wages and treatment. The work contains bibliographic references. Reading notes and maps provide further statistics and research leads.—PS

264. Moreno, Steve. Problems Related to Present Testing Instruments, El Grito, III (Spring, 1970), 25-29.

This brief article is concerned with the problems related to the use and effectiveness of traditional tests of intelligence, aptitude, and achievement on Mexican American children. Moreno first presents a review of some of the related research literature since 1932 and concludes that monolingual and bilingual Spanish-speaking children are handicapped by the standard testing instruments in the English language. He also concludes that the predictive validity of these tests is lost for Mexican American children. The author points out that although some organizations such as the California Department of Education are presently developing a Spanish version of an existing intelligence test, the premise behind such a test is that the children to be tested are monolingual in the language of the test. Given the fact that most Spanish-surnamed children are bilingual, such children will be penalized by a totally Spanish IQ test as much as they are penalized by one which is totally English. On the basis of these conclusions, the author makes several recommendations, including the development of tests to measure varying degrees of bilingualism and of curricula best suited to varying degrees of bilingualism, and also the establishment of special language development classes for those bilingual Mexican American children who are supposedly "functional" in English but lack the necessary language development to improve their socioeconomic status. An 18-item bibliography is included.—AP

265. Morin, Raul. Among the Valiant. Alhambra, The Borden Publishing Company, 1966. 290 pp.

This book is a collection of accounts about Mexican American military heroes. Most of the narrations deal with infantrymen in World War II, and an account of the author's own war experience is also included. The author suggests that the men in the war developed growing aspirations toward full social status and race pride. Morin's experiences illuminate the attitudes of many Mexican Americans toward themselves and toward the United States at that time.—CV

266. Moulton, Beatrice A. The Persecution and Intimidation of the Low-Income Litigant as Performed by the Small Claims Court in California, Stanford Law Review, XXI, No. 6 (June, 1969), 1657-1684.

The author contends that the efficiency and economy of the small claims court—originally established to benefit the working poor—operate at the expense of rather than the service of the contemporary poor. Even if the poor are aware the small claims courts exist and see their problem as a legal one, they often have an attitude that the legal system is unresponsive to their needs. This article reaffirms the conclusion of an earlier urban study that small claims courts function virtually as a collection agency for businesses and government agencies; studying four rural small claims courts, Moulton found that individuals comprised 93.3% of the defendants and only 16% of the plaintiffs. There is a discussion of the feasibility and ramifications of various reform proposals, such as eliminating business and governmental litigants, organizing the poor, allowing the use of counsel, and permitting lay advocates. Spanish-speaking people, who comprise only 9.1% of California's population, accounted for 35.5% of the defendants in the study.—SD

267. Moustafa, A. Taher and Gertrud Weiss. Health Status and Practices of Mexican Americans. Mexican-American Study Project Advance Report 11, Division of Research, Graduate School of Business, University of California, Los Angeles, 1968. 47 pp.

This report assesses the contemporary literature on Mexican American mortality rates, morbidity characteristics, mental illness, and health attitudes and practices. The section on morbidity characteristics—such as prevalence of chronic conditions, incidence and prevalence of specific diseases—is new information retrieved from a special tabulation of the 1954-1955 California Health Survey. The chapter on mental illness provides a review of the contradictory research results in this field. The inconclusive and limited findings about the health status and practices of Mexican Americans limits researchers to tentative conclusions, and the present authors are similarly confined by the paucity of data. To correct the "glaring deficiencies of information" the authors recommend that federal, state and local agencies collect health data on the Spanish-surname population rather than perpetuating the common "white-nonwhite" classification. The report provides a synthesis of current knowledge and makes suggestions on areas demanding investigation.—SD

268. Muñoz, Carlos. Toward a Chicano Perspective of Political Analysis. Unpublished paper delivered at the 66th Annual Meeting of the American Political Science Association, Los Angeles, California, September, 1970.

Muñoz contends that, due to the present status of the social sciences, no relevant research which can contribute toward the understanding and solution of Mexican American problems can be hoped for. The social sciences generally have failed to focus on the Chicano minority, he states, and political science in particular has almost totally ignored the Chicano. Even that little which has been written about the Chicanos has been based on a dominant Anglo perspective emphasizing an assimilationist viewpoint.

In attempting to suggest means whereby existing difficulties can be overcome and significant research concerning Chicanos can occur, Muñoz suggests that Anglo scholars are too far removed from the Chicano dimension of reality and that the responsibility for such research rests on the scholars from the Chicano community itself, who must develop new paradigms of research and analysis that will adequately deal with the problems of poverty, alienation, and political powerlessness. They must develop a Chicano perspective of political analysis which will not dichotomize action and intellectual endeavor, but which will be oriented toward the needs of the community.—BM

269. Murray, Sister Mary John. A Socio-Cultural Study of 118 Mexican Families Living in a Low-Rent Public Housing Project in San Antonio, Texas. The Catholic University of America Studies in Sociology, XXXVIII (Washington, D.C., 1954), 141 pp.

This study presents a description of Mexican Americans living in a situation of poverty. The focus is on assimilation of Anglo values in family relationships, religion, education, economic status and health practices. The author found the highest degree of assimilation in the acceptance of the value of education, although the Mexican Americans had a record of low achievement in this field because of language problems. Traditional family solidarity was apparently crumbling, partly because the Mexican American women's acceptance of Anglo familial norms, which give the woman more freedom and authority, resulted in parental clashes. The author believed that assimilation was to be equated with cultural improvement, taking for granted the superiority of Anglo culture.—RM

270. Nabokov, Peter. Tijerina and the Courthouse Raid, Albuquerque, University of New Mexico Press, 1969. 285 pp.

This is a chronicle of events leading up to and including the courthouse raid by Reies Lopez Tijerina and Alianza members in 1967. Written by a journalist located in the area, it presents in great detail an account of the legal and official actions surrounding the events of June 1967. It presents information concerning both sides of the controversy gathered from primary sources, interviews with some of the principals, and from a certain degree of personal involvement by the author in his capacity as a reporter.—CV

271. Nall, Frank C. Role Expectations, A Cross Cultural Study, Rural Sociology, XXVII, No. 1 (March, 1962), 28-41.

This study is based on the comparison of role expectations of high school students in Mexico and the United States. Mexican nationals looked forward to fulfilling particular occupations more than United States students, who thought in terms of collectivist group identity rather than of specific vocations. The Mexican

American students did not occupy an intermediate acculturative position; their outlooks ranged to both extremes of particularistic and collectivist expectations.—RM

272. Natalicio, Luis, and Diana Natalicio. The Educational Problems of Atypical Student Groups: The Native Speaker of Spanish, Urban Education, IV (October, 1969), 260-272.

In this article, the authors take as their starting point the premise that fundamental to the many problems that Mexican Americans must face is the language barrier that they confront in the educational system, the labor market, and society in general. Given this premise, the authors then proceed to argue for a comprehensive and long range program of teaching English as a second language beginning at the first grade level, stressing the training and retraining of teachers in TESL methodology and applied linguistics, and the cooperative involvement of both teachers and administrators in such special programs. The authors cite several linguistic sources to support their argument.—AP

273. National Advisory Committee on Farm Labor. Farm Labor Organizing, 1905-1967. New York, 1967. 40 pp.

This brief historical sketch deals with attempts at farm labor organizing in the United States. After comments on the National Labor Relations Act and its exclusion of farm laborers, the booklet examines unionization attempts in three different market situations. These discussions include California's seasonal migrant agriculture and the strikes in which many Mexican Americans participated, the Southern Tenant Farmers Union that was founded in Arkansas under the weight of the Depression, and the successful post-World War II unionization efforts in Hawaii's industrialized agriculture. Concluding sections treat the relationship of national labor unions such as the AFL-CIO to the farm workers and include short descriptions of recent organization attempts in different states.—SD

274. National Catholic Welfare Conference. The Spanish Speaking of the Southwest and West. Social Action Department, Second Report, Washington, D.C., 1944. 59 pp.

At this conference, representatives of various Catholic organizations discussed implementation of recommendations to combat discrimination against the Spanish-speaking. There is a section on education noting the importance of biculturalism and a discussion of the potentials and pitfalls of community organization.—SD

275. National Education Association, Department of Rural Education. The Invisible Minority: Report of the NEA-Tucson Survey on the Teaching of Spanish to the Spanish-speaking. Washington, 1966. 36 pp.

After a quick survey of Mexican American history and social conditions, the report focuses on the unsatisfactory results of ignoring Chicano cultural and linguistic traits in the schools and forcing Mexican American children to accept Anglo norms. Both educational and psychological damage is done by insisting that the Mexican American's cultural heritage is inferior, and by not taking this background into account in teaching methods (i.e., teaching in English to those who speak Spanish at home). The remainder of the report describes programs which use the Spanish language, teach the value of Mexican culture and experience, and engender a proud biculturalism.—RM

276. Navarro, Joseph. The Condition of Mexican-American History, The Journal of Mexican American History, I (Fall, 1970), 25-52.

This paper discusses the problems involved in the definition and extent of Mexican American history, considered here as the history of Mexicans in the United States from 1848 to the present. Navarro also examines and analyzes the usefulness and limitations of several works which deal with Mexican American history. He concludes by presenting specific suggestions concerning ways in which the critical and scholarly study of Mexican American history can be advanced through such means as searching for documents in United States and Mexican nation, state, and local archives, and following up with cataloguing, indexing, editing, annotating and publishing of these documents.—BM

277. New Mexico State Advisory Committee to the United States Commission on Civil Rights. The Civil Rights Status of Minority Groups in Clovis, New Mexico. May, 1969. 27 pp.

This report by the New Mexico State Advisory Committee shows that discrimination is firmly embedded in every facet of life in Clovis, especially in employment and educational opportunities. The largest minority group are Hispanos, and the city shows no sensitivity to cultural, educational or language differences between them and the Anglo population. There was no evidence of positive steps taken, particularly in employment practices, to eliminate discrimination.—RM

278. New Mexico State University. Conference on Teacher Education for Mexican Americans. Educational Resources Information Center, the Clearinghouse on Rural Education and Small Schools, Las Cruces, New Mexico, February, 1969.

Seven of the papers presented at this conference have been annotated and are listed below:

a. Carter, Thomas P. Preparing Teachers for Mexican American Children. 15 pp.

The author outlines several current approaches to solving the problems of education for Mexican Americans: "change the child," "change the educational institution," and "change the local society." After noting the promise and shortcomings of each standard approach, he falls back on another typical solution: "change the teacher." This technique has the advantages of being easier, less expensive, and less threatening to the majority of citizens. Depending on the extent to which teachers and teacher-preparation programs are altered, it may also effect change in some or all of the areas originally earmarked for revision.—PS

b. Kniefel, Yaneya Suárez. Programs Available for Strengthening the Education of Spanish-Speaking Students. 36 pp.

The author describes various federal programs, applicant eligibility requirements, and where to apply for the funds. The programs listed include those available for: the training of educational personnel for bilingual students, the education of bilingual students, and research on bilingualism. Suggestions for writing grant proposals and a list of special scholarships offered to bilingual students are also given.—SD

c. Lynch, Patrick D. Training Mexican American School Principals: An Analysis of a Program's Hits and Misses. 21 pp.

The monograph's report of training Mexican American administrators is incidental to its plea for restructuring university colleges of education.—PS

d. Ramírez, Manuel, III. Potential Contributions by the Behavioral Sciences to Effective Preparation Programs for Teachers of Mexican-American Children.
See annotation 188.

e. Rosen, Carl L. and Philip D. Ortego. Problems and Strategies in Teaching the Language Arts to Spanish-Speaking Mexican American Children. 21 pp.

The authors critically review some of the problems and potentialities of bilingual education. They feel the indiscriminate application of the traditional core curriculum to Spanish-speaking children has proved ineffective and inappropriate. There is an excellent discussion of problems hampering the successful teaching of English as a second language, including the confusion over the meaning of bilingualism and the need to research the proper timing of the introduction of a second language. A bibliography is included.—SD

f. Saunders, Jack O. The Blueprint Potentials of the Cooperative Teacher Education Preparation; Utilizing the Mexican Americans. 16 pp.

New Mexico State University operates an unusual work-study undergraduate teacher training program whose participants come from poor economic backgrounds. The author describes this program and the role and contributions of the Mexican American students who comprise half of the co-op teacher trainees.—SD

g. Van Meter, Ed and Alma Barba, eds. Proceedings of the Regional Conference on Teacher Education for Mexican Americans. 35 pp.

The New Mexico conference was the first of three held in 1969 with the purpose of initiating "improvements in the qualifications and supply of educational personnel working with Mexican-American students." This volume lists the extensive recommendations which emerged from discussions of the conference participants and gives the text of speeches delivered and abstracts of the seven papers presented.—SD

280. Nostrand, Richard L. The Hispanic-American Borderland: A Regional Historical Geography. PhD dissertation, University of California, Los Angeles, 1968.

In this study the author develops and elaborates on the "borderland" thesis first advanced by Bolton's The Spanish Borderlands, published in 1921. The thesis holds that appreciation and understanding of spatial dimension is essential to the study of the Hispanic population in America. Primary emphasis is placed upon regionalizing the Borderland and delimiting subregions on the basis of population density of Spanish surnames and Hispanic cultural intensity. Three methods are employed: cartographic plotting of surname data; regionalizing present-day data by distributional criteria, and historical analysis in order to trace the chronological development of the region over three and one half centuries. The end result is a mosaic of regional, historical profiles of eight subregional types in California, New Mexico, Arizona, Colorado and Texas. In addition to the gain in understanding of the cultural and geographic makeup of this area, the historical analysis of trends leads to twin conclusions for the future: continued increase of Hispanic population and territorial expansion of the Borderland.—MLB

281. Officer, James E. Historical Factors in Inter-Ethnic Relations in the Community of Tucson, Arizoniana, I (Fall, 1960), 12-16.

This is a brief account of the factors contributing to what the author considers the "generally cordial Anglo-Latino relations" in Tucson. He includes as important historical factors the mutual fight against the Apaches in the early period, intermarriage after the Civil War, and the emergence of Spanish-speaking businessmen giving prestige to the Spanish-surname community.—LH

282. Ortego, Philip D. Montezuma's Children, El Grito, III (Spring, 1970), 38-50.

In this article, the author discusses the educational problems facing Mexican Americans, commenting primarily on five areas: (1) the failure of existing educational programs, (2) intelligence testing, (3) the high dropout rate among Mexican Americans, (4) college and university enrollment, and (5) bilingual educational programs. The author is critical of the high percentage of Mexican American children assigned to special classes for the mentally retarded, the scarcity of Mexican Americans on college and university education faculties, and the limitations of English as a second language program. IQ testing is discussed both as an imprecise instrument and also as a socially pernicious instrument that can have a harmful and damaging effect on the lives of young Mexican Americans. The author links the high dropout rate of Mexican American students to testing and measurement, and he denies that their academic failure is due to low achievement or aspiration levels, but rather to inadequate school programs. Some figures on the extremely low college and university enrollment of Mexican Americans are presented, and the author suggests that this is in part due to an elitist and inegalitarian idea of the university that still pervades the thinking of most college professors and administrators. Ortego sees bilingual education as an attempt to articulate a Mexican American alternative in solving Mexican American problems, where Mexican Americans can see their roles in terms of their own cultural identity and linguistic heritage.—AP

283. —————————— Perspectives in Language, Culture, and Behavior, International Language Reporter, XV (Spring, 1969), 9-16.

In this essay, the author states that the dependence of much cultural-linguistic and psycho-linguistic research upon historical and traditional views has led to the reinforcement of widely held stereotypes concerning ethnic groups such as the Mexican Americans. He emphasizes the need for a more complex and searching study of language as a determinant in culture and behavior, and the cruciality of a more adequate understanding of language as a mediator of personality.—BM

284. Padfield, Harland and William Martin. Farmers, Workers, and Machines: Technological and Social Change in Farm Industries of Arizona. Tucson, The University of Arizona Press, 1965. 297 pp.

In this study the authors combined the disciplines of anthropology and economics to provide an integrated approach to their analysis of Arizona agriculture. They first describe the history and nature of the major Arizona crops (citrus, lettuce, and cotton) and present an economic analysis of the market structure. The authors then look at the labor market not from the viewpoint of theoretical supply and demand requirements, but from the vantage of the individual farm worker. To do so, they study the demographic characteristics, value patterns and cultural backgrounds of the important farm worker groups: Mexican Americans, Anglos, Negroes, and Indians. Traditional Mexican folk culture underwent differing transformations in three distinguishable Mexican American groups: the Texan, the Old Arizonian, and the Green Carder. In addition to information on the differing adaptations of Mexican Americans to the conditions posed by Arizona agriculture, the authors' theoretical approach yields conclusions about the effects of agricultural technological developments on the processes of social change.—SD

285. Palomares, Uvaldo Hill. A Study of the Role of Mobility in the Acculturation Process of Rural Migrant and Non-Migrant Disadvantaged Mexican Americans in the Coachella Valley. Unpublished PhD dissertation, University of Southern California, 1967.

The method of stratification which categorizes all economically disadvantaged Mexican Americans as constituting a single group, i.e. "lower class," is viewed by the author as being vague, unwieldy, and unrepresentative of the actual situation. The problem of such an orientation results in insufficient understanding of subgroup differences and in a "crude classification which labels but does not describe." Palomares advocates the need for studies which concern themselves with the degree and kind of intra-cultural differences within the Mexican American population. Through a review of the extant literature, the author has become convinced that the transient migrant farm workers constitute a significant subgroup, with distinct problems to overcome, within the larger sector of economically disadvantaged Mexican Americans. This dissertation focuses on the study of ecological, sociological, and psychological hypotheses as they are related to mobility. The mobility factor is considered as the key differentiating variable between the two populations, migrant and non-migrant Mexican Americans, and Palomares believes that his research data support the thesis that the mobility of the migrant Mexican American farm workers is a detrimental or handicapping influence in the acculturation process.—BM

286. ——————————, and Laverne C. Johnson. Evaluation of Mexican-American Pupils for EMR Classes, California Eduation, III (April, 1966), 27-29.

This is a brief report of research conducted by the authors, the purpose of which was to examine the findings of two types of intelligence tests administered by two examiners (the authors) of differing experience and ethnic background, on a sample of 50 Mexican American pupils, already referred by their teachers and screened by their principals for enrollment in classes for the educable mentally retarded. The tests used were the Wechsler Intelligence Scale for Children and the Goodenough-Harris (Draw-A-Man) Intelligence Test. The authors found a wide discrepancy in the scores on the two tests. Of the fifty pupils tested the number eligible for referral to EMR classes was 28 if using only the results of the WISC and 6 if using only the results of the G-H. The authors also studied the importance of the psychologist as a variable in the evaluation process. In one experiment of 68 referrals for EMR placement, a non-Spanish-speaking psychologist recommended that 73 percent of his referrals be placed in EMR classes, whereas a Spanish-speaking psychologist recommended 26 percent of his referrals to EMR classes. The authors conclude that it is likely that many Mexican American pupils in California who are placed in EMR classes as mentally retarded are incorrectly labeled.—AP

287. Panunzio, Constantine. Intermarriage in Los Angeles, 1924-1933, American Journal of Sociology, XLVII (March, 1942), 690-701.

This is a study of Los Angeles County marriage license statistics for the years 1924-1933, with reference to five ethnic minorities, among them first-generation (immigrant) Mexican Americans. The author found that 83 percent of the immigrant Mexicans had intramarried—that is, married either other immigrant Mexicans or native-born Mexican Americans. The greater proportion of marriages between Mexicans and people not of Mexican descent involved other Latins—persons of Central and South American, Spanish, and Italian birth.—RS

288. Paredes, Americo. Folk Medicine and the Intercultural Jest, in Spanish-Speaking People in the United States; Proceedings of the 1968 Annual Spring Meeting of the American Ethnological Society. Seattle, University of Washington Press, 1968, pp. 104-119.

This is an analysis of a collection of jests, tallas, recorded in Brownsville, Texas, at an evening gathering of Mexican American men. These tallas are parodies of the standard curandero stories, where the folk healer, instead of magically curing the patient, makes stupid and often obscene mistakes. At the same time, Anglo doctors are presented as cold and greedy. The tellers are middle-class men who are important in both cultural communities; while sufficiently assimilated to mock folk traditions, at the same time their strong Mexican identities allow them to ridicule Anglo characteristics.—RM

289. ——————. With His Pistol in His Hand—A Border Ballad and Its Hero. Austin, University of Texas Press, 1958. 247 pp.

Based on a famous border ballad, this study attempts to illuminate the attitudes and life style of the Mexicans living along the Texas-Mexico Rio Grande border in the early twentieth century. After first describing the history of the border region and the mutual stereotypes surrounding the Mexicans and the Texas Rangers, Paredes presents a formalized version of the legend of Gregorio Cortez. Through newspaper accounts, court records and personal interviews, he then examines the real life adventures of the hero Cortez. The second section of the book analyzes the development of the corrido, or Mexican narrative folk song, in the border area and examines the variants of the Gregorio Cortez ballad. Paredes analyzes the influence of Mexican balladry and Anglo culture on the border corrido; he also makes comparisons between the Cortez ballad and other legends of border heroes, for instance, those in Scottish and English ballads. The book evokes the ethos of the border Mexicans as revealed in their folk legends.—SD

290. Pasamanick, Benjamin. The Intelligence of American Children of Mexican Parentage: A Discussion of Uncontrolled Variables, Journal of Abnormal and Social Psychology, XLVI (1951), 598-602.

This is a critique of the 1950 study by Carlson and Henderson comparing the intelligence of Anglos and Mexican Americans. Especially criticized is the lack of attention to the problems of bilingualism and other environmental variables.—LH

291. Paz, Octavio. The Labyrinth of Solitude: Life and Thought in Mexico. Translated by Lysander Kemp. New York, Grove Press, 1961. 212 pp.

Octavio Paz presents a spiritual history of Mexico, heavily Freudian in interpretation. He equates Mexican history with the psychological, intellectual growth of a Mexican man; the nation is now in an adolescent stage of development, the time of beginning self-awareness and introspection. The Mexican shuts himself behind a mask to prevent the world from invading his privacy and his manhood; the ideal man is the one who can defend himself against all outsiders. Mexican history has always been a search for selfhood and for communion with others, a search stifled by sterile, alien forms such as the moribund Catholic Church and the French rationalism of the Independence movement. These forms are imposed by outsiders or by Mexicans infatuated with foreign models. The rejection of these alien elements causes the turn to solitude, the erection of the masks. Paz calls for the recognition of Mexico's ambiguous heritage, but believes that Mexico's situation is shared by the rest of the world; if the masks were removed, it would show all mankind solitary, together.

Paz treats Mexican Americans as people who are spiritually out of place: people who have lost their Mexican culture while they are prevented from becoming Anglo. This isolation can result in the Pachuco personality, the strong affirmation of individuality by simultaneously disguising and calling attention to the self. The Pachuco is a product of the society that rejects him, that allows him only the role of victim or of wicked hero.—RM

292. ——————. Posdata. Mexico, D.F., Siglo Veintiuno Editores, S.A., 1970. 149 pp.

According to the author this short work is a postscript to his earlier work, The Labyrinth of Solitude (1959). In this work, the author continues his exploration of Mexican culture with even more criticism and self-criticism than in his earlier work. He focuses mainly on explaining the meaning of recent youth rebellions. Even though he acknowledges the struggles of the Chicano, the black, the women's liberation movement, and the Hippies in the United States, as well as the rebellions in France, Italy, and West Germany, his main interest is the youth movement in Mexico since the tragic massacre of students in Mexico City in 1968. The more philosophical part of the essay is an incisive dialectical criticism of modern Mexico, its culture and what he calls its facade. What interests him is not so much the "national character" but what is hidden by that character—what is behind the mask of the "national character." In this work he delves deeper into the question of identity which he introduced in the second chapter ("Mexican Masks") of The Labyrinth of Solitude.—CV

293. Peak, Horace. Search for Identity by a Young Mexican-American in Clinical Studies in Culture Conflict, New York, Ronald Press Company, 1958, pp. 201-222.

This psychiatric case study describes the emotional distress which occurred in a young Mexican American, in part because his mother "passed for white" and rapidly advanced in socioeconomic status, away from supportive relatives. Subsequent ethnic shame was complicated by a Protestant religious affiliation and an accompanying superficial involvement in Anglo groups.

A recitation of culture conflict areas (e.g., Chicano time orientation, passivity, etc.) is followed by an analysis of a young man whose basic lack of personal and cultural identity produced a losing struggle for desperately desired status in the Anglo world. The article includes complete Thematic Apperception Test and Make-A-Picture-Story Test protocols.—PS

294. Peck, Robert F. Intelligence, Ethnicity and Social Roles in Adolescent Society, Sociometry, XXV (March, 1962), 64-72.

The hypothesis that Mexican American adolescents are discriminated against—i.e., are less "visible" in certain social roles than Anglos of the same intelligence—was borne out by results of tests on 1217 junior high school students. Intelligence was positively related to visibility (measured by classmate nominations) in such social roles as "brains," and "wheel." Anglos, however, were disproportionately nominated as visible both by their fellow Anglos and by Mexican Americans. The conclusion discusses whether traditional "passivity" keeps Mexican Americans from competing for leadership roles.—SD

295. Peña, Albar A. Report on the Bilingual Education Program, in U.S. Office of Education, National Conference on Bilingual Education: Language Skills. Washington, D.C., 1969, pp. 8-13.

In January of 1967 Congress amended the Elementary and Secondary Education Act of 1965 to include a Bilingual Education Program designed for the purpose of meeting the special educational needs of children from three to eighteen who have limited English-speaking ability, and who come from environments where the dominant language is other than English. Peña, the director of the U.S. Office of Education, Bilingual Education Programs Branch, outlines in this paper the administrative procedures, operational activities, and basic objectives of the program. The primary hypotheses being investigated through the various programs established throughout the nation include the following:

1. Children in bilingual education programs will progress better in school because of the provision of instruction in their mother tongue as well as in English for part or all of the curriculum.

2. Through bilingual education, non-English-speaking children will become more proficient in both English and their native language.

3. The children will be enabled to develop understanding and respect for their mother tongue and associated culture and thus greatly increase the likelihood of their developing a positive self-image and achieving satisfactory social and personal adjustment.—BM

296. Peñalosa, Fernando. Class Consciousness and Social Mobility in a Mexican-American Community. Unpublished PhD dissertation, University of Southern California, 1963.

By means of an empirical descriptive study, the author investigates aspects of social stratification in relation to class consciousness and social mobility among Mexican Americans in Pomona, California. He develops an index of social status and a sociocultural typology for Mexican Americans. The analysis is based on a research instrument consisting of an interview questionnaire constructed by the author and applied to a six percent random sample of Mexican Americans in Pomona. The author proceeded on the assumption that since the subjects of his study were being significantly affected by the related processes of urbanization, acculturation, and social mobility, increased understanding could be gained about the dynamics of social stratification among Mexican Americans by studying these processes in historical context and by relating them to the recognized characteristics of the people.—BM

297. ——————————. The Changing Mexican American in Southern California, Sociology and Social Research, LI, No. 4 (July, 1967), 405-417.

The author surveys the study of Mexican Americans by social scientists. He stresses the heterogeneity of the Chicano population and denies the validity of studies which describe it in terms of traditional Mexican folk culture. Peñalosa asserts that the Mexican American subculture in its most common form can best be explained as a variant of a United States subculture; Chicanos are partially Mexicanized Americans rather than partially Americanized Mexicans. For Peñalosa, this statement is substantiated by the wide divergence between the Mexican lower class and the Mexican-American lower class. All the popular images concerning the Chicano population are anachronistic, especially in Southern California; 85 percent of them are urban, 46 percent are semi-skilled or skilled workers and 22 percent are white collar workers. World War II was the turning point; it offered the Mexican American opportunities for increased horizontal and vertical mobility. The author concludes that the emergence of political activists and professionals of Mexican American descent will promote the further advancement of Southern California's largest minority.—RM

298. ——————. Social Mobility in a Mexican-American Community, Social Forces, XLIV (June, 1966), 498-505.
This is a sociological treatment of vertical social mobility in the Mexican American population of the city of Pomona in Southern California. To find correlations between certain selected characteristics and upward mobility, material was gathered in a series of structured interviews with a 6 percent sample from Mexican American neighborhoods which had been differentially ranked according to desirability. The author found that the second generation was most upwardly mobile and ranked highest on indices of socioeconomic status and acculturation when compared with immigrants and descendants of Spanish colonial settlers. Although acculturated, the second generation did not shed its ethnic identity or traditional religion, Catholicism. The authors conclude that the relinquishing of lower-class culture is more related to upward mobility than ethnicity.—RM

299. ——————. Toward an Operational Definition of the Mexican American, Aztlan, I (Spring, 1970), 1-12.
This is an attempt by a sociologist to map out some of the more significant and complex questions concerning the sociological study of the Mexican American population—questions whose answers are neither simplistic nor generalizations. The author provides some tentative answers and suggests some areas for future research, hoping that they will lead toward a more useful operational definition of the Mexican American. The questions are: (1) to what extent do Mexican Americans constitute a separate racial identity? (2) to what extent do Mexican Americans conceive of themselves as a separate ethnic group? (3) to what extent do Mexican Americans have a separate or distinct culture? (4) to what extent do Mexican Americans constitute an identifiable stratum in society? (5) to what extent is it realistic to speak of Mexican American communities? (6) to what extent are differences in historical antecedents reflected among Mexican Americans? and (7) to what extent are regional socioeconomic differences significant among Mexican Americans? The author's questions and tentative answers are suggestive of a possible groundwork for a new phase of Chicano sociology.—AP

300. —————— and Edward C. McDonagh. Education, Economic Status and Social-Class Awareness of Mexican-Americans, Phylon, XXIX (Summer, 1968), 119-126.
This is a study of the social class awareness of Mexican Americans. The authors interviewed a 6 percent random area sample of all adults of Mexican descent in Pomona, California. They used a social class index constructed from variables related to acculturation (schooling, language, age, generation) and economic status (occupation, income, residential area). The authors concluded that the Mexican Americans' perception of their group class structure and of their own

position within the structure was influenced more by acculturation factors than by economic status. (For a discussion of the relationship of economic status, particularly occupational level, to the authors' ranking of Mexican Americans' class position, see the annotation of their article entitled "A Socioeconomic Class Typology of Mexican-Americans.")—LH

301. ——————————. A Socioeconomic Class Typology of Mexican-Americans, Sociological Inquiry, XXXVI (Winter, 1966), 19-30.

This article creates a model to express class and value differentials within the Mexican American community. The Chicanos themselves described either a two or three layer society and tended to equate value orientations with economic status. That is, the Chicanos identified the "strivers" as middle class and those who "don't care" as members of the lowest class. The authors observed that acculturation to Anglo middle-class norms was necessary but not sufficient for a Mexican American to reach high socioeconomic status. In analyzing the class structure, the researchers found that occupational success was the key indicator of status gain; schooling and other forms of socialization-acculturation were preparatory to occupational success but were not indicators or guarantors of success. The authors developed a four-part social structure, with the lowest class those who were illiterate and had incomes under $4000, and the highest class those who were professionals with incomes over $9000.—RM

302. Phelan, John L. México y lo Mexicano, Hispanic American Historical Review, XXXVI (1956), 309-318.

In his review of trends in contemporary Mexican intellectual thought, Phelan places evolving definitions of national character in historical perspective. He points out the Mexican existentialists' debt to the German philosopher Heidegger, as well as the influence of Samuel Ramos' concept that Mexicans must rid themselves of inferior copies of European culture and create their own unique mestizo civilization.

Phelan observes that one controversial aspect of Mexican existentialism is its interpretation of indigenismo as the "most recent expression of the imitative tendency that has dominated the Mexican mind since the conquest." In this view, the mestizo is seeking a false sense of security by projecting himself into another culture. The new philosophers, Phelan adds, feel that historians must explain how the past conditions the future. Only by the historian's exploration of past frustrations can "future generations be liberated from these subconscious resentments which have thwarted Mexico's self expression."—SD

303. Phillips, Lester H. Segregation in Education: A California Case Study, Phylon, X (Winter, 1949), 407-413.

Phillips studied the issues involved in the 1947 Federal District Court ruling that ended the segregation of Mexican American children in the California school system. The decision of the Court constituted an important attack on the "separate but equal" rule established in the Plessy versus Ferguson case of 1896, and was one of a series of court rulings that later provided a precedent for the Supreme Court in its Brown versus the Board of Education decision of 1954.—RS

304. Pinkney, A. Prejudice Toward Mexican and Negro Americans: A Comparison, Phylon, 24 (Winter, 1963), 353-359.

Data were collected in 1952 from a city in western United States with a population of approximately 100,000. The purpose of the study was primarily to compare the attitudes of native white Americans in that particular city toward Mexican Americans and Negro Americans, and specifically to determine whether or not there were significant differences in the extent and nature of prejudice directed toward members of these two ethnic groups. The findings indicated that, on the whole, members of the dominant group approved of greater integration of Mexican Americans than of Negroes into the life of the community. In spite of this general difference in attitude, however, Pinkney notes that the status of the two minorities in actual practice is not significantly different.—BM

305. Pitt, Leonard. The Decline of the Californios: A Social History of the Spanish-Speaking Californians. Berkeley, University of California Press, 1966. 296 pp.

This is a survey history of the Californios, with emphasis on the contacts of the old Spanish settlers and their descendants with the Anglos who rapidly came to dominate the region. The bulk of the work deals with the period from the Bear Flag revolt through the droughts and floods that destroyed the Californios' pastoral, cattle raising economy. Pitt's account describes the Anglo settlers' racism, malice, greed, religious bigotry and chauvinism, while illegally seizing land, driving the Californios from the mines, and overturning the old political order. On the other hand, the weaknesses of the Californio leadership, and the lack of flexibility and foresight on the part of the rancheros contributed a great deal to the destruction of the upper class. Pitt emphasizes the aristocracy and the creation of the romantic picture of their life by Anglo writers such as Helen Hunt Jackson. This narrative history has some analysis, particularly of cultural conflict.—RM

306. Rael, Juan B. (ed.). Cuentos Españoles de Colorado y de Nuevo México. Stanford, Stanford University Press, 2 Vols. Vol. I, 559 pp., Vol. II, 819 pp.

These two volumes comprise perhaps the most complete collection of Spanish tales found in North America. The work contains 518 tales all in the original Spanish form in which they were once told and are still told in many parts of New Mexico and Colorado. In addition, the editor has included English summaries of each tale. These tales were collected over a ten-year period between 1930 and 1940 and were narrated to the editor by storytellers of varied ages and occupations, mostly "farmers, stock raisers, farm laborers, sheepherders, inhabitants of little rural communities..." of northern New Mexico and southern Colorado. The tales are divided into six categories: Cuentos de Advinanza, stories in which a riddle must be solved under penalty of death; Cuentos Humanos, "cuentos" and "chistes" or folk tales which deal with everyday life; Cuentos Morales, tales with a moral usually extolling the virtues of wisdom, truth and honor; Cuentos de Encantamiento, tales of enchantments, spells and witchery; Cuentos Picarescos, tales of adventurers, rogues and buffoons, and Cuentos de Animales, tales of animals much along Aesopian lines and often sharing the same origin. Within the six categories the tales deal with almost every facet of life and give a glimpse not only of traditions but often of the values of the Hispano culture in New Mexico and Colorado. The cuentos are presented in archaic Spanish form.—CV

307. Rainwater, Lee and David J. Pittman. Ethical Problems in Studying a Politically Sensitive and Deviant Community, Social Problems, XIV (1967), 357-366.

This article discusses the ethical concerns that were encountered in a broad anthropological study of a community. The authors report their solutions to such quandaries as when to report what information to which segment of the society, who is allowed access to the data, and the right of researchers to take sides in public controversy. Much of the outside society's pressure for interim research reports is attributed to vested interest in the findings. Whether to publish information that might be used against a minority group is explored. Blanket insistence on protecting informants' identity and confidentiality is challenged.—PS

308. Ramirez, III, Manuel, Identification with Mexican Family Values and Authoritarianism in Mexican-Americans, The Journal of Social Psychology, LXXIII (1967), 3-11.

This is a report of a study, the purpose of which was to assess the extent to which Mexican Americans identify with Mexican family values (as indicated by previous studies), and to determine the relationship between autocratic family ideology and authoritarian ideology in Mexican Americans. The sample for the study consisted of 140 middle-class, Catholic, college students, half of which were Mexican Americans (third generation) and half of which were Anglo Americans. All of the subjects were administered the California F Scale (for authoritarianism) and a Mexican Family Attitude Scale designed by the author. An analysis of the results indicated that Mexican Americans scored significantly higher on both scales, confirming observations in previous studies. The author's analysis of the data also showed that Mexican Americans do identify with Mexican family values, but show signs of "Americanization" in the form of decreased authority of the male.—AP

309. ——————————. Potential Contributions by the Behavioral Sciences to Effective Preparation Programs for Teachers of Mexican-American Children. ERIC, New Mexico State University, Las Cruces: February, 1969. 21 pp.

The author compares the personality characteristics of Mexican American and Anglo children. His attempt to isolate culture variables affecting school performance produces a "culture clash" hypothesis and suggests the need for preparation programs to make teachers aware of these cultural differences. The groups of children compared are controlled for age and socioeconomic status. Ramirez' methodology is explicitly detailed in the article.

The article contains specific recommendations for the use of anthropological methods in teacher training. Ongoing immersion in the students' communities is suggested, as are pragmatic field research projects (e.g., finding out who makes which decision in Chicano families). Such innovations in teacher training are expected to make "person perception" among students, parents, teachers, and school personnel a mutual reality.—PS

310. Ramos, Juan. Spanish-Speaking Leadership in Two Southwestern Cities: A Descriptive Study. Unpublished doctoral dissertation, Brandeis University, 1968.

This is a study of Spanish-speaking leaders in the cities of Phoenix, Arizona, and San Antonio, Texas. The author's analysis is based on data that were obtained from field interviews during the summer of 1967. The objectives of the study were set forth as: (1) the identification of Spanish-speaking minority group leaders in the two cities involved; (2) the determination of the social and leadership characteristics of these leaders; (3) the identification of their relationship patterns; and (4) the identification of their approach to problems. Ramos suggests that there are three identifiable sets of leaders of Spanish-speaking groups in the Southwest. In a kind of typology, he categorizes them as follows: "Latins," characterized by their influence in the Anglo community, but not in the Spanish-speaking community; "Mexican-Americans," those whose influence exists in both the Anglo and Spanish-speaking community; and "Chicanos," whose influence is absent in the Anglo community, but present in the Spanish-speaking community. The author analyzes the similarities and differences in background and orientation of the three types of leaders and discusses their respective approaches to the solution of the problems of the Spanish-speaking communities.—BM

311. Ramos, Samuel. Profile of Man and Culture in Mexico. Translated by Peter G. Earle. Austin, University of Texas Press, 1962. (Original Spanish edition, Mexico, 1934). 180 pp.

This is an essay on Mexican national character by a leading Mexican intellectual of his generation. Ramos analyzed Mexican personality in terms of the psychological theories of Alfred Adler. The Mexican, he argued, suffered from an inferiority complex which manifested itself in such anti-social character traits as distrust, resentment, aggressiveness, and haughtiness. This inferiority complex had deep historical roots. It was created in colonial times, said Ramos, when the creole (the European born in the New World) and the mestizo (the man of mixed blood) were treated as social inferiors by the ruling Spaniard. The complex became even more acute in the nineteenth century, after Mexico's independence, when creole leaders turned from Spain to other European nations, particularly France, as their cultural mentors. Implicit in the cultural borrowings that took place in the nineteenth century, said Ramos, was the belief that Mexico was inherently inferior to the old world, a belief which was strengthened by Mexico's apparent failure to become like Europe. Only since the Revolution of 1910-1917, argued Ramos, had Mexicans begun to look objectively at themselves. But the debate about what Mexico is, or should be, he suggested, was still phrased in false terms. Mexico could not withdraw into itself and create its own unique culture, as some wished it to do, for it was culturally a branch of Europe. But neither could the country become like the old world, for its European culture had grown up in a new environment. Mexico, said Ramos, had a creole culture; once Mexicans recognized this, and once they began to take legitimate pride in this culture, they would lose their inferiority complex and the negative character traits which went with it.—RS

312. Rechy, John. El Paso del Norte, Evergreen Review, II (Autumn, 1958), 127-140.

This is an account of El Paso and Juárez written by a Mexican American who grew up on the United States side of the border. Although an impressionistic memoir, written in the Evergreen Review "beat" jargon, the article describes many aspects of the border: prejudice, poverty, and Pachucos, as well as festivals, religion, and folk beliefs.—RM

313. Revelle, Keith. Chicano! A Selected Bibliography of Materials by and About Mexico and Mexican Americans. Oakland, California: Oakland Public Library, 1969. 23 pp.

This bibliography contains 80 briefly annotated entries of selected material dating between 1939 and 1968 divided under four general headings: (1) books, (2) newspapers, (3) periodicals, and (4) articles, reports, and speeches. The bibliography contains several regional and non-scholarly entries not usually included in other bibliographies.—AP

314. Revueltas, Jose. Los Motivos de Cain. Buenos Aires, Editorial Galerna,

1967. 115 pp.

First published in 1957, this novel is the story of Jack Mendoza, a Mexican American born in the United States, who only in his adult life begins to question his loyalties to the values of North American society. The conflict within a man who hates war but must fight for the United States in the Korean War explodes when the hero kills a North Korean prisoner who is half Mexican. After deserting the Army he finds refuge in Los Angeles, then in Tijuana, where he goes through the process of working out in his mind the inequalities which Mexican Americans face in the United States. He especially comes to question the legitimacy of giving his life for a country which denies him basic rights, liberties, and respect because of his "foreign" heritage.—CV

315. Riemer, Ruth. An Annotated Bibliography of Material on Ethnic Problems in Southern California (preliminary draft). Los Angeles, the Haynes Foundation and The Department of Anthropology-Sociology, University of California [1947], 60 pp.

This bibliography is an exhaustive compilation of documents concerning ethnic relations in Southern California. Mexican Americans are well represented along with other minority groups. Contents of the Works Projects Administration Files, a special collection in the University of California, Los Angeles Library, are described in detail.—PS

316. Rivera, Feliciano. A Mexican American Source Book with Study Guideline. Educational Consulting Associates, Menlo Park, California, 1970.

This bibliographical source book is geared toward the introduction of materials dealing with Mexican Americans in primary and secondary school curricula. This source book contains a study guideline and a selected bibliography of the history of Mexican American people. Also included are sections dealing with the Missions of California, a portfolio section, and illustrations of outstanding Mexican Americans. It concludes with the text of and a commentary on the Treaty of Guadalupe Hidalgo.—MLB

317. Robinson, Cecil. Spring Water with a Taste of the Land, American West, III (Summer, 1966), 6-15, 95.

Drawing heavily from his book, With the Ears of Strangers, Robinson uses the literature of the Southwest to explore cross-cultural contacts between Anglos and Mexicans in the region. He believes that the differences between the Southwest and the rest of the United States come from Mexican influences, and that the origins of the area's unique qualities are not appreciated.

The author feels that people in the United States have always seen Mexico and Mexican Americans in terms of a romantic myth or self-reassuring stereotype. The myth depicting them as idle, adventurous aristocrats was created largely by Gertrude Atherton and Helen Hunt Jackson. It had to be altered to allow for the presence of Mexican laborers after the 1930's, so the false dichotomy of Spanish and Mexican evolved. The later immigrants and the Mexicans were not seen as aristocrats, but rather as happy, humble agricultural workers.

Robinson describes the differences between Anglo and Mexican cultures. He stresses divergent attitudes toward the land, varying male-female roles, and differing emotional values. He finds Mexican traditions important in the architecture, speech, food, and the terminology of mining and cattle raising in the Southwest, although the influences have been denied. Finally, Robinson believes that the Mexican

American middle class is ceasing the imitation of Anglo attributes and is beginning to demand equal opportunity while maintaining the right to be different.—RM

318. ——————. With the Ears of Strangers: The Mexican in American Literature. Tucson, Arizona, The University of Arizona Press, 1969 ed. 338 pp.

This is a literary analysis of the image of Mexico and the Mexican in Anglo literature. It is primarily based on relatively minor writers from the Southwest. Robinson concludes that acceptance and appreciation of the Mexican has grown with the decline of the complex of racial and cultural ideas that formed Manifest Destiny and Anglo-Saxonism. Although the earliest Anglo writers saw the conflict of the Spaniard and Indian in Mexico as a precursor and a symbol of the history of all the Americas, the treatment of the Mexican himself has not been consistent. The first contacts were generated by westward expansion movements, and the resulting literature was full of racist and religious stereotypes. Gradually, an appreciation of the culture of the Mexican is growing, but this is often superficial and does not transcend stereotypes; the Mexican is admired for being simple, colorful, brave and humble. Southwestern literature, Robinson feels, has shown little understanding of the Mexican.—RM

319. Robles, Humberto. Los Desarraigados. Mexico D.F., Instituto Nacional de Bellas Artes, 1962. 159 pp.

This is a play, which was also made into a movie, which deals with the social and psychological problems of assimilation and acculturation of Mexicans and their children who live in the United States. The play deals with a family of Mexican immigrants and their children who are born in this country.

Although the play goes into the social and economic exploitation suffered by many Mexican immigrants, its main emphasis is focused on the identity problems of those of the younger generation, who, being ashamed of their heritage, embark on humiliating and self-destructive lives because of the irreconcilable lack of belonging in a culture and society they have chosen over that of their parents.

There are two story lines that merge into one basic statement—for the father of the family the concern is for the futility of expecting advancement in a society that considers him incapable and inferior; for the children the problem involves the difficulties of identification and the deprecation of the ways of their parents and their mother country. Some of the most poignant scenes deal with the nostalgia for the old country and the old values on the part of the parents.—CV

320. Rocco, Raymond A. The Chicano in the Social Sciences: Traditional Concepts, Myths, and Images. Unpublished paper delivered at the 66th Annual Meeting of the American Political Science Association, Los Angeles, California, September, 1970.

In this paper Rocco reviews and discusses some of the currently used works concerning the Mexican American, primarily concentrating on Carey McWilliams' book, North From Mexico, Octavio I. Romano's article, "The Anthropology and Sociology of the Mexican-American," and Deluvina Hernandez' monograph, "Mexican American Challenge to a Sacred Cow." Both Romano and Hernandez, reports Rocco, are critical of the acceptance by well-known social scientists of a stereotyped cultural model which represents the Mexican Americans as passive, apathetic, and unable to achieve because of their cultural background. These social scientists, according to Romano and Hernandez, have confused behavior indicative of culture with behavior which is conditioned by the social stimuli to which

Mexican Americans have been subjected.

Miguel D. Tirado is cited as one author who has pointed out distortion in the prevailing view of Mexican Americans as politically apathetic by attempting to show that many social scientists have a very confining conception of what constitutes political activity. Rocco concludes his paper by suggesting that in order to combat the stereotyping and bias which exist in the social sciences, it must be remembered that in the Mexican American community there exists an ideological context which differs significantly from the established order, and that therefore a perspective which also differs from the established social science paradigms must be developed. Only in this way can a realistic understanding of the significance of Mexican American political behavior be developed.—BM

321. Rodriguez, Armando. The Realities of Bilingual Education, in U.S. Office of Education, National Conference on Bilingual Education: Language Skills. Washington, D.C., 1969, pp. 14-21.

Bilingual education is defined in its broadest context as an educational process in which every child in school would be taught subject matter in his "mother" tongue while learning a second language, and then both languages would be used for instructional purposes. Historically, states the author, all movements toward bilingual education have been faced with a great deal of opposition, since the attitude of most schools has been that the sooner the Chicano was forced to speak English, the sooner he would become an American student—this attitude being enforced by the rule that no Spanish was to be spoken at school at any time. Rodriguez reports, however, that some significant forward movement has been made in recent years. One of the unifying themes of the 1967 Texas Conference for the Mexican American, for example, was the agreement that bilingual education must become a major responsibility of the Federal government in partnership with the states. Also, in 1968 the Bilingual Education Act was established, and under its auspices 65 proposals of local educational agencies for bilingual education projects were approved. The basic goal of all programs and projects concerning bilingual education, according to Rodriguez, is the realization and acceptance by all Americans of the cultural diversity and richness of difference in the United States.—BM

322. Rodríguez-Cano, Felipe. An Analysis of the Mexican American Migrant Labor Force in the Stockbridge Area. Department of Sociology, Michigan State University, East Lansing, Michigan (Available through Educational Resource Information Center), 1966. 97 pp.

This work describes demographic and behavioral characteristics of migrant workers located approximately 40 miles from Lansing, Michigan. The author analyzes the processes by which workers are recruited into the migrant stream and by which they make subsequent decisions. The report contains unusual information on how and why migrants move where they do, on their leisure time activities, and on the role which media play in shaping behavior.

Mexican American migrants in Michigan experience a strong feeling of alienation from the Anglo community. There is virtually no social participation, and economic interaction is limited by poverty. The socialization process creates a separate subculture of migrant workers. The author notes a growing tendency toward social change.—PS

323. Romano-V., Octavio Ignacio. The Anthropology and Sociology of the

Mexican-Americans: The Distortion of Mexican-American History, El Grito, II (Fall, 1968), 13-26.

This is a review article which criticizes the work of several prominent social scientists, including Ruth Tuck, Lyle Saunders, Munro S. Edmonson, Florence R. Kluckhohn and Fred L. Strodbeck, William Madsen, Celia S. Heller, and Julian Samora and Richard A. Lamana. Romano contends that they have all contributed to the development and perpetuation of a distorted, ahistorical, and stereotyped picture of Mexican Americans as passive, fatalistic, irrational, irresponsible, politically apathetic, and lacking in initiative and ambition. Furthermore, he states, they attribute these negative characteristics and conditions to the submersion of the Mexican Americans in a passive and unchangeable "traditional culture," and strongly suggest that their only hope for progress and betterment is through total acculturation into the Anglo way of life.

According to Romano, these observations and conclusions totally ignore such things as the pluralistic nature of the Mexican American people, and their actual history of extensive involvement in labor conflict over a period of several decades. In order to come to a more realistic understanding of the Mexican American people and their culture, he concludes, the currently accepted concepts of the "traditional culture" and the stereotyped picture of the "typical" Chicano must be entirely dropped, and a study of previously ignored elements in the historical culture of the Mexican Americans must be undertaken.—BM

324. ——————————. Charismatic Medicine, Folk-Healing, and Folk-Sainthood, American Anthropologist, 67 (1965), 1151-1173.

This paper utilizes findings drawn from a study of charismatic medicine among the Mexican American population in South Texas in an attempt to analyze the differences which exist between folk healers specifically in areas of influence and prestige. Charismatic medicine is defined as the successful interplay of the healer role as such with the individual personality of the healer, and a hierarchical spectrum of healers is formulated on the basis of sphere of influence. The spectrum ranges from the household and neighborhood influence of elder daughters, mothers, grandmothers, neighbors, etc., to the widespread influence of full-time town, city, or regional healers, and culminating in the extensive influence of international, religious folk-saints, and formal saints.

The specific case of Don Pedrito Jaramillo is presented as an example of a healer who rose in the healing hierarchy from a relatively unknown healer to ultimately receive the status of folk-sainthood, with influence which extended over a wide geographic area and affected major social segments of Mexican American life in that area. This degree of influence, contends the author, strongly indicates a fundamental manifestation of individual charisma. Since Don Pedrito performed his role in strict accordance with prescribed tradition, his experience is clearly suggestive of the existence of a type of conservative or renovative charisma in addition or in contradistinction to the generally accepted notion of charisma as being characterized by radical innovation.—BM

325. ——————————. Don Pedrito Jaramillo: The Emergence of a Mexican-American Folk Saint. PhD dissertation, University of California, Berkeley, 1964.

This is an anthropological case study of the folk-healing hierarchy within the context of Mexican American rural life in South Texas. The author illustrates the social and cultural factors which contributed to Don Pedro Jaramillo's ascension from a simple folk healer to a healer of international fame approaching sainthood. Don Pedrito's occurrence (1829-1907) is explained in terms of the "ideal culture," the world of folk healing and the folk healer himself. The "ideal culture" of La Raza is posited in terms of membership at the general, community, family and individual level. The curandero hierarchy is traced from the novice in the home to the fully vested healer. Don Pedro's roles, as a member of La Raza and folk healer and his fulfillment of them are analyzed. To explain Don Pedro's success, the author applies the Weberian concept of charismatic leadership which is linked to Foster's concept of "dyadic contrast." Although brief, Romano's chapter on The Ideal Culture of La Raza provides an illustration of a working definition of culture.—MLB

326. ——————. Donship in a Mexican-American Community in Texas, American Anthropologist, 62 (December, 1960), 966-976.

The primary purposes of this study involve the definition of a baseline concerning immigrant Mexican donship which will serve as a point from which change may be measured, and an indication of the importance of the concept of donship as a crucial aspect of research dealing with Mexican American acculturation.

The author explains that in the Mexican American community of Frontrera, where the data for the study were obtained, there are presently two main categories of men who are granted the respect term don. The first class contains those who are granted the title of respect on the basis of traditional usages and categories, such as the patrón, the Mexican consul, and specific men of wealth, political influence, or old age. The second category is made up of those who are accorded the position of donship as a result of the achievement of prestige and respect status, i.e. those men who have earned the good opinion of their neighbors, who are viewed by them as having solved the basic problems of life in their community, and who demonstrate the qualities of masculinity, authority, and independence.

Romano states that the stresses and conflicts between these two systems of donship comprise the essence of the dynamics of social life in the Mexican American community, and he suggests that donship, the process through which the male prestige system is perpetuated among Mexican immigrants in the United States, provides a very productive starting point for research dealing with social change and acculturation.—BM

327. ————————— (ed.). El Espejo—The Mirror: Selected Mexican-American Literature. Berkeley, California: Quinto Sol, 1969. 241 pp.

This volume is an anthology of selected works by eleven Mexican American writers and thinkers who express themselves variously through the means of short stories, essays, poetry, and a scenario. The essential thesis which seems to permeate the book is that of self-revelation and of attempting to discover and delineate the essential elements of life. In endeavoring to reveal the realities of Mexican American existence as they have been experienced and observed, the authors deal with such themes as barrio and migrant life, poverty, alienation, repression, and cultural and historical heritage. Possibly the general rationale of the anthology could be said to consist of the attempt to reflect Chicano self-knowledge and a definitive cultural identity.—BM

328. ——————. The Historical and Intellectual Presence of Mexican-Americans, El Grito, II (Winter, 1969), 32-47.

The author states that three principal historical philosophies or currents of thought were brought into the United States by the many Mexicans who fled northward during and following the Mexican Revolution. These three mainstreams of thought are designated by Romano as Indianism, which involves the idea of a return to origins and symbolizes opposition to cultural assimilation; Historical Confrontation, which consists of needs for autonomy, confrontation and articulation, and underlies such manifest action as that taken by Pancho Villa, by the labor protest movement of the Mexican Americans, by the separatism of the Pachucos, and by the present-day Chicano movement; and Cultural Nationalism, a Mestizo-based philosophy which emphasizes the multiple genetic and cultural origins of the Mexican Americans and contains humanistic and relativistic tendencies.

To these three historical philosophies has also been added a fourth, which can be called The Immigrant Experience. It is suggested that people of Mexican descent have adjusted to life in the United States in basically one of four main ways: Anglo-Saxon conformity, stabilized differences, realigned pluralism, and biculturalism. Romano stresses the idea that the vitality and freedom of the Mexican American people lie in great measure in the pluralism and multi-dimensionality encouraged by the complexity and multiplicity of historical processes which have gone into the "making of the mind of the Mexican American."—BM

329. Romero, Fred Emilio. A Study of Anglo and Spanish-American Culture Value Concepts and Their Significance in Education (Ed.D. dissertation, University of Denver, 1966), 266 pp.
This dissertation is an empirical study comparing "Anglo-American" and "Spanish American" culture value concepts in an attempt to determine where they conflict. It is also an attempt to determine the degree of acceptance of Anglo-American culture values by Spanish American students and the degree of teacher awareness of sociocultural differences as they affect the education of Spanish-speaking students. After reviewing the available social science literature on culture value orientations, the author hypothesized that Spanish American students at the secondary level had not, in general, accepted the Anglo-American culture value system, and that teachers, in general, were not sensitive to the sociocultural differences that seem to be extremely important in the education of Spanish-speaking students. The author then constructs a 25-item acculturation questionnaire and a 20-item teacher awareness scale. Both instruments were revisions of ones previously developed and used by other researchers. The author tested his hypotheses with 348 secondary school students in rural New Mexico and in urban Denver, Colorado (approximately half of the students were Spanish-speaking and half were Anglo), and the teacher awareness scale was administered to 82 Anglo teachers of these students. There was no differentiation among the Spanish-speaking students as to whether they had a Mexican background or a "Spanish" background, nor was there any differentiation as to socioeconomic status among the total group of Spanish-speaking and Anglo students. The findings indicated by the data led the author to conclude that the Spanish American students were demonstrating a high degree of acculturation, were complying with the dictates of the culture value system of the Anglo-American group, and were experiencing very little culture conflict while in school. He further concluded on the basis of statistical analysis of the data from the teacher awareness scale that teachers at the secondary level were sensitive to the sociocultural differences of

Spanish American and Anglo-American students. These findings were in contradiction to both the findings in the review of the literature and to the author's original hypotheses.—AP

330. Rosaldo, Renato. De Mayoria a Minoria, Hispania, LI, No. 1 (March, 1968), 18.
This is a reprint of Rosaldo's speech before the Forty-Ninth Annual Meeting of the American Association of Teachers of Spanish and Portuguese. The author enumerates those factors which distinguish the Spanish-speaking people from other immigrant minorities. The hispanic-Mexican, as the author prefers to designate them, are indigenous people whose roots in this country date back two hundred years and who, unlike European immigrants, persist in maintaining their culture. The process of assimilation has not taken place as rapidly with the hispanic-Mexican as it has among other minorities, due to the close geographical proximity to the mother country which continues to reinforce the culture with its constant flow of immigrants. Consequently the hispanic-Mexican has lacked cohesiveness in the past and thus has faced a dilemma: does he become Anglo or does he remain a foreigner in his own land? The author criticizes the school system for destroying the Spanish-speaking child in the process of teaching him English. The child negates himself and his family; he rejects his culture in order to acquire a new culture. To combat this, Rosaldo strongly recommends the establishment of bilingual programs.—MLB

331. Rose, Arnold M. and Caroline B. Rose (eds.). Minority Problems. New York: Harper & Row, 1965.
This book is a collection of essays dealing with problems facing minority groups today. The origin and nature of minority problems in the United States and in other parts of the world are explored. Among the topics discussed are: the range of various types of discrimination against minority groups; the response of minority groups to discrimination, specifically in regard to problems of identity and adjustment; some explanations of the causes of prejudice; and a consideration of various techniques which might be used to change and improve the situation.—BM

332. Rowen, Helen. The Mexican American. Washington, D.C.: U.S. Commission on Civil Rights, 1968. 70 pp.
This paper, written for the U.S. Commission on Civil Rights, is a survey of the kinds and scope of problems facing the Mexican American community today. The author presents a brief history of the Mexican American community, and reports on five areas where major problems exist: (1) civil rights and the administration of justice, (2) education, (3) employment, (4) public policies and agencies for assisting the Mexican American, and (5) the Mexican American's growing sense of identity. The author cites specific examples and personal experiences to illustrate major problems.—AP

333. ——————. A Minority Nobody Knows, The Atlantic, CCXIX (June, 1967), 47-52.
The author points up society's neglect of Mexican Americans and their problems, focusing on failures of the educational system to meet special cultural needs. She summarizes the current political activity of Mexican Americans throughout the Southwest.—PS

334. Rubel, Arthur. Across the Tracks: Mexican-Americans in a Texas City. Austin, University of Texas Press, 1966. 245 pp.

This anthropological study deals with Mexican American society in a small city in the lower Rio Grande Valley. The book is a product of the Hidalgo Country Project conceived by William Madsen and financed by the Hogg Foundation for Mental Health at the University of Texas (see Madsen, 1964—number 143). It focuses, however, on one type of community among the four surveyed in Madsen's book: the bicultural urban center. After a short historical introduction, the author describes the patterns of social relations in Mexican American society. He includes chapters on the political behavior and formal organizations of Mexican Americans as well as on the family and on interpersonal relations outside the family group. He gives special attention to beliefs about illness which he thinks often prevent Mexican Americans from taking full advantage of professional health services. In one of the final chapters the author develops a theory to explain the anxiety and disaffection which he perceives to be prominent in the social relations of Mexican Americans with individuals who are not members of their nuclear family. In the conclusion, as in the chapter on politics, he argues that Latin Americans—whether in Texas, Mexico, or Argentina—have their own very viable way of adapting to city life while continuing to emphasize "familial orientations and associations which are based on personal, rather than contractual relationships." He suggests that the social life of Mexican Americans in the community he studied will probably never be a mirror-image of that of Anglos.

Rubel obtained the data for his study primarily from "participant observation"—that is, from his own experience as a trained anthropologist, living in the community—and from interviews with "key informants," Mexican Americans whom he believed to be representative. He also used an open-ended questionnaire to elicit information about health and illness beliefs from a group of women who visited a health clinic.—RS

335. ——————. The Mexican-American Palomilla, Anthropological Linguistics, VII (April, 1965), 92-97.

This is an anthropological study of the role of amorphous friendship groups among Mexican American males. In South Texas, Rubel found that the informal male group or palomilla is very important during a young man's youth and early adult life.—LH

336. ——————. Social Life of Urban Mexican Americans. Unpublished PhD dissertation, University of North Carolina, 1962.

This is essentially the research and the first draft of his later book: Across the Tracks: Mexican Americans in a Texas City. Austin, University of Texas Press, 1966. 245 pp.—CV

337. Rulfo, Juan. The Burning Plain and other stories. Translated by George D. Schade. Austin, University of Texas Press, 1967. 175 pp.

These are short stories by a Mexican prose writer. Although none of the stories is set in the United States, one of them concerns a bracero's experiences. The story, "Paso del Norte," describes some of the problems of leaving Mexico, the peril of falling into the hands of unscrupulous "coyotes" who smuggle men over the border, and the disruption of the laborers' homes by the entire experience.—RM

338. Salinas, Luis Omar. Crazy Gypsy. Fresno State College, California,

Origenes Publications, 1970. 87 pp.

This is a collection of poems written by the author during the years 1964 to 1969. Many of the poems are on Chicano themes and several of them are written in Spanish.—AP

339. Samora, Julian. Conceptions of Health and Disease Among Spanish-Americans, American Catholic Sociological Review, XXII (Winter, 1961), 314-323.

This study emphasizes the role of religious belief in explaining the causes and cures of disease. Samora observed and interviewed Hispano villagers in New Mexico in 1959. He concluded that Hispano conceptions of health and disease are a combination of folk and scientific medicine.—LH

340. ——————————, ed. La Raza: Forgotten Americans. Notre Dame, Indiana, University of Notre Dame Press, 1966. 218 pp.

The essays collected here were written by Anglo and Mexican American scholars especially for this volume. Some of the articles present the results of original research, while others review research on a topic or argue a point of view. In discussing the demographic characteristics of the Mexican American population, Barrett analyzes data on age, sex, fertility, income, and education from the 1950 and 1960 censuses. The article by Sheldon on "Community Participation and the Emerging Middle Class" compares the backgrounds, values and life styles of a group of middle-class Mexican Americans in Los Angeles who were active in ethnic organizations with those of a sample of working-class Mexican Americans in the same city. George I. Sánchez focuses on the problem of educating Spanish-speaking people within a predominantly English-speaking population; he strongly criticizes the public school systems of the Southwest for attempting, in many cases, to suppress the speaking of Spanish among Mexican American students and advocates a bilingual approach to education. John R. Martínez studies the problems encountered by Mexican Americans in their attempts to organize for effective political action. Lawrence B. Glick surveys the extent of discrimination against Mexican Americans in areas such as education, housing, and employment. Reverend William E. Scholes reviews the history and current problems of the migrant worker. And, Reverend John A. Wagner assesses the role of the Christian Church (both Protestant and Catholic) in the Mexican American community. A concluding chapter by Herman Gallegos, Lyle Saunders and Julian Samora provides a survey of the important research which remains to be done on Mexican American society.—RS

341. ——————————— and Richard A. Lamanna. Mexican Americans in a Midwest Metropolis: A Study of East Chicago. Mexican American Study Project Advance Report 8. Los Angeles, Division of Research, Graduate School of Business, University of California, 1967. 140 pp.

This is a detailed study of the Mexican Americans in East Chicago, who have formed the only Chicano colony outside of the Southwest with a large percentage (11 percent) of the total community population. The authors analyze data and make time comparisons for such topics as family life patterns, employment and occupational status, the role of the church, internal group cohesion and political influence, and personal and social adjustment. The authors feel the high Mexican American residential segregation (80 percent lived in two subtracts) was due to desires to be close to the place of work, choice of neighbors, and discrimination;

however, in no block did the Mexican Americans make up more than 51 percent of the residents. Many patterns familiar in the Southwest—a young population with a subsequently high dependency ratio, low adult median educational level, poor school performance and a high dropout rate—were found in the Mexican American population of East Chicago. The authors felt that the election of a Mexican American mayor in 1963 was a turning point in Chicano political activity, but unless several factors, including continuing Chicano factionalism, can be overcome, the Mexican Americans will have only sporadic success at the polls and limited influence on the larger community. The authors define assimilation as a four-part process—accommodation and economic integration are followed by the cultural and social stages. They point out that accommodation was good because the Mexican Americans came to the area during a period of labor shortage; economic integration was initially successful but has been frozen at a basic level. Cultural assimilation is mixed, and depends on the recency of migration and age; except for employment organizations and unions, Chicano social integration is almost nonexistent. Group assimilation to Anglo society in the North has been very slow, the authors conclude, and East Chicago has served rather as a way station on the road to individual assimilation.—SD

342. ——————— and Richard F. Larson. Rural Families in an Urban Setting: A Study in Persistence and Change, Journal of Human Relations, IX (1961), 494-503.
    This is a follow-up of the 1939 study by Olen Leonard and Charles P. Loomis of El Cerrito—a small, isolated, Hispano village of 26 family units in New Mexico. The authors interviewed members of nine Hispano families who moved from El Cerrito to Pueblo, Colorado, a city of 100,000. They concluded that the migrants from El Cerrito did not face serious problems of personal and social adjustment because of several factors: the strength of religious and familial organizations, the small number of families moving to Pueblo, the absence of a physical ghetto, and the slowness of the migratory process.—LH

343. Sánchez, George I. Forgotten People: A Study of New Mexicans. Albuquerque, New Mexico, University of New Mexico Press, 1940. 98 pp.
    This pioneering work calls attention to the plight of the Hispanos, whom Sánchez calls "New Mexicans," the first white settlers in the area. Since the late sixteenth century they have fought for a bare subsistence in the harsh land of northern New Mexico. Sánchez states that the Hispano has always been ignored by the governing body, be it Spanish, Mexican, or the United States; he continues in large part to depend on the culture and technology of sixteenth century Spain. The Hispano's cultural limitations and ignorance of Anglo governmental forms combine to prevent him from taking full advantage of what services are offered—services which are usually not tailored to his needs in either their nature or their language. Prejudice forms the capstone to cultural inertia and mutual Anglo-Hispano ignorance in the rigid societal structure that keeps the Hispanos from improving their lot. Sánchez uses Taos county as a typical community in analyzing educational, agricultural and vocational problems and concludes with an account of prospects and a list of recommendations.—RM

344. ——————————. Group Differences and Spanish-speaking Children—A Critical Review, Journal of Applied Psychology, XVI (1932), 549-558.
    This article is a critical review of the literature prior to 1932 on the

intelligence testing of Spanish-speaking children. Sánchez tabularized the results of the major studies showing low abilities of Spanish-speaking children, with information on the measures used in each study, the size of the sample, and the type of interpretation given to the results of each study by the author, that is, whether he generally attributed the low scores to heredity, environment, or language difficulties. Sánchez rejected the labeling of these differences between the scores of Spanish-speaking and Anglo children as racial differences, and he preferred to refer to them as group differences because of the extent of non-hereditary influences involved. The author also comments that some far-reaching suggestions and interpretations of test results have been made without due regard to this fact. A 40-item bibliography is included with the article.—AP

345. ——————————. Bilingualism and Mental Measures—A Word of Caution, Journal of Applied Psychology, XVIII (1934), 765-772.

In this early article, the author presents an argument against the superficial and unanalytical use of intelligence measuring instruments. The author states that there have been several abuses and errors in the use of mental tests, with the gravest errors being made in the treatment of the problems of the bilingual. The author believes that "a test is valid only to the extent that the items of the test are common to each child as they were to children upon whom the norms were based." With regard to Spanish-speaking children, the author states that the problem is much more complex than a simple translation of mental tests into Spanish. Sánchez also comments on the role of the investigator's attitudes in interpreting test results, the sometimes malicious use of test results to further a doctrine of Nordic superiority, and the responsibility of the public schools "of supplying those experiences to the child which will make the experiences sampled by standard measures as common to him as they were to those on whom the norms of the measures were based."—AP

346. —————————— and Howard Putnam. Materials Relating to the Education of Spanish-Speaking People in the United States: an annotated bibliography. Austin, University of Texas, Institute of Latin American Studies, 1959. 74 pp.

Most of the entries in this bibliography are about persons of Mexican descent, but the stress on bilingualism as a major factor in education might recommend its use to other Spanish-speaking groups. In addition to the usual citations of books, articles, pamphlets and bibliographies, the authors include references for courses of study developed and used in school systems throughout the United States. Unpublished theses and dissertations, mostly from the University of Texas, are also cited.—PS

347. Sanchez, Luisa Guerrero. The Latin-American of the Southwest. Backgrounds and Curricular Implications. PhD dissertation, University of Texas, Austin, 1954.

This study takes the perspective of positing the necessity of examining the origins, culture, and other factors impinging on Mexican American children in order to comprehend their educational problems. Utilizing an acculturation-assimilation model it is shown that the unacculturated child has tended to internalized norms and attributes which ascribe a superior status and moral worth to his Anglo counterpart. This "superior-inferior" relationship creates problems for Anglo classmates and teachers as well as for the Mexican child himself. Addressing school teachers, administrators and other educators, the study points out that without proper appreciation of the cultural heritage of the Mexican American the educational system can do much harm to the self-image of the minority child as well as doing little to educate. Citing studies demonstrating the validity of the "self-fulfilling prophecy" at work in the classrooms, this study warns teachers against approaching the child with preconceived stereotypes as this tends to reinforce the child's own ambivalence as to his status, thus conditioning the child to scholastic performance far below his capabilities. Rather than seeking to eradicate the child's cultural heritage through the educational system the author recommends greater utilization of the Mexican Americans' unique historical background in order to maximize the efficacy of the learning process.—MLB

348. San Diego City Schools. Bibliography of ESL/Bilingual Teaching Materials. San Diego, California, 1969.
This bibliography consists of the compilation of a list of materials for use in bilingual classes on elementary, secondary, and adult levels of education. Included are lists of materials, such as books, visual aids, and recorded information, for the teaching of English as a foreign language and for the teaching of Spanish. There are also suggested reading lists designed to assist teachers in the understanding of the theory and application of bilingual instruction and to provide them with a certain amount of background dealing with the culture of Spanish-speaking Americans.—BM

349. Saunders, Lyle. Cultural Differences and Medical Care: The Case of the Spanish-Speaking People of the Southwest. New York, Russell Sage Foundation, 1954. 245 pp.
This work, based on a combination of sociological and anthropological data, is a study of the effect that Mexican American cultural patterns have on the acceptance of Anglo medical practices. Saunders sees Chicano political and social organizational activity as proof that those involved have been acculturated.—RM

350. ————————— and Olin E. Leonard. The Wetback in the Lower Rio Grande Valley of Texas. Austin, University of Texas Press, 1951. 92 pp.
This is a social survey of the status of the wetback (illegal Mexican immigrant) and of the factors that promote his existence in the Rio Grande Valley. The wetbacks are young men, usually farm workers from central Mexico, who are lured to Texas by hopes of higher pay. Most expect to return to Mexico as soon as they have some earnings; many have repeatedly sneaked over the border. There is a strong Anglo political bloc which defends the wetbacks because they are a cheap, docile labor force; their illegal status can be used as a constant threat to keep them in line at low wages. The Border Patrol cannot stop the migration for logistical reasons, as well as because of the pressures that are brought to bear not to interfere with traffic in profitable labor. The local Mexican Americans resent the immigration because it undercuts them economically and forces them into migrant labor, although they defend the wetbacks as members of La Raza. The wetbacks are subject to Anglo prejudice, but many Texans say the wetback labor makes the Valley's agriculture profitable and that "Americanizing" the wetback would ruin him—that is, it would make him demand higher wages.—RM

351. Schmidt, Fred. After the Bracero: An Inquiry into the Problems of Farm Labor Recruitment. Los Angeles, Institute of Industrial Relations, University

of California, 1964. 138 pp.

In this study, Schmidt came to the conclusion that urban workers could be successfully used to stabilize the farm labor market if the importation of foreign labor was eliminated; these findings challenged the assumptions of many agribusinessmen.

352. ——————. Spanish Surnamed American Employment in the Southwest. Washington, D.C.: U.S. Government Printing Office, 1970, 247 pp.

This study provides statistical information on the job patterns that prevail among Americans of Spanish heritage in the southwestern part of the United States. The report presents evidence demonstrating severe discrimination in the employment of Spanish-surnamed Americans. They are, according to the author, both underrepresented and underutilized in the labor force. Pertinent historical background is analyzed in an attempt to provide insight into how and why these discriminatory job patterns have come about.—BM

353. Schramko, Linda Fowler. Chicano Bibliography: Selected Materials on Americans of Mexican Descent. (Revised ed.). Sacramento, California: Sacramento State College Library, 1970.

This list of approximately 1,000 items concerning Mexican Americans is the result of a survey of the holdings of the Sacramento State College Library as of Spring, 1969. It includes books, periodical articles, master's theses, and doctoral dissertations, either dealing directly with Mexican Americans or providing pertinent background information. The entries are arranged alphabetically within the broad subject categories of education, health and psychology, historical background, literature and fine arts, and social life and problems. A more detailed subject index is also included at the end of the work. In addition, a listing of current Chicano periodicals is provided.—BM

354. Scroggs, Otey. A History of Mexican Agricultural Labor in the U.S. 1942-1954, PhD dissertation, Harvard University, 1957.

This study provides a description of the historical aspects of the problems and the role of Mexican labor in American agriculture. The author describes the defacto wetback program and other labor importation programs as parts of the most recent phase of the "perennial seasonal agricultural labor problem." In this context, the author asserts that the farm labor force has always been composed largely of recent immigrants either because they were unskilled or were barred from industrial employment by racio-ethnic discrimination. The effects upon Mexican agricultural workers in the United States caused by World War I and World War II, Mexican socioeconomic conditions, farm mechanization, American immigration policy, and specifically the Bracero Program are discussed. The author also discusses the effect of Mexican workers on the domestic farm labor force. "No resident group was more profoundly affected by the employment of braceros and the wetback influx than was the Mexican American population, which suffered most in terms of unemployment and social disorganization." He states that the migration northward across the border has had the effect of setting in motion another northward movement, involving tens of thousands of Mexican Americans who could not survive at wages based on the presence of large groups of foreign workers.—LN

355. ——————. Texas, Good Neighbor? Southwestern Social Science

Quarterly, XLIII, No. 2 (September, 1962), 118-125.

This article explores Mexico's attitude toward the discrimination practiced against Mexican Americans in Texas. It is a historical account of Mexican pressure on the United States in testing with these issues.—LH

356. Sena, Jaime Rivera. Chicanos: Culture, Community, Role—Problems of Evidence, and a Proposition of Norms Towards Establishing Evidence, Aztlan I (Spring, 1970), 37-51.

In this article, the author discusses current evidence for the existence of a Chicano culture, and attempts to build a societal model for the Chicano based on the evolution of Chicano culture as emergent from the forced death of the culture of Mexico in the United States. The first steps in the author's analysis are to expand and update current common conceptualizations of "culture" and "community," and then to describe the current societal models at work in the "melting pot" concept of acculturation and assimilation in American society. It is the author's view that "dominant" cultural groups hold less control over Chicanos than Chicanos realize. Sena formulates two norms as indigenous to Chicano culture: (1) the norm of non-materialistic achievement as primary, and (2) the norm of cooperation of effort and the sharing of resources toward mutual achievement. These norms serve both as evidence for the existence of Chicano culture and also as a source of conflict with the dominant normative framework of American society, one which the author describes as marked by ruthlessness, impersonality, and self-centeredness.—AP

357. Shannon, Lyle W. The Study of Migrants as Members of Social Systems, in Spanish Speaking People in the U.S.; Proceedings of the 1968 Annual Spring Meeting of the American Ethnological Society. Seattle, distributed by the University of Washington Press, 1968. pp. 34-64.

This is a comparative study of Mexican Americans, Negroes and Anglos in Racine, Wisconsin. The author concludes that many minority group members who accepted dominant cultural values and acquired the accompanying attributes—such as education, work experience, and high aspirations—did not automatically attain success. Demands within the ethnic groups as well as external constraints made it difficult for minority group members to take advantage of opportunities. However, Negroes and Chicanos who have less exposure to the dominant cultural traditions (which favor an active attitude toward the world) reflected a more passive attitude toward change than other members of their groups. Shannon found a direct relationship between active value orientations and high levels of aspiration and (by projection) attempts to succeed in Anglo cultural terms.—RM

358. —————— and Elaine M. Krass. The Economic Absorption of Immigrant Laborers in a Northern Industrial Community, American Journal of Economics and Sociology, XXIII (January, 1964), 65-84.

This is a study of the urban adjustment of Mexican Americans of Southwestern rural origin living in Racine, Wisconsin. Data from interviews of Mexican American and Anglo heads of households or their spouses conducted in 1959 were used to determine the importance of social antecedents as a factor in economic absorption. The variables considered were geographic origin, place of socialization and education, years of education, and first place of work. Present occupation of males and total annual income for families in 1958 were used as the two measures of economic absorption. Although a significant proportion of the disparity in occupational levels between Mexican Americans and Anglos could be attributed to educational antecedents and initial work experience, these factors could not account for all of the variation.—LH

359. ——————— and Kathryn Lettau. Measuring the Adjustment of Immigrant Laborers. Southwestern Social Science Quarterly, XLIV (September, 1963), 139-149.

The authors try to measure the degree of "adjustment" of Mexican Americans to life in an industrial community in northern Illinois. They studied a random sample of Mexican Americans and Anglos from predominantly Mexican American neighborhoods. They considered both external criteria (income, occupational level, and material standard of living) and internal criteria (subjective feelings of satisfaction or dissatisfaction) as measures of adjustment. They found that among the Mexican Americans there was no correlation between external and internal indicators. The Mexican Americans did not have the same material level of the Anglos, but both groups tended to express satisfaction with their lot. The Mexican Americans, many of whom had been migrant laborers before moving to the industrial community, apparently felt that their present life was an improvement over what they had experienced previously. Among Anglos there was a slight negative correlation between occupational level and satisfaction; those in the higher levels tended to be somewhat less satisfied than those in the lower levels.—RS

360. ——————— and Patricia Morgan. The Prediction of Economic Absorption and Cultural Integration among Mexican-Americans, Negroes, and Anglos in a Northern Industrial Community, Human Organization, XXV (Summer, 1966), 154-162.

This report of a three-year study of immigrant labor in Racine, Wisconsin, compares the economic absorption and cultural integration of Anglos, Mexican Americans and Negroes. The article describes the authors' search for relevant antecedent sociological and intervening social-psychological factors. With data gathered from personal interviews, elaborate statistical tables predicting occupational level and world-view (the measures of economic absorption and cultural integration) were constructed. The tables permit not only a three-way comparison between Anglos, Mexican Americans and Negroes but also comparisons of the relative importance of such variables as antecedent experiences, present status, and present associations.—LH

361. Shapiro, Harold A. The Pecan Shellers of San Antonio, Texas, Southwestern Social Science Quarterly, XXXII (March, 1952), 229-244.

Shapiro gives a history of the conditions and problems of laborers in the pecan-shelling industry of San Antonio, Texas, in the 1930's and 1940's. The Southern Pecan-Shelling Company of San Antonio dominated the national pecan industry in the 1930's, and during one peak season employed 10,000 workers. The laborers, primarily immigrant Mexicans, were paid extremely low piece-rates for their work and conditions led them to strike for better wages in 1938. The walk-out was partially successful, but the national Fair Labor Standards Act had more dramatic benefits, forcing the Southern Company and other operators in San Antonio to raise wages to $.25 an hour. This increase in labor costs, however, made it more economical for the Southern Company to turn to machinery, following the path that most of its competitors in other states had taken in the late 1920's and early 1930's. As a result of mechanization, employment in the industry in San Antonio declined drastically; by 1941 the Southern Company's labor force had fallen to 600 people.—RS

362. Sheldon, Paul. Mexican-Americans in Urban Public Schools—An Exploration of the Drop-out Problem, California Journal of Educational Research, XII (January, 1961), 21-26.

This is a report of an investigation of 2,062 high school youths who left school for any reason (including graduation) during the period from 1955 to 1957. The youths were from three Los Angeles high schools of differing ethnic compositions and in areas of differing socioeconomic status. Mexican Americans made up 46 percent of the total sample. On the basis of the analysis of data taken from the cumulative school record folders of each of the students, the author made the following conclusions: (1) Mexican American senior high school students of Los Angeles are more likely to drop out than students of other ethnic groups (31 percent of the sample as compared to 18 percent of the non-Mexicans); (2) areas of low socioeconomic status furnish a disproportionately high number and percentage of dropouts; (3) differences in dropout rate between males and females were not significant; and (4) the students who dropped out tended to have low ratings by teachers on scales of behavior, with the Mexican Americans having lower ratings than students of other ethnic groups.—AP

363. Shibutani, Tamotsu and Kian M. Kwan. Ethnic Stratification: A Comparative Approach. New York, MacMillan Company, 1965. 596 pp.

The book combines an array of social science and historical works to outline a broad theory for the study of ethnicity and ethnic group relations. The authors present a wide spectrum of approaches, ranging from cultural pluralism to strident nationalism, stressing that essentially political positions underlie attitudes about ethnicity. Both the processes which sustain separate groups and those which integrate them are examined.—PS

364. Shotwell, Louisa R. The Harvesters—The Story of the Migrant People. Garden City, New York, Doubleday and Company, Inc., 1961. 213 pp.

Several aspects of the national migrant farm labor problems are covered in this book, which attempts to clarify many of the complex issues involved. Short journalistic case histories of individual migrant families alternate with historical accounts and discussion of the contemporary migrant labor situation. The author briefly traces the evolving role of immigration from the 1860's, the farm labor union movement, and the nature of migrant health, education, housing and transportation problems. Other topics include the day haul system, the function of crew leaders and contractors, and the history of the Migrant Ministry of the National Council of Churches, one of the few private agencies attempting to deal with migrant problems on a national basis.

There is a discussion of state and federal legislative attempts to cope with the difficult and interrelated problems of migrants. The author urges a comprehensive attack upon these problems coupled with anticipatory planning so the migrant worker can compete in the skilled farm labor market that will result from mechanization. References for quotes and statistics are not given; there is, however, a short annotated bibliography.—SD

365. Siegel, Bernard J. Defensive Structuring and Environmental Stress,

American Journal of Sociology (to be published September, 1970).

This essay explores the reactions of members of certain societies who view their environment as being hostile. These groups, who perceive themselves as being exposed to prolonged environmental stress which they cannot meet directly and aggressively, tend to react with considerable regularity by the use of a specific type of adaptation which Siegel terms "defensive structuring." In an attempt to preserve their cultural identity in the face of external threats from their environment, they practice such elements of defensive adaptation as elite authoritarian control over members, endogamy, cultivation of symbols of cultural identity, and early socialization for impulse control.—BM

366. ——————. Social Disorganization in Picuris Pueblo, International Journal of Comparative Sociology, 6 (September, 1965), 199-206.

This study points out that the communities of Picuris and Taos, in spite of an extensive period of common cultural history, exhibit great differences in cultural vitality. Social disorganization and extensive cultural loss have occurred in Picuris, whereas in Taos the commitment to traditional value orientations has continued and has even been intensified. The reasons for these differences, suggests Siegel, may lie in the different impact of stress because of environmental change as it affected each of the pueblos. Increasing encirclement by Spanish Americans and Anglos seems to have developed in Taos a strong feeling of urgency in adapting to a perceived threat to cultural survival, thus actually resulting in the strengthening of the conventional power system. Picuris, on the other hand, being removed from the centers of development, has lacked any sense of urgency as far as the protection of their traditional systems of belief and behavior are concerned. The result has been considerable disruption of social organization, loss of cultural vitality, and the emergence of pervasive anomie in the generation of young adult males.—BM

367. Simmons, Marc. Spanish Government in New Mexico. Albuquerque, University of New Mexico Press, 1968. 216 pp.

This monograph, based on archival research, is concerned with Spanish governmental institutions and practices in New Mexico in the late colonial period, primarily the eighteenth century. An important argument put forward by the author is that, contrary to much scholarly opinion, New Mexico was closely tied to the central colonial government in Mexico, and through it, to Spain. A change in policy by the central government would result in commensurate alterations in New Mexican policy. The author conjectures that economic and social patterns, like administrative practices, were echoes of Mexican values. This is a study of a comparatively neglected field, and suggests a possible recasting of the usual image of the socially and politically isolated Hispanos of New Mexico.—RM

368. Simmons, Ozzie G. The Mutual Images and Expectations of Anglo-Americans and Mexican-Americans, Daedalus, XC (Spring, 1961), 286-299.

Simmons delineates the expectations and ideologies that Anglos and Mexican Americans use to define each other. The study is based on a sociological survey of a town in the Rio Grande Valley of Texas. The author concludes that the Anglos possess ambiguous attitudes toward Chicanos. Anglos accept the United States creed, so they say that Mexican Americans must be afforded full acceptance and equal status, usually contingent on the Chicanos' having gained a command of Anglo ways and occupational and financial success. However, Anglos also often believe that the Chicanos are a homogeneous, inferior group, unclean, criminal and immoral.

Mexican American opinions of Anglos reflect Anglos' views as well as the Chicanos' subordinate status. Some Chicanos, Simmons feels, have a very defensive attitude toward themselves, while they see Anglos in images both favorable—industrious, ambitious—and unfavorable—cold, mercenary, exploitative. Mexican American attitudes toward Anglos are less elaborate than Anglo views of Chicanos; Mexican Americans do not have to justify the present intergroup relations. Anglos feel justified in withholding equal status as long as the Mexican American is different, while the Chicanos refuse to give up all of their culture and believe that acculturation will not be rewarded by a change of attitude.—RM

369. ————————— and Robert C. Hauson. The Rural Migrant in the World of Work, Proceedings, XI, Interamerican Congress of Psychology, Mexico City, December, 1967. 20 pp.

The thrust of this article is to test a sociological model to deal with the mechanisms used by rural migrants in finding urban employment. The test cases the authors chose were Mexican Americans; there is a description of attempts to find work, aimless drifting, and ultimate dependence on social networks of acquaintances.—RM

370. Simpson, Lesley Byrd. Many Mexicos. Berkeley, G.P. Putnam and Sons, 1961 ed. 334 pp.

In this history of Mexico the author stresses that there are "many Mexicos"—many widely divergent geographical areas, life styles, and cultural traditions. The emphasis in the book is on the Spanish colonial days and the clashes between the Indians, creoles, and Spanish, which Simpson believes clearly foreshadowed the Independence movement. The book closes with a look at the economic and agricultural problems of the 1950's.—RM

371. Sjoberg, Gideon, ed. Ethics, Politics, and Social Research. Cambridge, Massachusetts, Schenkman Publishing Company, Inc., 1967. 358 pp.

This collection of articles presents vital questions about the ethics involved in social science. Individual authors examine the influence exercised by institutions which fund research, researchers' personal bias, the impact of political ideology in research design and application, latent and manifest racism, external pressure groups, and the researcher's relationship to the people he studies. The discussions represent all disciplines. The issues raised are international in scope, but most cases refer to the United States. No pat solutions appear, nor is any point of view espoused.—PS

372. Smith, M. Estellie. The Spanish Speaking Population of Florida, in Spanish-Speaking People in the U.S.; Proceedings of the 1968 Annual Spring Meeting of the American Ethnological Society. Seattle, distributed by the University of Washington Press, 1968. pp. 120-133.

This is a survey of four Spanish-speaking groups in Florida: Puerto Ricans, Mexican Americans, and Cubans who came to the United States before and after Fidel Castro came to power. The findings stress the wide range of cultural differences found within the linguistic category. There is a discussion of Mexican American migrants based on interviews with one migrant group. The central point of the work is a plea for a set of anthropological research guidelines.—RM

373. Solé, Carlos A. Bibliografía Sobre el Español en América: 1920-1967. Washington, D.C.: Washington University Press, 1970. 175 pp.

This is a bibliography on Spanish linguistics which focuses primarily on dialectology. In addition to works on the various countries of Latin America, the author provides a section which lists works dealing with the Spanish linguistic zones or regions in the United States. The list includes works on the Southwest in general and individual sections on Arizona, Colorado, New Mexico, Florida, and other areas.—BM

374. Sommers, Joseph. After the Storm—Landmarks of the Modern Mexican Novel. Albuquerque, University of New Mexico Press, 1968. 208 pp.

In this study, the author examines four novels which he considers landmarks of the post-revolutionary period in Mexico. The novels are Al filo del agua (The Edge of the Storm) by Agustín Yáñez in 1947, Pedro Párama (1955), and two novels by Carlos Fuentes, La región más transparente (Where the Air is Clear) in 1958 and La Muerte de Artemio Cruz (The Death of Artemio Cruz) in 1962. The author believes that with these four major works a new level of maturity has been reached for the modern Mexican novel which transcends the novel of the Revolution and strikes a balance between national preoccupation and universal values. Sommers examines the structure, narrative technique, style, and world view in each of these novels. He also includes an introductory chapter on the novel of the Revolution and a final chapter putting the novels in a larger context and discussing what implications they have for the future of the novel in Mexico.—AP

375. Sommers, Vita S. The Impact of Dual-Cultural Membership on Identity, Psychiatry, XXVII (November, 1964), 332-344.

This article contains a series of psychiatric analyses of the responses of male minority group members, including a Mexican American, to the strains of dual cultural membership. The author assumes that Mexican Americans will respond similarly to others who are in the same culturally ambiguous position. The individuals used in the test cases all were born into poverty, were exposed to childhood frustrations, and suffered a turbulent adolescence. One of the most vital determining factors in the subjects' psychology was the childhood experience of prejudice directed at the parents by others. The child's view of how his parents were valued in the community at large was very important to the growth of his own self-identity. The perceived discrepancy between the way the parents ought to be and actually were treated often led to beliefs that the parents were inferior, to a rejection of the parental culture, and to the adoption of values and behavior patterns in opposition to the child's early training. Psychoses can develop from these stresses, resulting in a defensive way of life and a preoccupation with the status and self-esteem reached by embracing Anglo attributes. The behavior sometimes becomes a caricature of Anglo norms; and the difficulties are exacerbated by the conflict between the newly adopted values and the remaining loyalties to the parental ethnic culture.—RM

376. Soukup, James R. Party and Factional Divisions in Texas. Austin, University of Texas Press, 1964. 221 pp.

This book is a report on the role of alliances and interest groups in Texas politics. It contains one section on Mexican American political activity. The author states that Chicanos tend to be Democrats and until recently were manipulated to support conservative candidates. When Chicanos are organized and free to express their true beliefs, they are liberal in outlook and are more concerned about civil rights than economic programs.—RM

377. Southwest Educational Development Laboratory, Proceedings—National Conference on Educational Opportunities for Mexican Americans. April 25-26, 1968. Austin, Texas: Southwest Educational Development Laboratory, 1968.

This is a report of the activities of the first national conference of this type ever held. It was sponsored by the U.S. Office of Education and held in Austin, Texas. The conference was attended mostly by teachers and administrators and some university personnel. The purpose of the conference was to review and discuss recent legislation relative to the education of the Mexican American, and the conference focused on new programs in bilingual and migrant education. The report contains abstracts of addresses delivered at the conference by speakers from the U.S. Office of Education, and also reports on several discussion groups and demonstrations.—AP

378. Spilka, Bernard and Lois Gill. Some Non-Intellectual Correlates of Academic Achievement Among Spanish-American Students, School Counselor, XII, No. 4 (May, 1965), 218-221.

Sixty high school juniors and seniors were given a battery of tests in this study, including measurements of IQ, achievement, hostility and anxiety adaptation. The authors concluded that achieving girls and underachieving boys came from homes where the mothers were demanding and dominating. Achievement was also related to conformist behavior.—LH

379. Spota, Luis. Murieron a Mitad del Rio, Mexico D.F., B. Costa-Amic, 1969. 261 pp.

First published in 1948, this novel follows the exploits of three Mexican workers who enter the United States illegally and seek to earn money by performing migrant labor. Spota portrays the dulling effect that migrant labor has on the human psyche, and delineates the moral and spiritual degeneration which he contends takes place in a competitive capitalistic economic system. This is especially true, he contends, of lower class, uneducated, rural people who get caught up in the obsession to make money in a society where money is the center of life.—CV

380. Steiner, Stan. La Raza: The Mexican Americans (New York, Harper & Row, 1968).

In this work the author describes in a historical context the plight of the Mexican American in his fight for social justice and economic equality. La Raza is divided into three areas of geographic and thematic interest: Part one tells of the land grant struggle headed by Reies Tijerina in New Mexico; part two shifts to the urban environment of East Los Angeles and the efforts to dramatize and remedy the conditions of the barrios, and part three focuses on César Chávez and the attempts to unionize the migrant workers in the grape fields. Steiner gives particular emphasis to the symbolic aspect of La Huelga, for example, the songs, the theatrical group, El Teatro Campesino, and, of course, the personality of Chávez himself. In the epilogue, the author describes Corky Gonzales who is now the leader of the Denver Crusade for Justice. Steiner's book is an attempt to portray two main currents presently emerging within the Chicano movement: First, the increasing awareness of the existence of their community within the dominant Anglo culture and socioeconomic institutions, and second, the recognition of the need for identity and consciousness of self among Chicano youth which could lead to a new activism and new ideological perspectives on the role of the Chicano in American society.—MLB

381. Stoddard, Ellwyn R. Comparative Structures and Attitudes Along the United States-Mexican Border. Conference on Urbanization of the United States-Mexican Border, El Paso, Texas, June, 1968. (Available through Educational Resource Information Center.) 35 pp.

This article suggests that comparative, cross-cultural research could reveal a great deal about the problems of acculturation, since people in different countries must adjust to varying national structures and institutions. Case studies of urbanization and political structure, disaster relief, law enforcement systems and applications, and self-identity problems are presented as indicative of promising research areas. Stoddard concludes his article with a statement on the need for research which can be used in policy-making and in social action.—PS

382. ——————. Comparative Structures and Attitudes Along the U.S.-Mexico Border, in Ellwyn R. Stoddard (ed.). Comparative U.S.-Mexico Border Studies, Occasional Papers No. 1, Border-State University Consortium for Latin America, May, 1970, pp. 1-38.

The term "U.S.-Mexican Border" is defined respectively as a geographical region, a legal-political entity, a cultural milieu, and in relation to a focus on the Mexican American people. The historical antecedents of contemporary border research are outlined, and the current use of the comparative method approach is delineated in terms of research in the specific areas of political structure and urbanization, disaster relief, law enforcement, and self-identity.—BM

383. ——————. The U.S.-Mexican Border as a Research Laboratory, Journal of Inter-American Studies, 11 (July, 1969), 477-488.

The research cited in this report concentrates on various empirical studies with which the author has been involved or concerned. These studies, grouped into the three main categories of Political Leadership and Social Structure, Comparative Disaster Studies, and Studies of Self Identity, are briefly summarized and discussed in order to illustrate the kinds of possible contributions which might be made by empirical border research. Stoddard explains that the types of findings engendered by such research are applicable in at least two significant ways: in supporting or questioning basic assumptions made about Latin American culture, and in helping to locate bias and ethnocentrism in the interpretations of Latin American institutions and values made by United States scholars. It is suggested in conclusion that the kind of empirical research illustrated in this report should be considered as a valuable extension of the traditional historical approach to Latin American Studies.—BM

384. Stone, Robert C., et al. Ambos-Nogales: Bicultural Urbanism in a Developing Region, Arizona Review of Business and Public Administration, XII, No. 1 (January, 1963), 1-29.

This is the first in a series of articles focusing on the twin cities Nogales, Arizona, and Nogales, Sonora. An overview of economic and ethnic patterns is provided along with historical and geographic backgrounds. Nogales' population is

80 percent Mexican and bilingualism pervades much of public life. This community study is informative, detailed, comprehensive, and covers ethnic group relations.—LH

385. Strauss, Anselm L. Mirrors and Masks: The Search for Identity. New York: The Free Press, 1959.

In this work Strauss suggests ways of theorizing about and doing research on the social processes from which identity emerges, and about the symbolic and cultural foundations of its structure. He stresses the importance of the influence of social organization upon individual behavior and individual personality structure. The significance of language in human action and identity, and the indeterminancy of identities in a context of continual social change are also discussed in depth.—BM

386. Summer, Margaret L. Mexican American Minority Churches, USA, Practical Anthropology, X (1963), 115-121.

This is a study of the effects of joining a Protestant church on the social contacts of a Mexican American. The author concludes that Chicano Protestants retreat from the life of the barrio, with the degree of withdrawal determined by the strictness of the sect joined. However, Protestant church membership did little toward furthering integration of Mexican Americans into groups of Anglo Protestants. The author believes that "indigenous" churches are not good agents of assimilation and calls for cooperation and sponsorship between English- and Spanish-speaking churches.—RM

387. Suttles, Gerald D. The Social Order of the Slum: Ethnicity and Territory in the Inner City. Chicago, University of Chicago Press, 1968.

This is a study of four ethnic groups—Italian, Mexican American, Puerto Rican and Negro—in a Chicago slum. The author observes that Mexican Americans occupy a median position between the Italians and Negroes on nearly every social measurement. One of Suttles' conclusions is the importance of territorial boundaries—the delineations of neighborhoods which sometimes supersede usual ethnic areas and identities. The author believes, for instance, that the Mexican American and Negro adolescents of one neighborhood would ally to combat invaders of either ethnic group from another neighborhood. The main methodology used, that of the Chicago school of participant-observer, is not sufficient to support this thesis; no confrontation similar to the example took place while the author was in the neighborhood.—RM

388. Swadesh, Frances J. The Alianza Movement: Catalyst for Social Change in New Mexico, in Proceedings of the 1968 Annual Spring Meeting; American Ethnological Society. Seattle, distributed by the University of Washington Press, 1968. pp. 162-177.

This is a history and explanation of the social role of Reies Tijerina and the Land Grant movement in New Mexico. It is a direct answer to Nancie González' The Spanish-Americans in New Mexico (Mexican American Study Project Advance Report 9), which characterized Tijerina and his followers as a cultural revitalization movement (in Anthony Wallace's term, a returning to the practices and values of the past to solve current problems).

Swadesh argues that revitalization movements are internal in nature, transforming a culture to make it more satisfying. Tijerina's crusade is external because it tries to change conditions by directly challenging the controls exercised by Anglos. Also, it is not a nativist cult because religion is not central to its vitality, nor is it completely culturally exclusive, since Anglos have been participants and its targets are often Hispano politicians.—RM

389. ——————————. Hispanic Americans of the Ute Frontier From the Chama Valley to the San Juan Basin, 1694-1960. PhD dissertation, University of Colorado, 1966.

This is an anthropological study of the Hispanic communities of the Tierra Amarilla Grant since 1694. Through the utilization of structural analysis and the perspective of ethnohistory, the author attempts to broaden understanding and appreciation of the historical context of the area that is of concern today due to the activities of Reies Tijerina. Using a variety of anthropological theories of cultural change and social structural transformation, the study examines the hypothesis which proposes that hispanic communities in which strong frontier traditions are institutionalized are capable of further cultural evolution without cultural disintegration and loss of identity. A system of analysis composed of three types of structural and cultural transformation is developed: Cyclic, Substitutive and Transitional. By comparing the atypical pattern of social relations of these New Mexico communities with more common Latin American communities, the study supports the theoretical view which holds that similar structural characteristics tend to produce similar patterns of cultural divergence and adaptability regardless of the geographical location of the community.—MLB

390. Talbert, Robert H. Spanish-Name People in the Southwest and West. Fort Worth, Texas, Leo Potishman Foundation, Texas Christian University, 1955. 90 pp.

This sociological survey based on the 1950 census presents many of the demographic characteristics of the Spanish-speaking population and compares their social situation to that of the "white and nonwhite" populations. The work focuses on Texas; the questions pursued are geographical distribution, education, marital and economic status and housing.—RM

391. Taylor, Paul S. An American-Mexican Frontier: Nueces County, Texas. Chapel Hill, University of North Carolina, 1934. 329 pp.

This 1934 study is based on quotes from Texas Anglos and Mexican Americans that give opinions on many questions, usually about social interaction between South Texas ethnic groups. Taylor concentrated his efforts on problems of employment, education and racial prejudice, and demonstrated clearly the racism and social stereotypes which determined the forms of social interaction. He also described the rather violent history of the Nueces region, especially the armed clashes that continued almost to the turn of the century and endowed both groups with fears and hatreds that survived into the early 1930's. The attitudes the book illuminates are Anglo insistence that Mexican Americans are inferior, and an almost apologetic withdrawal on the part of the Mexican Americans in the face of Anglo prejudice.—RM

392. ——————————. The Mexican Immigrant and the Problem of Crime and Criminal Justice, in U.S. National Commission on Law Observance and Enforcement, Report on Crime and the Foreign Born, X, Washington, D.C., 1931.

199-243.

This study is based on the material collected by Taylor for his general works on Mexican immigration, using court records and school populations for statistical data. He found considerable diversity in law observance among Mexican Americans in different localities. While in the total statistics Mexican Americans accounted disproportionately for arrests for narcotics and crimes of violence, in some communities this did not hold true. Taylor criticized the use of records of arrest and conviction to evaluate the criminality of an ethnic group because the police and courts often show prejudice against minority group members, who are politically and economically helpless before the law.—RM

393. —————————. Mexican Labor in the United States: Bethlehem, Pennsylvania. University of California Publications in Economics, VII, No. 1 (Berkeley, University of California Press, 1931), 1-24.

In his briefest study of Mexican labor in varous geographical regions of the United States, Taylor examined the position of the Mexican Americans who were attracted to the steel mills of Bethlehem, Pennsylvania. Spurred by labor shortages in the industrial recovery after the post-World War I depression, steel companies began recruiting large numbers of Mexicans (primarily recent immigrants) from San Antonio in 1923; during two months alone over 900 were transported North. The Mexican Americans rapidly dispersed from the Bethlehem colony in search of better jobs; by 1930, only 84 Mexican Americans were employed by Bethlehem Steel. As in all his studies of Mexican labor, Taylor discusses employment and social relations. He found no public or school discrimination, but there was prejudice in labor relations. It was exercised primarily by the immigrant European foremen, not by the Anglo superintendents; Taylor observes that discrimination by ethnic group was prevalent in the industry before the Mexicans arrived. Acculturation, although slow, was more rapid than in Texas; the Mexicans learned English and adopted Anglo dress more quickly.—SD

394. —————————. Mexican Labor in the United States: Chicago and the Calumet Region. University of California Publications in Economics, VII, No. 2 (Berkeley, University of California Press, 1932), 26-280.

In this detailed study of the Mexicans who migrated to the Chicago region after World War I, Taylor covered, among other topics, the economic market and labor relations, occupational advance, saving, spending and ownership patterns, and the standard of living. Many Mexicans were recruited for railroad work and entered industry as the war progressed; the majority of them "leapfrogged" over the border regions and went directly from central Mexico to the Midwest. Taylor examined the Mexican penetration as well as that of other ethnic groups into different industries and found that in 1928 Mexicans comprised 43 percent of the track labor on the major railroads and 12.1 percent of the employees of eight of the largest industrial plants. In addition to using available statistics in such areas as employment, school attendance and housing patterns, Taylor expanded his study with interviews to determine Anglo and Mexican American attitudes. Taylor found that the attitudes of employers about Mexicans varied with the type of work involved and seemed related to the industry's dependence on Mexican laborers. Taylor observed that the Mexican Americans felt steady employment was as important as a high wage rate.—SD

395. —————————. Mexican Labor in the United States: Dimmit County,

Winter Garden District, South Texas. University of California Publications in Economics, VI, No. 5 (Berkeley, University of California Press, 1930), 294-457.

In this study Taylor explored the status of Mexican labor in one of the United States' major production areas of winter vegetables, the Southwestern portion of Texas. Taylor traced the development of intensive agriculture in the region and the history of the Mexican American presence. He then analyzed the labor market and presented attitudes (gathered from interviews with the workers and the growers) about the effects of "cheap labor" and about labor relations. Interestingly, many small growers and tenant farmers who worked for others expressed a common antipathy toward the large producers; these landowners, they charged, imported Mexican labor to keep prices low and consequently depressed the earnings of the small farmer who depended disproportionately on his own labor. Taylor elicited frank expressions of prejudice; a board of education member observed that the Mexican Americans were provided with a school building to prevent complaints from the Mexican consul. In addition to school attendance statistics, Taylor also provided data on property leasing and ownership, amount of urban employment, and residential segregation.—SD

396. —————————. Mexican Labor in the United States: Imperial Valley. University of California Publications in Economics, VI, No. 1 (Berkeley, University of California Press, 1928), 1-94.

In this study Taylor again offered the results of his research into such topics as the history of Mexican Americans in California, the nature of the labor market and working conditions, standards of living, and school and residential segregation. As is true of his other works on Mexican labor in the United States, he combines presentation of the available statistics with interviews revealing Anglo and Mexican American attitudes. Taylor observed that discrimination in businesses was most apparent when personal service was involved—for example, in restaurants and beauty parlors—and least evident when commodities were sold. Taylor concluded that the "Mexican laborers of the valley are on the whole a class apart...the coincidence of class, racial and cultural differences...combine to maintain a social ostracism, which in its turn reinforces and stabilizes the differences." He felt the Mexican migration to the Imperial Valley differed from previous European labor-class immigration to the United States because the Mexicans worked in rural areas and Anglos viewed them with a "strong consciousness of racial difference."—SD

397. —————————. Mexican Labor in the United States: Migration Statistics, I-IV. University of California Publications in Economics, VI, No. 3 and XII, No. 1-3 (Berkeley, University of California Press, 1929-1934).

Taylor's volumes on migration statistics represent an additional aspect of his early contribution to the Mexican American labor picture. In the first report he compared the statistics on Mexican border crossings for 1910-1928 and found grave discrepancies between the figures published by the United States and by Mexico. Taylor's critique of the sources of error in the data includes a discussion of the difficulty of estimating illegal entries into the United States.

The second and third monographs examined seasonal fluctuations in Mexican American and Negro migration from Arizona into Southern California and from this area northward to California's Central Valley. In the fourth study Taylor used unpublished Mexican government data to look at the repatriation of Mexicans in 1930-1933. He also studied the origins in Mexico of immigrants in different regions of the United States and found wide variations: the northeastern part of Mexico contributed 87 percent of the Mexican Americans in the Winter Garden district of South Texas but only 17.6 percent of the Mexican American population in California's Imperial Valley; immigrants from Mexico's central plateau made up barely 13 percent of the Mexican American population in the Winter Garden district but comprised 75 percent of the Mexican Americans in the Chicago region.—SD

398. ——————. Mexican Labor in the United States: Racial School Statistics, California, 1927, University of California Publications in Economics, VI, No. 4 (Berkeley, University of California Press, 1929), 259-292.

Taylor reports the geographic distribution of Mexican American, Negro and Japanese school children with data tabulated from a special census of public and Catholic elementary schools. Unlike the state enrollment figures gathered in September, this census was taken in February during the slack agricultural period when migratory families, significantly Mexican Americans, should be "at home." Among other comparisons, the breakdown by county revealed the heavy concentration of minority groups in Southern California, which accounted for 83 percent of the total Mexican American state enrollment, 68 percent of the Negro total, and 44 percent of the Japanese totals.—SD

399. ——————. Mexican Labor in the United States: Valley of the South Platte, Colorado. University of California Publications in Economics, VI, No. 2 (Berkeley, University of California Press, 1929), 97-235.

The history and socioeconomic condition of the Mexican American laborers in the sugar beet fields of Colorado are examined by Taylor in this work. There are data similar to that presented in Taylor's other studies, including tables on sugar beet production and labor costs, changes in the ethnic composition of the migrant labor force, county welfare expenditures, and school attendance. Taylor observed that those few Anglos who made a distinction between the Hispanos and the Mexican Americans felt that the Hispanos as a class were better educated and spoke better English and Spanish but almost no Anglos could distinguish between individual members of the two groups. As long-time residents of the area, Taylor noted that the Hispanos felt superior to the Mexican Americans and were displeased because Anglos did not distinguish between them and the recent immigrants. The Mexican Americans, in turn, resented the Hispanos' superior attitude, and there was occasionally friction between members of the two groups.—SD

400. Tebbel, John and Ramon E. Ruíz. South by Southwest: The Mexican American and His Heritage. Garden City, New York, Doubleday and Company, 1969. 120 pp.

In this work the authors emphasize Mexican political and intellectual history. The book gives an account of Mexican and United States military and diplomatic clashes.—RM

401. Texas Advisory Committee to the United States Commission on Civil Rights. Employment Practices at Kelly Air Force Base, San Antonio, Texas. June, 1968. 17 pp.

This report by the Texas Advisory Committee attempts to establish that broad and glaring inequalities exist in the distribution of supervisory and higher grade positions among the civil service employees of Kelly Air Force Base. Based on employment records, it finds that minority group workers, Mexican Americans and Negroes, are concentrated in the lower job strata with little possibility of advancement. In part this is due to the self-perpetuating practices of the Anglo managerial and foreman class. The report observes that Mexican Americans are skeptical about the good faith of management officials and the value of the Equal Employment Opportunity programs on the base.—RM

402. Tharp, Roland G., and Arnold Meadow, Susan G. Lennhoff, Donna Sattefield. Changes in Marriage Roles Accompanying the Acculturation of the Mexican American Wife, Journal of Marriage and the Family, XXX, No. 3 (August, 1968), 404-412.

In this study of Mexican American wives in Tucson, Arizona, the authors confirmed the hypothesis that there is a trend toward family equalitarianism in acculturating groups. Using an area and cluster sampling technique, the researchers first collected the responses of 250 Mexican American wives to a standardized questionnaire. Two subgroups representing the extremes of acculturation (fluent English-speaking versus little or no English facility) were then given intensive personal interviews. The authors justified using language ability as the measure of acculturation by noting the correlation they found in their sample between English fluency and other indicators of assimilation. English-speaking was correlated with higher levels of education, birth in the United States, youth, high occupational level of the husband, and, especially, with residence in an ethnically mixed neighborhood rather than a Mexican American barrio.

Among the significant differences between the two groups, the authors found that the wives who spoke Spanish and little or no English believed more strongly that the husband should be the "boss" in the family and that children should be raised strictly. These wives also denigrated their personal status, had fewer recreation activities with their children, and were more concerned with the duties of their role as housekeeper than the wives who spoke fluent English. The authors warn, however, against attributing these role changes solely to the experience of acculturating Mexican American wives; they note that all lower class women have been found to undergo similar role changes as their family prosperity level increases.—SD

403. Tirado, Miguel David. Mexican American Community Organization—The Key to Chicano Political Power, Aztlan I (Spring, 1970), 53-78.

This article is a historical analysis of past Mexican American efforts at community organization, which attempts to refute the commonly held assumption that the Mexican American minority has been politically apathetic and slow in developing community action organizations. The author chronicles the history of Mexican American community organizations from about 1910 to the present, including the early "mutualistas" and protective societies, the League of United Latin American Citizens (LULACS), the Mexican Congress, various Unity leagues, the Community Service Organization (CSO), the American G.I. Forum, and the Mexican American Political Organization (MAPA). A central part of Tirado's analysis is an attempt to discover and isolate the ingredients of these organizations which have tended to promote stability and vitality in Mexican American political organization. Tirado has isolated five elements: (1) most successful Mexican American community organizations in the past have been multifunctional, willing to serve many different functions for their membership; (2) they have tended to make provision for some kind of involvement of the entire family; (3) they have been able to capitalize on a single area issue crisis approach, mobilizing grass roots support around a series of crisis issues; (4) they have emphasized personalistic consensual leadership, often guarding against dictatorial leadership by decentralizing their structure; and (5) they have been able to attract supporters through the effective use of ethnic symbolism.—AP

404. Tireman, L.S. Bilingual Children, Review of Educational Research, XI (June, 1941), 340-352.

This article is a review of the literature on bilingual education in the United States during the years from 1932 to 1941. The author reviews the literature on the psychological and sociological aspects of bilingualism, including the influence of bilingualism on school adjustment and verbal intelligence, the influence of environment and experience on test results, and the use of Spanish translations of intelligence tests. The author also discusses the curriculum needs of bilingual students and reports on several experimental schools under way during the period. A 73-item bibliography is included.—AP

405. Tobias, Henry J. and Charles E. Woodhouse (eds.). Minorities and Politics, Albuquerque, University of New Mexico Press, 1969, 131 pp.

This is a brief study of five movements: the Jews in Tsarist Russia, the separatist movement of the French Canadians in Quebec, the cultural and social survival of the Pueblo Indians, the Negro in Albuquerque, New Mexico, and the irredentist Alianza movement of New Mexico. The aim of the authors is to survey how minorities see politics as relevant to their interests and how they have attempted to exploit political means in behalf of these interests. They ask questions: (1) How do minorities become involved with politics in a quest for cultural identity or in an effort to preserve identity? (2) How do minorities become involved in a quest for cultural identity as a result of their political involvement?

The history of the Alianza and actions in which it was involved are outlined by Frances Swadesh. The Alianza movement is seen as a breakaway from local political forms—as an incipient protest and civil rights movement operating in hostile surroundings with goals which are virtually unattainable. The section dealing with the Alianza gives sources on Mexican reaction to the land reclamation movement.—CV

406. Topete, Jesús. Aventuras de un bracero. Mexico City, Editorial Amexica, 1949. 143 pp.

This is an account of the author's experiences as a bracero in the United States. Topete spent six months in 1944 working in the potato fields near Stockton, California. Defenseless in a foreign country, and unaided by the inspectors from the Mexican government who were supposed to protect him, the bracero had to accept what his employer offered. In Topete's experience, this included a wage rate substantially lower than that given to native United States labor (although greater than that which he could have expected in Mexico) and earnings which were quite uncertain because of frequent days without work. The bracero, says Topete, also encountered poor housing, inadequate food, dangerous working conditions, and violations of his labor rights. Topete, however, notes that the experiences and earnings of the bracero varied considerably.

Chicanos are criticized for having become Anglicized, for knowing little about Mexico, and for feeling superior to Mexicans. Anglos as a group are neither condemned nor praised, but United States society is criticized for its materialism and for its prejudice toward the Negro and the Mexican.—RS

407. Trueba, Alfonso. California: Tierra Perdida. Mexico, D.F., Editorial Campeador, II Volumes, 1956, 1958, Vol. I (93 pp), Vol. II (199 pp.).

This is a short two volume history of California and its loss by Mexico to the United States. It covers the period of California history from the time of its settlement by Spanish explorers to the acquisition of the territory by the U.S. In this concise history Trueba treats the establishing of the missions by the Franciscans, the Russian "period," the turmoil of civil war after Mexican Independence and the battles against United States forces at Monterrey, San Pedro, Natividad and San Pascual, all of which set back American attempts at annexation before the war of 1846. The author also discusses the factors which kept California so separated from the Mexican central government and made its fall into American hands almost inevitable.—CV

408. Tuck, Ruth D. Not With the Fist: Mexican-Americans in a Southwest City. New York, Harcourt, Brace and Company, 1946. 234 pp.

The author feels that the majority group attitudes derive from the demands of surviving in a frontier society. An idealized version of this Old West heritage was proudly maintained in the small community of "Descanso," producing intolerance of anyone (in this case, Mexican Americans) perceived as "weak" in the constant life struggle.—PS

409. Turner, Ralph H. and Samuel J. Surace. Zoot Suiters and Mexicans: Symbols in Crowd Behavior, American Journal of Sociology, LXII (July, 1956), 14-20.

This is a study of the connotations that were given to identity terms when the group identified was clashing with the dominant society. In the World War II Zoot Suit Riots between military personnel and Mexican American zootsuiters, the term "Mexican" did not gain pejorative connotations. The authors believe this was because the pleasant tradition of a romantic Spanish past was an important belief in Southern California. Instead, all animosity was aimed at the symbol of the zoot-suiter. He was a man outside the societal system with no traditions and an alien appearance; he was therefore "fair game."—RM

410. Ulibarri, Horacio. Educational Needs of the Mexican-American. New Mexico State University, University Park, April, 1968, Available through Educational Resources Information Center. 21 pp.

In this article, Ulibarri evaluates the appropriateness of the typical education available to Mexican Americans in terms of occupational success, citizen participation, and personality factors. Ulibarri shows that education is inadequate. Functional illiteracy and subsequent unemployment (or underemployment) is high because bilingualism is not taken into account in school programming. Active citizen participation (e.g., insistence on civil rights and challenges to the status quo) does not grow out of the assimilationist approach taught by schools. A survey of what Mexican Americans believe about themselves reveals very negative self-stereotypes, which are reinforced by subtle discrimination in the school system. The author suggests remedying these disparities through bicultural education.—PS

411. Ulibarri, Richard O. American Interest in the Spanish Southwest,

1803-1848. PhD dissertation, University of Utah, 1963.

The author traces the history of American interest in the area that today comprises the American Southwest, from the time of the Louisiana Purchase until the conclusion of the Mexican War in 1848. Feeling that American expansion into both Texas and California has been discussed elsewhere, the author chooses to concentrate primarily on expansionary activities into New Mexico. While most readers will find the chronicles of various adventurers, mountain men and diplomats to be primarily of historical interest only, the chapter on the development of Manifest Destiny doctrine as an ideological rationale for commercial expansion seems appropriate to contemporary concerns of Mexican Americans. Tracing the origins of this expansionist ideology back to the birth of the American Republic, and especially to Thomas Jefferson, this study gives attention to the mixture of racist and economic elements in American policy. Ulibarri also discusses racial themes that justified expansion at the expense of Mexico on the basis of a "superior" Anglo-Saxon culture bringing progress and enlightenment to backward northern Mexican provinces.—MLB

412. United States Commission on Civil Rights. The Mexican American. Prepared by Helen Rowan, Washington, D.C., 1968. 69 pp.

This is a short introduction to many aspects of Mexican American life. It dwells primarily on the types of problems Chicanos face and suggests solutions. Starting with a general description of the Chicano population, the author then explores briefly questions of civil rights and justice, education and relations with public agencies. In all the topics treated there is a look at the cultural clashes, misunderstandings and prejudices that complicate Chicano-Anglo interactions and exacerbate social problems.—RM

413. ————————. Stranger in One's Land. Washington, D.C.: Clearinghouse Publication, No. 19, May 1970. 49 pp.

This publication is an account of the United States Commission on Civil Rights hearing held in San Antonio, Texas in December of 1968, as reported by California journalist Ruben Salazar. Major areas of concern explored were educational and bilingual suppression, economic deprivation, discrimination in employment, and inequities in the administration of justice, as each applied to the Mexican American minority. More specificity than is usual in such conferences prevailed at the San Antonio hearing. In each area of concern, precise names and institutions accused of insensitivity toward Mexican Americans were dealt with and specific solutions were suggested.—BM

414. ————————. Mexican Americans and the Administration of Justice in the Southwest. U. S. Printing Office, March, 1970. 135 pp.

This document is the official report of the Commission on Civil Rights presented to the Congress and the President of the United States. The Commission documents its extensive field investigations and hearings throughout the Southwest during 1967 and 1968. In the Commission's introductory letter to the Congress and to the President, the members of the Commission outline some of their conclusions as follows: "Our investigations reveal that Mexican American citizens are subject to unduly harsh treatment by law enforcement officers, that they are often arrested on insufficient grounds, receive physical and verbal abuse, and penalties are disproportionately severe. We have found them to be deprived of proper use of bail and of adequate representation by counsel. They are substantially underrepresented on grand and petit juries and excluded from full participation in law enforcement agencies, especially in supervisory positions." What follows in the report is the documented evidence that led the Commission to these conclusions, along with a list of specific recommendations to remedy the many injustices that they found. The appendix includes a study of the Grand Jury selection system in California, and the underrepresentation of minority-group individuals on such juries.—AP

415. United States Congress, Senate. Hearings before the Special Subcommittee on Bilingual Education of the Committee on Labor and Public Welfare. Washington, D.C., United States Government Printing Office, 1967. 681 pp.

At hearings held in Washington, D.C., Texas, California and New York, the subcommittee heard a wide variety of testimony from state and local public officials, professional and administrative school personnel, and representatives of Mexican American organizations. Also included are resolutions of various regional conferences, detailed information on existing bilingual and special educational programs, tables of Mexican American education statistics, and texts of various journal articles on bilingual education. This was the first bill on bilingual education introduced in Congress; bilingual programs became the revised Title VII of the Elementary and Secondary Education Act of 1965.—SD

416. U.S. Office of Education. National Conference on Bilingual Education: Language Skills. Washington, D.C., 1969.

This document is a report of the conference on bilingual education held at the University of Maryland in June of 1969. The objectives of bilingual education were defined as consisting of helping all children to realize their full potential in a linguistically and culturally pluralistic society, and the specific goals of the conference were listed as the identification of the variables crucial to the building of a successful bilingual language program, the identification of gaps in the present body of knowledge about bilingual education, and the establishment of goals for future research efforts. Included in the conference report are seven papers, presented by specialists in bilingual education, which deal with the theory, rationale, and practice of bilingual education programs. In the concluding section of the report, specific research priorities in the areas of basic research, language acquisition, teacher preparation, assessment, and methods and materials, are discussed and recommended.—BM

417. United States Department of Labor, The Bureau of Labor Standards. The Community Meets the Migrant Worker, Bulletin 221, Washington, D.C., 1960. 59 pp.

This government publication was designed to promote understanding of the migrant workers and their social situation. It explains the migrants' crop following patterns and suggests the community services they need: day care centers, schooling, child labor protection, health services and emergency relief. There are also suggestions about areas of the migrants' lives which need improvement: housing, transportation to farming areas, incomes and social security. The pamphlet describes programs undertaken by some states, towns and service organizations to provide for these needs and to try to integrate the migrants into the community. Mexican American migrants are not dealt with specifically.—RM

418. United States National Commission on Law Observance and Enforcement. Report on Crime and the Foreign Born, X, Washington, D.C., 1931. 416 pp.

This is a study by a team of criminologists and sociologists who investigated the popular notion that recent immigrants contribute disproportionately to the criminal population. The data used were gathered from the court records and statistics on commitment to corrective institutions of several states and larger cities. The conclusions reached in examining these data were that: in proportion to their percentage of the population, the foreign born committed considerably fewer crimes than the native born; the foreign born most closely approached native white rates in crimes of personal violence and were greatly exceeded by them in numbers of crimes for gain. Several studies of the Mexican American crime rate, by Paul Taylor, Max S. Handman, and Paul L. Warnshuis, were included; the Taylor study is annotated separately.—RM

419. Upham, W. Kennedy and David E. Wright. Poverty Among Spanish Americans in Texas. College Station, Texas, Texas A&M University, Department of Agricultural Economics and Sociology and Texas Agricultural Experiment Station, 1966. 55 pp.

This work is based on the census report of 1960 and is a statistical comparison of the economic and educational position of Mexican Americans in Texas with the Anglo and nonwhite population of the state. The authors focus on the relationship of families below the $3000 per year poverty line to education, family size, unemployment, and urban or rural residence. The report shows the disadvantaged position of Chicanos in Texas, which has the highest percentage of poverty-stricken Mexican Americans.—RM

420. Vaca, Nick C. The Mexican-American in the Social Sciences: 1912-1970, El Grito, III (Spring, 1970), 3-24.

This is Part One (1912-1935) of a major four-part study, and it provides a review of the major social science literature on the Mexican American during this period. In the Introduction, the author traces the roots of the social science study of the Mexican American, arising out of the Mexican conflict with Texas in 1846 and the wave of new immigration to the United States beginning in 1882. The author presents a background of the concern over unrestricted immigration (mainly from southern and eastern Europe) and the rise of the doctrine of Nordic superiority leading to the Immigration Act of 1924 and subsequent attempts to restrict the immigration of Mexicans. The author then reviews the most significant literature on the Mexican American in the fields of psychology (1922-1935) and sociology (1912-1935), quoting primary sources throughout the review. In psychology, the central theme of this early literature dealt with the inherent inferiority of the Mexican, both in intelligence and capabilities. In sociology, the central concern was a debate over whether the "problems" of the Mexican immigrant were a result of his cultural heritage or the socioeconomic conditions he faced in the United States.—AP

421. Valdes, Daniel Tapia. A Sociological Analysis and Description of the Political Role, Status, and Voting Behavior of Americans with Spanish Names. Unpublished PhD dissertation, University of Colorado, 1964.

This study is based on data derived from historical documents, census reports, election materials, and results of a panel study concerning an opinion survey. The analysis focuses on questions concerning the historical development of the political role and status of Americans with Spanish surnames at local and state levels in areas in which they constitute an important segment of the population; the extent of change in the political role and status of Spanish-surnamed Americans; the role of ethnicity in this change, and the importance of ethnically oriented propaganda in the effect of such change. The author uses the theoretical concept of "ethnic consciousness" as a principal variable in his analysis of the pattern of specific political behavior among American Hispanos. He attempts to operationalize "ethnic consciousness" by subjecting it to certain behavioral research procedures such as the selection of a concrete sphere of action (the 1963 mayoralty election in Denver), the reduction of the application of the concept specifically to Hispanos in Denver, and by the use of statistical techniques for measuring degrees of ethnicity.—BM

422. Valdez, R.F. The Fallacy of the Spanish Surname Survey, Journal of the California Teachers Association, LXV, No. 3 (May, 1969), 29-32.

Valdez points out the error of the prevalent assumption that Spanish-surname surveys yield fairly accurate counts of the Mexican American population. He stresses that the characteristics of rural and urban Mexican Americans vary greatly, as do the attributes of Spanish-surnamed United States citizens from Europe and South America. Valdez feels that because of their fallacious interpretation of these surveys, school administrators (as well as other public officials) ignore the great differences that exist and act as though all Spanish-surnamed children had identical language and educational "problems." The author concludes that the money and time expended on statewide school surveys of Spanish-surnamed children could be better spent on local district attempts to determine the precise educational problems they face. Valdez offers personal observations to substantiate his arguments.—SD

423. Valdez, Luis, Sister Mary Prudence and César Chávez. Tales of the Delano Revolution, Ramparts, V (July, 1966), 37-50.

These are three personal accounts, one a poem by Sister Mary Prudence, of the Delano grape strike at its inception in 1966. All are written from the perspective of the participants in the strike, both Anglo and Mexican American. The "tales" by Valdez and Chávez also include background on the strike.—LH

424. Valentine, Charles A. Culture and Poverty: Critique and Counter-Proposals. Chicago, University of Chicago Press, 1968. 189 pp.

This essay is an important challenge to the current "culture-of-poverty" concept. The author reiterates anthropology's definition of culture as "the entire way of life followed by a people" and urges that those studying any culture remember "to distinguish carefully between cultural patterns and external conditions, whether environmental or historical." In contradiction to many theories which blame the fact of continued poverty on the poor (because of their self-perpetuating "culture of poverty"), Valentine suggests "that the cultural values of the poor may be much the same as middle-class values, merely modified in practice because of situational stresses."

In addition to this theoretical statement, Valentine gives a critique of traditional analyses (E. Franklin Frazier, Daniel P. Moynihan) and introduces some new conceptualizers (Kenneth Clark, Charles Keil, Thomas Gladwin). He then proposes some alternative approaches to the study of poor people and complex societies. Valentine concludes with a specific, pragmatic plan for social action in the United States.—PS

425. Vasquez, Richard. Chicano. New York, Doubleday & Co., 1970. 376 pp.
This novel traces the story of a family named Sandoval through four generations, from its roots in a village in northern Mexico during the revolution of 1910 to the present-day barrio in East Los Angeles. In tracing the family from generation to generation, the author describes the poverty and exploitation of the people in northern Mexico, the life of the rural poor trying to establish roots in California, and of some of the Mexican Americans living in East Los Angeles and the problems they face—problems of poverty, education, acculturation, relations to the dominant Anglo society, and the crisis of cultural identity.—AP

426. Vega, Jose J. Nuestra America, Galve, S.A. Mexico D.F. 1969.
Nuestra America consists of a series of historical essays concerning the transfer of European civilization and Christianity to this continent by Spaniards and Mexicans since the 16th century. Vega divides the Spanish epoch into three stages: The Discovery, The Exploration, and The Colonization of the territories which later comprised much of the present United States. In the sections dealing with The Discovery and The Exploration, the author tells of the great deeds and contributions of such Spaniards as Ponce de Leon and Hernando de Soto in exploring new territories from Florida and the Carolinas, and from the Atlantic seaboard across to Arizona and New Mexico and California on the Pacific. In the concluding section on the period of colonization, the author details the historical development on the principal Spanish and Mexican territories and the important contribution of Spaniards and Mexicans to the economic progress of the Southwest.—MLB

427. Villarreal, Jose Antonio. Pocho. Garden City, New York, Doubleday and Company, 1959. 235 pp.
This is a novel about a Mexican American boy growing up in the Santa Clara valley of California. Richard Rubio is a pocho, a second generation Mexican American, who is acculturated to many Anglo values. He partially rejects his family, renounces Catholicism, accepts school, and associates with a group from mixed ethnic backgrounds. However, he values and honors his Mexican origins, and the author makes a point of showing that Rubio sees many things as a Mexican. Obviously in part autobiographical, the novel discusses many of the problems faced by a Mexican American who tries to acculturate to the dominant society; the problems are both imposed from without, such as prejudice, and result from internal strife, such as the clash of traditional family mores with Anglo culture.—RM

428. Waddell, Jack O. From Dissonance to Consonance and Back Again: Mexican American Correctional Processes in a Southwest City, in Spanish Speaking People in the U.S.; Proceedings of 1968 Annual Spring Meeting, American Ethnological Society. Seattle, distributed by the University of Washington Press, 1968. pp. 135-144.
Waddell used Leon Festinger's cognitive dissonance model to explain the behavior of Mexican American convicts. The Mexican Americans had been given paroles, and the author wanted to study how they would resolve the difference between their value systems. In his experience, Waddell noted that the Mexican

Americans rejected their parole stipulations, preferring to return to prison rather than change their life style or abandon friends. However, the author does not argue that this type of behavior is limited to Mexican Americans; nor does he define the core values of Chicanos which the parolees are said to choose.—RM

429. Wald, Richard A. The Effect of Cultural Influences on Mexican-American Consumers. Unpublished monograph, Institute for Business and Economic Research, San Jose State College, 1970.

The author attempts to provide factual information about Mexican American families in an urban environment, and especially to measure the influence of cultural patterns on economic behavior. Wald discusses basic attitude, value, and behavior patterns of Mexican Americans, based on cultural and historical factors, and states that the consumer behavior of Mexican Americans is determined largely by their cultural attitudes. They have, he states, a special set of needs and desires that the market must recognize.—BM

430. Warner, W. Lloyd and Leo Srole. The Social Systems of American Ethnic Groups. Yankee City Series, III, New Haven, Yale University Press, 1945. 312 pp.

This book expresses the assimilationist point of view concerning the immigrant. The authors argue that the United States political organization, industrial economy, public education and class system will ultimately destroy ethnic identification. The speed at which this will occur will be determined by the degree of difference between the ethnic group and the dominant society in terms of race or color, religion, and language. In this analysis, an English, Protestant immigrant would merge easily and quickly into United States society, while a Mexican American who is mestizo, Catholic and speaks Spanish would be assimilated very slowly. Inferior status would also vary directly with the ethnic group's difference from Anglo society; the Mexican American, for example, would experience considerable subordination.—RM

431. Watson, James B. and Julian Samora. Subordinate Leadership in a Bi-cultural Community: An Analysis. American Sociological Review, XIX (1954), 413-421.

The authors analyzed leadership among the Spanish-speaking people of a bicultural community in Southern Colorado. They found a deficiency of leadership in the Hispano population, both in inter-ethnic and intra-ethnic affairs. The authors discuss the conditions that they believe primarily cause this deficiency; among them are the unadaptability of the traditional form of leadership (that of the patrón) to the social and economic changes experienced by the community and the necessity for effective leaders to be familiar with the language and legal and social ways of the dominant Anglo culture. In addition, the Hispanos often are suspicious of "successful" group members—those who have acquired an extensive education and might be potential leaders—and tend to regard them as "agringados" (too much like Anglos). Finally, Anglo society often absorbs potential Hispano leaders and decreases their motivation to serve the Spanish-speaking community. The authors suggest that these causes of inadequate leadership among Hispanos in the community they studied may operate to some extent among Spanish-surname people throughout the Southwest.—RS

432. Weaver, Thomas. Social Structure, Change, and Conflict in a New

Mexican Village. PhD dissertation, University of California at Berkeley, 1965.

This study endeavors to describe the social structure, to analyze the causes and effects of culture change, and to discuss the social correlates of situations of conflict in Abajo, a Spanish American village of northern New Mexico. It is observed that kinship arrangements exist on both micro and macro levels, focusing respectively on patriarchal and bilateral elements of kinship. Specific historical events are described and analyzed as forces for change in the cultural patterns of Abajo, and three particular types of conflict are identified and discussed.—BM

433. Wheeler, Stanton. See Brim, Orville G., Jr. and Stanton Wheeler, Socialization After Childhood: Two Essays.

434. Williams, Robin M., Jr. Strangers Next Door: Ethnic Relations in American Communities. Prentice-Hall, Inc., New Jersey, 1964. 391 pp.

This book treats the nature of ethnic relations in the United States. Both personality and societal variables are considered in explaining the phenomena of ethnocentricity and prejudice. Discrimination is explained largely in terms of low interaction between ethnic groups and feelings of social distance. The discussion of change and conflict is brief, but the social process is seen as moving toward integration.

Research for the book was done in 17 small cities, including several in the Southwest. Mexican Americans are among the ethnic groups specifically treated in the numerous tables as well as in the general discussion.—PS

435. Witherspoon, Joseph Parker. Administrative Implementation of Civil Rights. Austin, University of Texas Press, 1968. 543 pp.

This is a study of the operation of human rights commissions, a common state and local approach to the exploration of racial and ethnic problems. The author concludes that the commissions have not been used to their full potential and offers proposals to eliminate their weaknesses. Witherspoon also recommends civil rights legislation to coordinate federal, state and local agencies. The emphasis is on Negro-white relations, not Chicano-Anglo. However, many of Witherspoon's illustrations and conclusions apply equally to all minorities, since he focuses on organizational approaches, not cultural differences.—RM

436. Wolf, Eric R. Sons of the Shaking Earth. Chicago, The University of Chicago Press, 1959. 256 pp.

This is an introduction to the ancient Indian cultures of Mexico and Guatemala and the interaction of the Indian and the European after the Spanish conquest. The book focuses on the pre-Colombian and the Colonial periods, but two concluding chapters bring the discussion of the hacienda, the Indian community and the mestizo up to the present. The author, an anthropologist, integrates material from many disciplines, including ecology, genetics, linguistics and history.—RS

437. Womack, John, Jr. Zapata and the Mexican Revolution. New York, Alfred A. Knopf, 1968).

Womack's documented study of Zapata and the revolutionary period in Mexico analyzes Zapata both as a man and as a symbol to the Mexican people. Writing in the Verstehen mode of historical analysis, Womack treats Zapata not as a hero apart from his followers, but as a leader in intimate relation to the Mexican people, prominent in history "because the villagers of Morelos put him in charge and persistently looked to him for guidance, and because other villagers around the Republic took him for their champion." This populist perspective is followed throughout the book beginning with a prologue titled "A People Chooses a Leader," and ending with the epilogue, "A People Keeps Faith" in which the state of Morelos is analyzed as a microcosm revealing the revolutionary dynamic underlying Zapatismo. Womack explains that Zapatismo is not merely the identification of a people with a great leader, but is more importantly representative of a revolutionary upheaval in which the masses of the people come to understand the impossibility of continuing their lives under existing social and economic conditions without breaking the ties that bind them to their ancestral lands.—MLB

438. Woods, Sister Frances Jerome. Cultural Values of American Ethnic Groups. New York: Harper & Brothers, 1956.
The hypothesis upon which this book is based is that a knowledge of cultural values and an appreciation of their significance to those who hold them is often essential for the effective practice of such professions as social work, educational counseling, psychiatry, etc., as they involve contact with members of ethnic groups. Such knowledge and appreciation would provide the professional worker with at least a minimal ability to differentiate between such things as personality disorder and cultural differences, and would assist him in understanding the personal conflict which arises when an individual is faced with incompatibilities between ethnic group values and American cultural values. In order to show the extensive and pervasive influences of variations in the culture patterns of ethnic groups, the author has drawn upon examples from case records, personal documents, records of interviews, and from secondary sources, and has systematically examined basic values, roles, and attitudes as they are viewed in connection with American, Oriental, Mexican, European, Jewish and Negro ethnic groups in the social setting of the United States.—BM

439. ——————. Mexican Ethnic Leadership in San Antonio, Texas. The Catholic University of America Studies in Sociology, XXXI (Washington, D.C., 1949), 122 pp.
This work emphasized that the Mexican American community generates both leaders and organizations that focus on achieving ethnic aims. The author felt there were two types of true leaders: the radicals who protest forcefully against Anglo prejudice and have mass followings, and the conservatives who emphasize the ethnic group's responsibility for self-improvement and concentrate on cooperation with other ethnic groups. A third type, the "coyotes," are not true leaders but men who pretend to be benefactors but exploit their fellow Mexican Americans. The book describes the Mexican American class structure and the process of recruitment for the different types of leadership.—RM

440. Woodward, Dorothy. The Penitentes of New Mexico. PhD dissertation, Yale University, 1935.
The Penitentes are a religious Confradia or Confraternity centered in the northern counties of New Mexico. The society is unusual in that it still practices bodily penance for sins, including public flagellation and actual dramatization of the Biblical story of the Passion and Crucifixion. The study traces the history of the society from the days of the Spanish conquerors and colonists until contemporary

times. After considering and rejecting several theories of the society's origin, the author demonstrates that the most satisfactory explanation lies in an examination of the Penitentes as a defense mechanism which protects the members from surrounding Indian and Anglo cultures. With their social organization headed by the absolute rule of the Hermano Mayor, the Penitentes became a self contained society possessing considerable power in state and local politics in New Mexico.—MLB

441. Wright, David E., Jr. Occupational Orientations of Mexican American Youth in Selected Texas Counties. Texas A&M University, 1968, Available through Educational Resources Information Center. 167 pp.

This is a report of research undertaken to determine the occupational aspirations and orientations of low-income Mexican American high school sophomores in four Texas counties. Making a distinction between what is desired and what is expected, the author finds that Chicano youth aspire to high level jobs, mostly in the "low professional" category. They expect, however, to achieve less than they want. The minute sex-based differences suggest that young Chicano women view themselves as equal competitors for employment.

The report questions the long-standing notion of "class bound expectations." Wright claims, rather, that his findings validate Robert Merton's theory that all members of United States society, irrespective of their position in the social structure, share the same high success goals. In the conclusion, the author explores the implications of this theory for policy-making and social action.—PS

442. Young, Donald. Research Memorandum on Minority Peoples in the Depression. New York, Social Science Research Council, 1937. 252 pp.

This memorandum discussed the impact of the Depression on minority groups (Mexican Americans, Indians, Negroes, Orientals, and European immigrants), as distinct from the total United States population. Intra-group differentiation received special attention. Forced repatriation of braceros was covered as one instance of post-Depression nativism.

The study also described the state of minority-oriented research in the late 1930's, making some general comparative comments, posing questions, and delineating areas for future research. It suggested unusual source materials appropriate to the investigation of specific problems.—PS

443. Zeleny, Carolyn. Relations Between the Spanish Americans and Anglo Americans in New Mexico: A Study of Conflict and Accommodation in a Dual Ethnic Situation, PhD dissertation, Yale University, 1944.

This study is concerned with the overall pattern of relations between Hispanos and Anglos in New Mexico. It analyzes the chief conflicts between the two groups and the accommodative process through which they are resolved, and discusses the modus vivendi that has been established and by which they live and interact. Zeleny concludes that while there has been little assimilation of the Hispanos, the conflicts between the two groups—Anglos and Hispanos—have been settled by two forms of accommodation: (1) adjustments through the use of political instrumentalities, for example the use of the courts to settle land disputes, and (2) "unconscious adjustments" or automatic accommodations which lead to patterned relationships. She posits that unlike the Negro in the South, the Hispano in New Mexico has not been subordinated and enjoys beneficial political and social status equal almost to that of the Anglo. She contends that the emergence of a milieu in which she views the Spanish American as enjoying a favorable political status in New Mexico is a result of the interrelatedness of governmental mechanisms and unconscious adjustments in the general pattern of inter-group relationships in New Mexico.—CV

444. Zurcher, Louis A., et al. Value Orientation, Role Conflict and Alienation from Work: A Cross-Cultural Study, American Sociological Review, XXX (1965), 539-548.

The authors attempt to substantiate the hypothesis that the value orientation "particularism" is influenced by cultural background. Particularism is the tendency to relate to family and friends rather than to institutions and casual acquaintances. The authors hypothesized that Mexicans would be more particularistic than Anglos and Mexican Americans would fall in between the two extremes, although tending toward the Anglo values. A study of bank employees in Nogales, Sonora, and Nogales and Tucson, Arizona, supported the proposition. A further assumption that particularism would result in alienation from the work situation (which is universalistic) also was substantiated. Although the correlation was low, the authors point out that other factors, such as pay rates, could have compensated for the conflict in the work situation between particularism and universalism.—RM

SUBJECT INDEX

C/S

FIELD INDEX

1. Anthropology

Acculturation, 19, 135, 140, 175, 197, 199, 217, 222, 223, 326, 349, 366
Assimilation, 140, 197, 269
Biculturalism, 328
Charisma, 324
Compadrazgo, 253
Cultural change, 13, 109, 132, 172, 199, 215, 243, 432
Cultural contrast, 203, 222, 325, 334, 336, 389, 440
Cultural pluralism, 140
Cultural values, 138, 144, 155, 325, 334, 336, 349, 389, 440
Culture, 55, 70, 161, 185, 189, 204
Culture of Poverty, 172, 213, 424
Culture retention, 111
Curanderismo, 196, 223, 288, 324, 325
Discontinuity, 19
Donship, 326
Ethnicity, 55
Family, 175
Farmworkers, 284
Folk medicine, 66, 196, 223, 288, 324, 325, 334, 336, 339
Folklore, 289
Hispanos, 243
Identity, 132, 365, 366, 385
Innovation, 13
Kinship patterns, 432
Mexican culture, 125
Mexico, 436
Migration, 207
Palomilla, 335
Penitentes, 32, 183, 440
Poverty, 132, 155
Religion, 325, 339, 386, 440
Social change, 13, 326, 385
Social class status, 138
Social science models, 323, 424
Social science research, 307, 323, 371, 424
Socialization, 19
Stereotypes, 323
Subcultures, 129
Teacher training, 203
Urbanization, 157
Xenophobia, 169

2.   Economics

Agricultural industry, 238, 239, 284, 394, 395, 396
Agricultural labor market, 110, 394, 395, 396
Agricultural mechanization, 187, 284
Borderlands, 33
Bracero program, 208
Braceros, 59, 187
Consumer behavior, 162, 429
Cultural change, 109
Culture of Poverty, 213
Discrimination in employment, 352
Emigration of Mexicans, 59
Employment, 41, 115, 168, 177
Employment patterns, 252
Farmworkers, 59, 110, 126, 158, 187, 238, 239, 284
Immigrants, 158
Immigration, 126, 228, 358
Immigration patterns, 33, 128
Immigration policy, 59, 156
Labor unions, 205
Manpower training, 157
Migration, 47
Poverty, 109, 155, 254
Unionism, 187, 205
United States-Mexican relations, 33
Urban workers, 205
Urbanization, 157, 358, 384
Wetbacks, 194

3.   Education

Acculturation, 15, 75, 82, 115, 150, 329
Alienation, 75
Aspirations, 441
Assimilation, 88, 115, 410
Bibliography, 101, 102, 141, 159, 160, 346, 348
Bicultural education, 410
Biculturalism, 117, 275
Bilingual education, 9, 10, 53, 63, 112, 117, 246, 295, 321, 416
Bilingualism, 9, 12, 36, 63, 64, 81, 104, 112, 117, 150, 159, 165,
       166, 184, 193, 211, 212, 225, 264, 272, 282, 295, 321, 345,
       404, 410, 416

4.   History

5. <u>Law</u>

10. Psychology

11. Public Health

12. Sociology

CHICANO PERIODICALS

Arizona:

CORAJE
Post Office Box 383
Tucson, Arizona 85705

EL PAISANO
Post Office Box 155
Tolleson, Arizona 85353

California:

AZTLAN: CHICANO JOURNAL OF THE SOCIAL SCIENCES
AND THE ARTS
UCLA Mexican American Cultural Center
Los Angeles, California

BASTA YA
Post Office Box 12217
San Francisco, California 91312

BRONCE
1560 34th Avenue
Oakland, California 94601

BRONZE
142 Pickford Avenue
San Jose, California 95127

CARTA EDITORIAL
Post Office Box 54624
Terminal Annex
Los Angeles, California 90054

CON SAFOS, REFLECTIONS OF LIFE IN THE BARRIO
CON SAFOS, Inc.
Post Office Box 31085
Los Angeles, California 90031

CHICANO TIMES
719 Delgade
San Francisco, California 94118

CHICANISMO
MECHA—Stanford University
Post Office Box E
Stanford, California 94305

EL ALACRAN
MECHA—California State College
Long Beach, California 90801

EL CHICANO
4021 First Avenue
San Bernardino, California 92410

EL GRITO, A JOURNAL OF CONTEMPORARY MEXICAN
AMERICAN THOUGHT
Quinto Sol Publications, Inc.
Post Office Box 9275
Berkeley, California 94709

EL HISPANO
630 Ninth Street
Sacramento, California 95814

EL MACHETE
MECHA—Los Angeles City College
Los Angeles, California

EL MALCRIADO
Post Office Box 130
Delano, California 63215

EL POCHO CHE
Post Office Box 4426
Berkeley, California 94704

EL POPO
Post Office Box 1876
Pacoima, California 91331

EL POPO
MECHA—California State College, San Fernando
Northridge, California 91324

EL TECOLOTE
1292 Potrero
San Francisco, California 94110

EL TRAVIESO
3045 E. Whittier Blvd.
Los Angeles, California 90024

ES TIEMPO
MECHA—Foothill College
12345 South El Monte Avenue
Los Altos Hills, California 94022

INSIDE EASTSIDE
Post Office Box 63273
Los Angeles, California 90063

JOURNAL OF MEXICAN AMERICAN HISTORY
Box 13906
Santa Barbara, California 93107

LA CAUSA
4715 E. Olympic Blvd.
Los Angeles, California 90033

LA LUCHA
655 Castro Street
Mountain View, California 94040

LA OPINION
1436 S. Main Street
Los Angeles, California 90015

LA PALABRA
Post Office Box 4879, Station C
San Jose, California 95126

LA PRENSA LIBRE
2973 Sacramento Street
Berkeley, California 94702

LA RAZA
3571 City Terrace Drive
Post Office Box 31004
Los Angeles, California 90031

LA VERDAD
Post Office Box 13156
San Diego, California 92113

LA VIDA NUEVA
5337 E. Brooklyn Avenue
Los Angeles, California 90022

LA VOZ
Community Service Organization
2820 Whittier Blvd.
Los Angeles, California

LA VOZ DEL PUEBLO
2732 Durant Avenue
Berkeley, California 94704

NEW-MISSION-NUEVA
2204 Bryant Street
San Francisco, California 94110

REGENERACION
Post Office Box 54624, Terminal Annex
Los Angeles, California 90045

SALAZAR TRIBUNE
9237 Whittier Blvd.
Pico-Rivera, California 90660

SAL SI PUEDES
423 North Milpas Street
Santa Barbara, California 93103

THE FORUMEER
435 Hubson Street
San Jose, California 95110

Colorado:

EL GALLO
1567 Downing Street
Denver, Colorado 80218

New Mexico:

EL GRITO DEL NORTE
Route 2, Box 5
Espanola, New Mexico 87532

EL PAPEL
Post Office Box 7167
Albuquerque, New Mexico 87104

Texas:

COMPASS
1209 Egypt Street
Post Office Box 8706
Houston, Texas 77009

EL AZTECA
701 Santa Gertrudis
Kingsville, Texas

EL DEGUELLO
Post Office Box 37094
San Antonio, Texas 77537

EL GOLPE AVISA
Post Office Box 2321
Waco, Texas

EL INSURGENTE
1816 Springfield Avenue
Laredo, Texas 78040

EL REBOZO
Post Office Box 37207
San Antonio, Texas

EL YAQUI
Post Office Box 52610
Houston, Texas 77052

HOY
701 Santa Gertrudis
Kingsville, Texas

I N F E R N O
719 Delgado Street
San Antonio, Texas 78207

L A R A Z A N U E V A
2815 W. Commerce
San Antonio, Texas

L A R E V O L U C I O N
Post Office Box 1852
Uvalde, Texas

L A V O Z D E L O S L L A N O S
1107 A Avenue G
Lubbock, Texas

L O S M U E R T O S H A B L A N
1903 Bruni Street
Laredo, Texas 78040

T H E V A L L E Y O F T H E D A M N E D
2020 Santa Rita Avenue
Laredo, Texas 78040

Y A M E R O
Post Office Box 1044
McAllen, Texas 78501

Other States:

A D E L A N T E
2019 Summit Street
Kansas City, Missouri 64108

L A D O
1306 N. Western Avenue
Chicago, Illinois 60622

L A G U A R D I A
635 S. 5th Street
Milwaukee, Wisconsin

L A V O Z M E X I C A N A
Post Office Box 101
Wautoma, Wisconsin 54982

N O T I C I E R O   H I S P A N O
1337 Van Buren
Gary, Indiana

N U E S T R A   L U C H A
110 NW 5th Avenue
Delray Beach, Florida 33444

V I V A
Post Office Box 2181
Kansas City, Kansas 66110

C/S